NEW FISCAL AND ECONOMIC STRATEGIES
FOR GROWTH
IN DEVELOPING COUNTRIES

NEW FISCAL AND ECONOMIC STRATEGIES FOR GROWTH IN DEVELOPING COUNTRIES

S. S. KOTHARI

Delhi
OXFORD UNIVERSITY PRESS
Bombay Calcutta Madras
1992

Oxford University Press, Walton Street, Oxford OX2 6DP

NEW YORK TORONTO
DELHI BOMBAY CALCUTTA MADRAS KARACHI
KUALA LUMPUR SINGAPORE HONG KONG TOKYO
NAIROBI DAR ES SALAAM
and associates in
BERLIN IBADAN

© Oxford University Press 1992
ISBN 0 19 562931 0

Phototypeset by All India Press, Kennedy Nagar, Pondicherry 605001
printed by Rekha Printers Pvt. Ltd., New Delhi 110 020
and published by S. K. Mookerjee, Oxford University Press,
YMCA Library Building, Jai Singh Road, New Delhi 110001.

To the memory
of my father
Shiva Singh Kothari

Preface

Optimum development of the country's enormous potential and resources postulates fundamental changes in the structural framework of policies and the formulation of new strategies of growth—fiscal and economic—to facilitate transition from a command economy to a 'market-friendly' one. The Soviet model of planning and policies largely adopted by the Government since the fifties, with concomitant controls on investment and allocation of resources, production, consumption, and distribution resulted in economic distortions and retarded the momentum of development. Liberalization in various fields became inevitable to unshackle the economy and release pent up energies for accelerated multi-dimensional growth. The book has grown out of this conviction. The new strategy, which has a practical orientation, is its subject.

The book also incorporates various suggestions on economic management, fiscal policy, and tax structure I have made from time to time to the government, in parliament and outside. Successive governments have been responsive to innovative thoughts. Some of the ideas have percolated into government policy and been implemented; for instance, the backward areas tax rebate was mooted and submitted to the Lok Sabha by me in the form of a Private Member's Bill. The government subsequently accepted the suggestion. The Fourth Plan (1969–74) does not contain the word 'monitoring' anywhere. It was in 1969 that I suggested to the then Prime Minister, Mrs Indira Gandhi, that 'simultaneous monitoring' of expenditure was necessary; what the government was doing at that time was tantamount to post-mortem examination. The concept was accepted, although its implementation even after two decades leaves much to be desired.

Growth economics relating to development of underdeveloped economies is well accepted as a specialized subject of study but the greater part of the literature has been devoted to the Latin American and African experience. It was in this context that I felt that a book analysing the principal issues and problems facing

India and Asian countries, and highlighting their experience and the evolution of appropriate fiscal and economic policies, would be useful alike to the general reader, the professional economist, and student.

The first draft of the book was written between 1987 and 1990. The original framework has been retained, but extensive modifications have been effected and additional material included to reflect the wide-ranging changes in economic and fiscal policies of the government and in the international economic environment. In July 1991, government announced the New Industrial Policy, giving an edge and thrust to the policy of liberalization. An overview of the new policy has been provided in the last chapter; and reforms upto July 1991—taken as the cut-off date for tax rates and legal provisions—have been dealt with in the book.

Substantive changes with wide ramifications and import have occurred in the erstwhile Soviet Union and Germany since this book was written. References in the text to the Soviet Union relates to the USSR as it existed prior to the country's reorganization into a number of independent and semi-autonomous states, and those to East and West Germany as they were constituted prior to unification into a single united Germany.

It is difficult to individually acknowledge my intellectual indebtedness to various authors who have made a seminal contribution to the development of growth economics and fiscal policy in under-developed economies. Their books are listed in the Bibliography.

I am greatly indebted to Prof. Alak Ghosh who read the preliminary draft and gave valuable advice and guidance. K. S. Mehta offered useful suggestions, particularly in regard to institutional finance. Prof. Rakhal Datta reviewed the mathematical models and P. K. Bhattacharya tax calculations. H. K. Kaul, Librarian, India International Centre, gave wise counsel and unstinted cooperation in the use of the Centre's Library for research. My thanks are due to all of them.

I should also like to thank the *Statesman* for permission to include in the book in modified form the article 'Equity and Growth' first published by them. Two other articles, 'Fiscal Policy' and 'Foreign Capital and Investment Climate', published in the *Economic Times* and *Times of India* have been adapted for inclusion in the book. For the chapter on International Economic

Environment in particular, the *World Development Reports* and various issues of the *Economist*, London were most useful.

I am most grateful to officials of Oxford University Press for their valuable advice and support which enabled the publication of the book.

I have to thank my daughters Madhulika and Sangita, and my wife Rajkumari for their constant support that enabled me to complete the task.

Centre of Economics and Taxation Studies,   S. S. KOTHARI
21, Old Court House Street,
Calcutta 700 001
2 April 1992

Contents

Chapter 5–Challenges and Strategies for Developing Economies in the Nineties

Chapter 6–Elements of Growth: Crucial Role of Capital Formation

Chapter 7–New Initiatives for Growth

Chapter 8–Control of Inflation: Friedman's Monetarist Approach Versus Supply Side Factors

Chapter 9 – Agricultural Breakthrough: Social Welfare, Justice, and Equity

Chapter 10 – Liberalization and Sectoral Growth

Chapter 11 – Internal and External Indebtedness: Scenario in the Nineties

Chapter 12 – Foreign Capital and Investment Climate

Chapter 13 – Role of Technology for Growth: Japan's Strategy – A Success Story

Chapter 14 – Institutional Finance

Part II Fiscal Policy for Growth in Developing Economies

Chapter 15 – Fiscal Policy and Plan Finance

Chapter 16–Tax System for Developing Economies

Chapter 17–Evaluation and Reform of the Indian Tax Structure

Chapter 18–Corporate Tax Reform

Tables

PART I

STRATEGIC FRAMEWORK OF POLICIES FOR GROWTH WITH EQUITY

1

Introduction

This book seeks to familiarize the reader with the macroeconomic aspects of the framework of economic policies and the principal issues and problems confronting developing countries in their efforts to stimulate the development of their economies and improve the standards of living of the people. The study analyses recent changes in India's economic policy and performance and their implications for economic growth in the nineties. The focus is fiscal and economic liberalization and transition towards a market economy. It is our contention that recent liberalization of taxation, private investment and corporate policies has helped in improving the overall economic performance in the eighties, and further liberalization and rationalization of economic policies in general, and fiscal policy in particular, will enable the economy to perform even better in the nineties.

The book succinctly surveys the principal doctrines and ideas of leading growth economists. It is an amalgam of basic principles, critical analysis of the existing policy framework and state of the Indian economy; and suggestive of remedial measures and strategies that could accelerate the momentum of growth in developing economies. The principles and strategies are largely applicable to most developing countries of South and South-East Asia, but the major part of the discussion is *with particular reference to India.* We have not attempted to dilate upon all the problems of growth of developing economies, but certain aspects, considered to be of vital importance for stimulating growth, have been discussed in detail. It is also necessary to emphasize that as different countries are in varying stages of development, generalizations have their limitations. We have largely dealt with problems and issues particularly relevant to economies which, in terms of Walter Rostow's stages of economic growth, are in the transitional stage, heading towards take-off, or in the stage of self-sustaining growth.

Part I begins with a survey of the international economic environment in the eighties and the perspective for the early nineties, together with a brief survey of the progress of the Indian economy and its economic balance sheet—its strengths, weaknesses, and future prospects. The historical perspective of the development of capitalism and eclipse of socialism, evolution of the welfare state or mixed economy, and the revival of liberalism, have been broadly analysed, together with the Keynesian Revolution. We begin with Adam Smith's doctrine of the 'invisible hand' and the self-regulating nature of the economy and, after broadly traversing the wide expanse of economic thought of over 200 years, we return to liberalism and the ideas of monetarists like Friedrich Hayek and Milton Friedman, who endorse the doctrines of Adam Smith and plead for reduced state intervention and increased liberty. The wheel appears to have turned full circle. Finally, our historical survey concludes with the question: was Mill a better prophet than Marx?

The challenges and strategies for developing economies in the nineties are highlighted, and need for revision of the role of the public sector in certain economies in the transition and take-off stages, and advantages of privatization, are discussed. The basic assumptions of a liberal economy are critically examined from a theoretical and analytical point of view, and thereafter we proceed to discuss the Indian experience of liberalization. The crucial role of capital formation, the causes and critical inputs for growth, and the necessity to break the underdevelopment equilibrium and the vicious circle of poverty in underdeveloped economies, are discussed. The theories and propositions of leading growth economists—W. Arthur Lewis, Nurkse, Schumpeter, Galbraith and others—and a simple version of the well-known Harrod–Domar Model of growth are presented. The reader is given a bird's eye view of Rostow's Stages of economic growth. In Chapter 5, the strategy of growth is broadly spelt out.

We may, however, indicate the limitations of this work. Much of the analysis relates to the industrial sector, although it accounts for only a portion of the output, investment and employment in the economy. While inter-sectoral linkages between industry, agriculture and the services sector are strong and multi-dimensional, and progress in various sectors is interdependent, the truth is that the index of progress and growth in the modern world is the degree of industrialization that has occurred; the developed countries are those that have passed through the second and third phases of the industrial revolution. We have however dealt with various aspects of inter-sectoral linkages, the agricultural breakthrough in the form of the Green Revolution, and the need for its extension to the rest of the country.

We discuss in Chapters 7 to 13 the new initiatives taken by government to accelerate growth: liberalization and rationalization of policies, reduction in controls and taxes, and promotion of social welfare and equity. The need to stimulate the inflow of foreign investment capital, which is accompanied by modern technology, is emphasized. The role of technology for growth and the Japanese experience of this are highlighted. Any discussion of the growth scenario in the nineties would be incomplete without reference to the internal and external indebtedness of the country and budgetary deficits. Both plan and non-plan expenditure need to be monitored and reduced, so that an internal debt trap and inflation may be avoided. The foreign exchange crunch, exacerbated by the Gulf crisis, and the necessity to increase exports and reduce their import-intensity, have been discussed in Chapter 11. The current inflationary situation, with the Wholesale Price Index crossing double digit figures, and its socially explosive implications, have been discussed and remedial measures suggested. Milton Friedman's monetarist approach *vis-à-vis* supply-side factors are also analysed, particularly with reference to the Japanese case study. Finally, we conclude Part I with a discussion of the commendable role of financial institutions in the country's economic development.

Part II deals with fiscal policy for growth in developing economies. The criteria for evaluating fiscal policy are discussed; the structural budgetary deficiency is highlighted; the adequacy of resources for financing plans assessed, as also the role of deficit financing and its inflationary implications. An appropriate tax system for developing economies is indicated; besides, the Indian tax structure, both personal and corporate, is evaluated, while canons of taxation for developing economies are discussed. Two new canons, based on empirical evidence, are projected. We discuss, in Chapter 20, a new theory enunciated by us, incorporating the

Corporate Nucleus Capital (CNC) Super-Multiplier, which constitutes an instrument of fiscal policy, useful for promoting investment through corporate tax cuts.

Both in the developed countries in the West and the 'advanced' developing countries of the world, taxes have been drastically cut. This is the field where fiscal imperatives and government actions have transcended economic theories and doctrines; and older generation economists find difficulty in adjusting their ideas and thoughts to the realities of the situation. Even in Sweden and the UK, which were at one time bastions of high taxes, taxes have been pruned or are in the process of being reduced. Japan and West Germany traditionally had low tax structures and this contributed to their speedy post-War recovery and reconstruction.

Prof. J. A. Kay,[1] of the London Business School and Member, Meade Committee on Tax Reform (UK), writing in *The Economic Journal*, says that tax reform is on the political agenda almost everywhere. This is a part of 'a much wider reliance on market forces rather than state intervention in economic policy generally. Lower direct tax rates...have been introduced in both the personal and the corporate sectors.' Tax rates have been sliced in the highest income brackets and the number of brackets have been reduced. Even the Laffer Curve, which at one time was derided, is now finding respectability. Prof. Kay admits that the Laffer Curve correctly draws attention to the possibility that reduction in the rates of certain taxes might induce increased tax revenue rather than their diminution. We have advocated, both in Parliament and outside, that high taxes have an adverse effect upon growth, and that lowering of taxes has a beneficial effect upon work, production and incomes; and revenues eventually do not suffer on account of reduced taxes. All new ideas take time to be accepted. The next generation of economists would probably regard high taxes above 60 per cent as an anachronism and an idea only of historical interest.

Finally, we deal with current economic perceptions and future perspectives in the country in Chapter 21 entitled 'Equity and Growth: Both Essential for Economy'. The Planning Commission's approach to the Eighth Plan was to rely on a trade-off between employment and growth, but there was a clear need for a synthesis of the two approaches. The last chapter incorporates an overview of the New Industrial Policy initiated by the Finance Minister in July 1991.

ECONOMIES OF SOUTH AND SOUTH-EAST ASIA

The basic challenge that faces not only the Indian economy, but most developing countries in South and South-East Asia, is to substantially reduce the yawning gap in per capita incomes between the developed and developing countries and improve the standards of living of the people, provide them with employment and alleviate poverty. A revolution of rising expectations has occurred. The evolution of new strategies of growth and modification of the structural framework of policies are imperative if people's aspirations are to be fulfilled.

The progress made in the eighties by the Newly Industrializing Economies (NIEs) like South Korea, Taiwan, Hong Kong, Singapore, and Thailand—despite several constraints that have developed—are sterling examples of what can be achieved. What is necessary is the will and capacity to absorb modern technologies, skills, and foreign capital. The country should be prepared to adopt new strategies and liberalize policies, and increase productivity and savings. Incentives should be provided to stimulate work, production, and incomes; besides, the pattern of resource allocation should be varied, and exports stimulated through curbs on domestic consumption. A kaleidoscopic survey of the principal economies of South-East Asia shows that prudent macroeconomic management and a continuing process of structural reform enabled them to avoid macroeconomic imbalances; they emerged largely with modest fiscal deficits and manageable levels of external debt. While economic reforms and expanding international trade have contributed to high growth performance, the gains have been partially neutralized by high population growth—the bane of most Asian countries.

Growth in GDP for Asian developing countries[2] amounted to 9.3 per cent in 1988 and is estimated at about 7.6 per cent in 1989. Increase in fixed investments exceeded 12 per cent in 1988 in East Asian countries, and exports in terms of volume expanded by over 9 per cent. However, the economies of some of the poor countries of South Asia have not fared well, particularly due to internal political disturbances and natural calamities: civil strife in Sri Lanka and Burma (Myanmar), and severe floods in Bangladesh. Further afield, Laos faced droughts, which accentuated poverty; Indonesia suffered economically due to adverse external terms of trade owing to the fall in oil prices and increasing debt service burden.

Certain common problems face most South and certain South-East Asian countries like Indonesia, Laos, the Philippines and Papua New Guinea. High pressure of increasing population neutralizing growth; dualistic societies with islands of affluence and widespread poverty, necessitating programmes for poverty alleviation, rural development, and provision of improved health, education and housing facilities; shortage of foreign exchange and high external debts. The imperative need is, (a) to attract foreign equity investment and induction of modern technology to improve international competitive capacity; (b) to stimulate the generation and mobilization of savings, and the volume of investment and exports; (c) to improve the structure of political and economic institutions and achieve stability; and (d) to improve the working of public sector enterprises and ensure a return flow of funds to the budget from surpluses generated.

The strategic framework of policies for stimulating growth for each country would inevitably have to be adapted and modified in consonance, *inter alia*, with its stage of economic development, structural framework and natural resources, the pattern of its import and export trade, and the mosaic of its existing fiscal, industrial and economic policies. While export-led growth, for instance, may yield spectacular results for certain NIEs like South Korea, Taiwan, Thailand and Malaysia, such a pattern of growth may not be feasible for countries like India and Pakistan. However, as stated, there is a basic homogeneity in regard to constraints and problems of growth for most developing economies in South and South-East Asia, and the economic strategies of growth discussed in this work are broadly applicable, with suitable adaptation, to most countries in the region.

REFERENCES

1. J. A. Kay, 'Tax Policy: A Survey', *The Economic Journal*, March 1990, Royal Economic Society/Basil Blackwell Ltd., Oxford, pp. 18, 35.
2. Source of Figures (SOF): *The World Bank Annual Report 1989*, World Bank, Washington, p. 114.

2

International Economic Environment

The international economic environment sharply deteriorated in 1980–2 as a consequence of the second oil shock in 1979. The industrial market economies experienced the unusual phenomenon of inflation, accompanied by unemployment and stagnation. Anti-inflationary policies initiated by various countries triggered a severe recession, the impulses of which reverberated through the developing countries. The recession lasted for about three years. Thereafter, in 1983, the process of recovery in the industrial economies manifested itself and subsequently gathered momentum.

On the whole, the decade of the eighties witnessed healthy growth in the industrial world. However, a sharp and distinct downturn in economic activity occurred in 1990 as a by-product of the Gulf crisis. The magnitude of the recession, however was not as great as the earlier depression. With the ceasefire of 28 February 1991, signs of revival are again discernible and economic forecasts predict a rise in national income, production, and demand in mid-1991 and 1992. With export-led growth, the NIEs, like South Korea, Thailand, Malaysia, Hong Kong, Singapore, and Taiwan, as also China, recorded phenomenal increase in their GNP, production and exports in the eighties. However, during 1990 and 1991, their economies faltered due, *inter alia*, to international recession, protectionism by western countries and Japan, and inflation and infrastructural bottle-necks.

The international economic environment during the eighties was hardly favourable to the stimulation of internal growth in GDP in most third world countries. Many developing economies, particularly in Latin America and Sub-Saharan Africa, not only failed to generate the momentum of growth achieved in industrial countries, but their real incomes declined in absolute terms. The World Bank's verdict is telling: 'For many of the World's poor, the 1980s was a "lost decade"—a disaster indeed.'[1] The performance of the

Indian economy during the eighties, however, despite an adverse international climate, was impressive, of which more later.

INDUSTRIALIZED COUNTRIES

The industrialized economies made significant progress during the eighties. While increase in output recorded high levels, and close to the potential, inflation continued to be restrained. Real GDP increased on an average by 3 per cent per annum during the period 1980–9 and by 3.6 per cent in 1989. Investment rose by 20.9 per cent per annum and 21.5 per cent of GDP, and exports grew by 4.8 per cent and 7.6 per cent in the respective periods. World trade continued to expand. Unemployment which had soared to high levels during the recessionist phase of 1980–2, also abated substantially, while productivity increased.

Deceleration in business activity in most industrial economies occurred in 1990. The UK and US economies faced sizeable recession, as also various OECD countries. West Germany, however, received an impetus in demand and economic activity consequent upon unification with East Germany; while the Japanese economy remained strong with surging production levels. The global recession gathered momentum and its tentacles spread; GNP actually declined over a wide spectrum of industrialized countries during the last quarter of 1990: in the UK −3.8 per cent, Sweden −0.6 per cent, Canada −4 per cent and the USA −1.6 per cent. Germany and Japan, however increased their national output by about 4.5 and 4.7 per cent in 1990. Unemployment intensified in the various OECD countries, while it diminished by about 1.2 per cent in Italy and 1 per cent in Germany; it remained pegged at about 2 per cent in Japan.

In the UK, USA, Australia, and several industrialized countries, corporate entities have been reducing employment, cutting excess capacity and limiting capital expenditure in order to combat recession. Reflecting unoptimistic expectations, an all round fall in investment, business activity, production, and profits was in evidence. Marginal industrial units have turned sick and some of them have closed their shutters. Inventories have accumulated, order books are partially empty, and as lack of demand spreads in ever-widening circles, the economies have been facing a slump. It is significant that consumer prices did not synchronize with the downturn in business activity in most industrial countries and maintained high levels in 1990: UK 9.3 per cent, USA 6.1 per cent, Sweden 10.9 per cent, and Australia 6 per cent. Germany, however, controlled its inflation at 2.9 per cent, while Japan recorded a modest 3.8 per cent increase in consumer prices over the year.

The cease-fire in the Gulf on 28 February 1991 provided a boost to the investment climate in most industrial economies. Gulf peace should stimulate recovery in the USA and UK—albeit less speedily for the latter—on account of prospects of a low level of oil prices and receding chances of exorbitant increase, and accrual of most reconstruction contracts in Kuwait to US and UK companies, which should stimulate business, economic activity, and employment. Optimism exists that during the second quarter of 1991 in the USA and the third quarter in the UK, output and recovery should gather momentum.

Interest rates have been declining and monetary expansion is taking place. The stock exchanges, which anticipate and presage economic recovery, have turned buoyant, and the corporate sector is able to raise capital through public issues. Equity offers have almost doubled in the first quarter of 1991, as compared to the previous year, in America. Its dependence for finance upon banks is reduced. Only 25 per cent of the funds borrowed by companies and households in the USA emanate from the banking sector. Pessimistic forecasts about a serious credit crunch and prolonged recession no longer hold good. The economies are reviving, albeit slowly. The forecasts made by *The Economist* indicate moderation in recession and signs of recovery in mid-1991 and 1992 in leading industrial countries of the world. This is indicated by the Table given below:

TABLE 2.1— *GNP Forecast for Leading Industrialized Countries*
GNP—Percentage Increase

Country	1990	1991	1992
UK	−1.3	−1.3	2.1
USA	0.5	−0.4	2.6
Canada	−1.0	−1.1	3.0
Australia	0.6	0.7	2.7
France	1.8	1.9	2.6
Germany	4.5	2.6	2.2
Japan	4.7	3.5	3.9
Holland	3.4	2.2	2.6

SOURCE *The Economist*, 20 April 1991.

Desynchronization of the principal industrial countries, as emphasized by *The Economist*,[2] which had assisted in obviating deep and prolonged global recession, would now decelerate the recovery. West Germany and Japan recorded a growth rate of about 4.5 per cent in 1990, and the buoyant conditions in these economies contributed to the sustenance of world demand, when the USA, UK, Canada, Australia and other industrial economies were struggling in the throes of a slump. Now, as the USA and UK are progressing along the road to economic revival, the economies of Germany and Japan are slowing down. With growth rate pared by almost half in 1991 over the previous year, exports to these countries are likely to be depressed. Slow recovery, however, is not always to be deprecated. A sudden boom could trigger inflation, leading to monetary restraints; the consequent setback to revival could be serious.

Thanks to the inherent strength of the German economy, its trading partners—Holland, with exports to Germany equivalent to 15 per cent of its own GDP, Belgium 12 per cent, and Australia 11 per cent—are expected to record satisfactory performance in regard to output and growth. During the recession period of 1990, their economies have been holding up, with almost buoyancy in output. GNP in Holland increased by about 3.4 per cent, when most other OECD countries including the USA, were struggling with less than half this growth rate and deceleration in business activity.

NEWLY INDUSTRIALIZING ECONOMIES

The years 1980–9 have witnessed wide variation in growth among the developing countries of the world. While at one end of the spectrum, countries in East Asia, including China and NIEs like South Korea, Taiwan, Malaysia, and Thailand have increased growth of real per capita GDP by 6.7 per cent, and those in South Asia, including India and Pakistan, by 3.2 per cent, at the middle and other end of the spectrum, countries in Eastern Europe, the Middle East, North Africa and Latin America have registered low per capita growth rates, or even negative rates as in the case of Sub-Saharan Africa. East Asian countries have also increased their share of developing economies' real incomes from 22 per cent in

1960–5 to 37 per cent in 1988–9; the corresponding share of other third world countries has fallen.

Some East Asian countries faced difficulties in the early eighties due to world recession, but they extricated themselves through stimulated exports and internal macroeconomic adjustments. Most of these countries had built up strong world trade positions and current account surpluses at the beginning of the eighties; besides, their fiscal balances were also healthy. This enabled them to withstand shocks in the form of high world interest rates and the Gulf war. They succeeded in maintaining stability and sustained growth.

The progress achieved by certain South-East Asian countries (and China) between 1965 and 1988 is shown by the Table given below:

TABLE 2.2 — *GDP of Certain South-East Asian Countries and China*
(GDP Increase)

Country	1965–80	1980–88
South Korea	9.6	9.9
Thailand	7.2	6.0
Indonesia	8.0	5.1
Malaysia	7.3	4.6
Singapore	10.1	5.7
Hong Kong	8.6	7.3
China	6.4	10.3

SOURCE *World Development Report 1990*, Tables on pp. 180, 181.

However, after five years of sustained growth, the economies of most of these countries are expected to slow down: GDP growth in Singapore is expected to decline from 8.3 per cent in 1990 to 5.2 per cent in 1991, Thailand from 10 per cent to 7.4 per cent, Malaysia from 9.4 per cent to 8.3 per cent, and South Korea from 9 per cent to about 6.5 per cent in the respective years.[3] With rapid growth of these economies, various pressures on macro-balances and infrastructure increased. The large trade surpluses accumulated during 1986 to 1988 were replaced by trade deficits. Inflation gathered momentum in most countries and the infrastructure proved inadequate to cope with the expansion of the economies. This became particularly evident in China, Thailand and South Korea. The actual inflation rate in South Korea may be double the official rate of 9 per cent.

Inevitably, the world recession in 1990 adversely affected the exports and foreign exchange earnings of these countries. This has been compounded by increasing protectionism and trade barriers by industrialized countries. Take the case of South Korea. Japan, Europe, and the USA raised barriers against its exports. Japan forced a 'voluntary export restraint' (VER) agreement—ironically, it had itself been subjected to VERs by the USA—on South Korea in respect of knitwear exports by fixing quotas. Europe suppressed Korean electronics exports through anti-dumping laws, while the USA applied Super 301 provisions. It is estimated that the difference between the trade surplus in 1988 and trade deficit in 1990 would be about 10 per cent of South Korea's GNP.[4]

DEVELOPING AND OTHER ECONOMIES

Most developing countries in Latin America and Sub-Saharan Africa, and other developing economies have recorded unimpressive overall growth rates. Increase in population in excess of growth in GDP in many cases has brought about a decline in per capita incomes, as a result of which poverty has been accentuated. While GDP increased during the 1980s by 1.6 per cent in Latin America and the Caribbean, and 1.0 per cent in Sub-Saharan Africa, per capita incomes declined by 0.6 per cent in the former region and 2.2 per cent in the latter. High and volatile interest rates and adverse terms of trade, particularly in respect of primary commodities, diminished real incomes in these countries. Large-scale deficit financing in the wake of reduced availability of foreign loans, excessive government spending, and unstable exchange rates in the case of highly indebted middle-income countries, contributed to severe inflation. In certain Latin American countries, inflation exceeded 100 per cent on an average between 1980 and 1987, while it was about 5 per cent in East Asia and 8 per cent in South Asia. Inflation adversely affects investment, inflow of capital and revenues; it exacerbates foreign exchange problems and its proper allocation, and makes the adjustment process difficult.

The large magnitude of internal and external debts of these countries is attributable to sustained sizeable public sector deficits and borrowings, leading to macroeconomic imbalances. Certain countries like Mexico, Venezuela, Jamaica, and Equador have introduced structural reforms, deregulating their financial systems, restructuring the public sector, reducing protective tariff barriers, and opening up their economies to foreign and domestic investment. Some other countries like Argentina, Brazil, Uruguay, and Peru are reducing their fiscal deficits as a component of their stabilization programmes. The objective in both cases is to stimulate allocative efficiency in both public and private sectors and to bring about macroeconomic stability through control of inflation. Contrary to the general trend, some countries like Chile, Columbia and Paraguay have recorded higher per capita incomes in 1990 as compared to those in 1980. The structural reforms undertaken by these countries to stimulate recovery and growth, have been supplemented by fiscal discipline and macroeconomic stability. Average inflation over the decade is less than 25 per cent—moderate in comparison to the hyper-inflation in certain Latin American countries—while the average growth rate during the period 1980–8 amounted to 1.9 per cent, 3.4 per cent, and 1.7 per cent respectively for these three countries.[5]

According to a World Bank study,[6] while debt relief and external aid are imperative to buttress the economies of Sub-Saharan Africa, the countries themselves must continue effecting structural adjustments, including 'reforms to rationalize the incentive system, develop domestic infrastructure, diversify the productive base, and improve the efficiency of investment'. This would stimulate investment and achievement of growth of export volume of more than 3 per cent per annum.

EASTERN EUROPE

Cataclysmic political changes have swept through the Soviet Union and other East European countries. As communism collapses they are struggling to evolve market economies. The pangs of transition to capitalism, in the form of decline in production and shortage of goods, inflation, and unemployment, are proving to be severe. Even in East Germany, despite unification, output and consumer spending have declined, and unemployment is on the rise. The economies of Poland, Hungary and Czechoslovakia are facing inflation of about 40 per cent per year. The governments are striving to achieve structural reform—with privatization a high priority on the agenda—in an effort to achieve sustained growth in output, incomes, and jobs. Assistance to Eastern and Central Europe by the World Bank, and on a bilateral basis by financial institutions—largely for projects and trade by the latter—is proposed. Despite international goodwill and assistance from industrial economies, the task of transformation of these economies is not easy, and in any case is likely to take considerable time.

MIDDLE EAST, NORTH AFRICA, AND OTHER DEVELOPING EUROPE

High-income oil exporting countries have, on the whole, not fared badly in 1989, as due to a combination of higher prices and greater demand, the value of oil exports in 1989 increased by about a third over that in the previous year. However, during 1980–9, the GDP of countries in the Middle East, North Africa, and other developing economies like Turkey, Greece, and Yugoslavia increased by 2.9 per cent only as compared to 6.3 per cent in the period 1965–80. Per capita GDP grew by less than one per cent over the decade, a very unsatisfactory performance. Close linkage exists between economic growth in developing economies and the policies and steady growth of industrialized countries. Deceleration of growth in the latter has wide-ranging effects on developing economies: demand for imports of their goods diminishes to the detriment of exports and foreign exchange earnings, and the tendency towards protectionism and higher tariff barriers is accentuated; the quantum of aid and assistance inevitably suffers erosion; higher interest rates make the debt service burden more onerous and declining commodity prices adversely impinge upon exporters with deteriorating terms of trade. Not surprisingly, the poorest countries suffer most in such circumstances.

Various factors contributed to an adverse international environment for the third world countries:

1. The world recession in the early eighties, critically affected economic development, particularly in countries which were burdened with considerable foreign debts contracted during the seventies. The international trading environment deteriorated. International commodity prices declined sharply due to a diminishing

volume of imports by industrial countries. This resulted in stagnation of the exports of developing countries and adverse terms of trade. The average commodity prices almost continuously declined and were about one-third lower in 1989 as compared to 1980. For poor countries, like Ghana which greatly depends upon export of cocoa beans and Papua New Guinea largely dependent on the export of copper and coffee, the sharp decline in prices of primary commodities severely impinged upon their foreign exchange earnings and current account balances.

2.   Decline in multilateral concessional assistance at a time when the cost of importing oil had escalated, compounded the difficulties of third world countries and forced them to take recourse to commercial borrowings at high rates of interest. This resulted in a net transfer of resources on a global basis from the developing to the developed countries in the form of debt servicing. A consequence of the sharp diminution of foreign concessional aid, and in 1983 of commercial borrowings, was that many developing countries, particularly in Latin America, resorted to deficit financing and currency expansion. Inevitably, inflation gathered momentum.

3.   In combination with world recession and worsening terms of trade, an escalation in real interest rates brought about the debt crisis. Such rates were almost six times higher than in 1974–9; they were triggered and sustained by 'a decline in industrial country savings, by lack of progress in dealing with global current account imbalances, and by large swings in the major currencies, perhaps accompanied by greater uncertainty regarding future exchange rate movements' (World Bank).[7]

4.   Increasing trade barriers—tariff and non-tariff—and protectionist policies of leading industrial countries since the mid-1970s, and particularly during the eighties, had an adverse impact upon expansion of developing countries' volume of exports and foreign exchange earnings. The future outlook—what with the near stalemate in GATT talks, moves towards formation of trade blocks, increased protectionism, managed trade, and free use of VERs—is hardly a good omen for a healthy international trade environment for developing countries. Actually, the danger is that the multilateral, rule-based approach to trade under GATT may be jeopardized.

A successful adjustment process contributes to the resolution of difficulties. This, however, postulates macroeconomic stability and low inflation, controlled deficit financing, and small budgetary deficits and a realistic exchange rate. The microeconomic environment should also be favourable to new investment, inflow of foreign investment capital, and absorption of modern technology. Many of the third world countries, particularly in Latin America and Sub-Saharan Africa, were faced with severe macroeconomic constraints which rendered it difficult for them to make the necessary adjustments, and their growth rates suffered.

Strategy for Reduction in World Poverty

The *World Development Report 1990* has focused attention on the widespread phenomenon of poverty that has defied easy solution. More than one billion people (about one-third of the population of developing countries) had an income below $370 per capita per annum in 1985. The World Bank has suggested a two-faceted strategy:[8] 'pursuit of a pattern of growth that ensures productive use of ... labour [and] ... widespread provision to the poor of basic social services, especially primary education, primary health care, and family planning'. This has to be reinforced by 'well targeted transfers, to help those not able to benefit from these policies, and by safety nets, to protect those who are exposed to shocks'. It is emphasized that while international aid is necessary to support and sustain the developing country's own efforts, it should be interwoven with the country's plans and development programmes directed at growth and reduction in poverty in order to be really effective.

Prospects of Growth of Developing
   Countries in the Nineties

The developing countries are expected to grow in terms of real GDP growth rates at 5.1 per cent (per capita 3.2 per cent) during the period 1989–2000, as compared to 4.3 per cent (per capita 2.3 per cent) during the eighties (1980–9). Improved performance during the nineties could take place provided the international economic environment, comprising certain factors indicated below, is favourable:

    (a)   external aid increases by about 3 per cent a year in

consonance with a similar increase in the growth-rate of industrial countries;

(b) external shocks and world recession do not recur, and the present recession (1990–1) is not prolonged;

(c) the Gulf crisis is largely resolved and oil prices remain in the vicinity of $18 ($\pm$ $5) per barrel;

(d) real interest rates decline to between 3 and 4 per cent over the decade as compared to the 5.5 per cent average over the eighties;

(e) real commodity prices gradually stabilize and record some rise; in any case, the decline is not accentuated;

(f) constructive restructuring of domestic budgetary policies and regulatory framework, the financial sector, and trade, tariff, and protection policies is effected by the developing countries themselves; and finally,

(g) the industrialized countries make an earnest effort—the Brady initiative in 1989 marks a good beginning—to reduce the debt burden on developing countries and effect a multilaterial lowering of the barriers to world trade.

The extent to which these postulates are realized, would largely determine the outlook for growth of the third world countries.

There has been a decline in the availability of external finance, which assists developing countries to augment their rate of investment as a proportion of GDP. With severe constraints of resources and high investment requirements for accelerating growth and alleviating poverty, foreign aid assumes great significance for developing countries. But the overall size of the pool of exportable funds in countries with surplus capital and the competing claims of different countries in the pool determines the availability and cost of external finance. While the former has declined, cost has escalated during the eighties, thereby adversely affecting the developing countries. However, apprehension that aid to Eastern Europe may lead to diminution in the quantum of assistance to developing economies has been allayed by the World Bank.

Even in an adverse international environment, developing countries can accelerate the pace of development through effective domestic macroeconomic policies. Certain countries, including China, Turkey, Columbia, Indonesia, and Thailand, have recorded commendable economic growth because of sound policy frameworks. Budgetary deficits should be controlled and public spending fructuous by avoiding wastages and leakages; the tax system should be efficient and productive of revenues at minimum economic cost; public enterprises should yield surpluses and there should be increased decentralization in governmental activity. The industrialized countries should adopt positive steps to reduce their trade imbalances. This would restore stability in financial markets the world over. Private investment and consumption would increase, and inflation and real interest rates could be controlled.

With a higher level of export demand, lower interest rates and improved commodity prices, as also a larger quantum of foreign aid and reduced net resources outflow, the developing countries could record higher growth. The developing countries must intensify efforts to control population so that increase in GDP is not neutralized by increase in population, and is adequately reflected in higher per capita incomes.

The prospects for the international trading system in the nineties are hardly encouraging as pressures continue to mount. As *The Economist*[9] sees it,

if over the next few years, liberal trade gives way to managed trade, if the global economy does splinter, as some fear, into separate trading blocks, and if the recent revival of protectionism accelerates, the economic losses could eventually put all three oil shocks to shame. The last great cycle of recession and protection reached its climax in the Great Depression of the 1930s.

Moves are afoot for the formation of three blocks, the European Community, the Americas, and the Asia Pacific Region with Japan as the kingpin or central force. If the Uruguay round of talks fails, the stability of GATT and its very existence may be threatened. This is unfortunate, for GATT has been striving to establish an open multilateral system of trade negotiations and significant international liberalization of trade, with reciprocity, non-discrimination, and transparency as the guiding norms; and these principles have in the past stood in good stead in promoting international trade and industrial development. Much of the remarkable economic progress during the second half of the century is attributable to growing trade and GATT which promoted it.

During the seventies, however, the traditional industrial sectors of Western developed economies faced increasing competition from developing economies in the context of a modified pattern of comparative advantage. A new wave of protectionism resorted to by America and other industrialized countries not only militates against developing countries' efforts to stimulate their exports—which is vital to increase their momentum of growth—but also contributes to a diminution of productivity and growth in their own economies. Free and liberalized trade, like mercy, is 'twice blest'; it benefits the poverty-ridden developing countries and it also benefits the rich industrialized countries themselves. These ideas, however, are being ignored on short-term considerations and internal group pressures. The rate of growth of international trade has not matched the increase in global output owing to widespread protectionism in some form or other. Through so called 'voluntary export restraint' (VER), powerful governments have compelled other countries to restrict certain exports of goods to their country. Most of these VERs and similar arrangements, over 300 in number—relating to textiles, electronic goods, automobiles, steel, machinery, and other goods—have been used as instruments to protect the US and European markets, often against exports from Japan, South Korea, and other NIEs, as also India and certain Latin American countries.

The USA adopted under the OTCA[10] the practice of invoking a new section, Super 301, under which countries are charged with a wide range of so-called unfair trade practices and threatened with trade retaliation if they did not arrive at an agreement with the US Trade Authority within a specified period. India, Japan, and Brazil were named in 1989, although the last two were later removed from the list; and 25 other countries were warned that they were under observation. The Super 301 is patently inequitable because America unilaterally decides what is unfair trade practice; and it violates GATT principles in that it would not reciprocally lower its own trade barriers; it is dicriminatory against a particular country whose imports are liable to be barred; and it lacks transparency, in that some non-tariff impediments to trade flows would be set up. Other countries, including the European Community, take advantage of loopholes in GATT under the garb of 'safeguards', anti-dumping, and countervailing duty rules to shut out exports.

The developing countries have also resorted to protectionism, largely in defence of their weak exchange positions. Article 18 of GATT permitted them to impose trade restrictions to protect their balance of payments. It is doubtful whether on balance, the third world countries gained out of protective tariffs; they lost the benefits flowing from free trade and inevitably faced trade barriers to their exports in developed countries. It is indeed an irony that both developing countries and the USA—one of the most prosperous countries—are moving in the same direction towards protectionism. The industrial countries are raising protective barriers to free trade and promoting what is termed a 'strategic trade policy' or opting for 'managed trade'. The third world countries, with perception of self-interest and some pressure from IMF authorities, realize the usefulness of multilateral liberalization and free trade; a north–south division has emerged, with the south pressing for less protectionism by the developed countries and freer flow of their exports to them. Brazil, Mexico, and Chile have recently reduced tariff barriers and exposed their markets to competition from abroad. Since the current accounts position of most developing countries is vulnerable, it is for the powerful industrial economies to strive to ensure the success of multilaterial negotiations under the auspices of GATT. This would be in global interest, and enure to the benefit of all.

PROGRESS OF THE INDIAN ECONOMY IN AN ADVERSE INTERNATIONAL ENVIRONMENT

It is significant that despite an adverse international economic environment during the 1980s, and severe drought during 1987–8, the Indian economy moved into a higher growth orbit, from 3.5 per cent in 1965–80 to 5.5 per cent in 1980–90, during the periods of the Sixth and Seventh Plans. It was a sterling performance and particularly creditable because growth was achieved at the cost only of single digit inflation.

The following Table broadly reflects the progress of the Indian economy during the last few years (see Table 2.3).

As we proceed, the progress during the last five years will be further discussed. We shall also consider the challenges facing the Indian economy during the nineties.

TABLE 2.3—*Major Indicators for the Indian Economy*
(Percentage change over previous year)

Item	1980–81	1985–86	1986–87	1987–88	1988–89 (P)	1989–90 (Estimated)
Growth in GDP at 1980–1 prices	7.4	5.1	3.8	3.6	10.6	4.5
Agricultural production	15.6	2.4	–3.7	–2.1	20.8	1.5
Industrial production	4.0	8.7	9.1	7.5	8.8	8.3
Electricity generated	5.9	8.5	10.3	7.6	9.5	10.8
Wholesale Price Index (1970–1 = 100) on point to point basis	16.7	3.8	5.3	10.6	5.7	9.1
Imports (At current prices)	37.3	14.7	2.8	10.9	25.9	25.6
Exports (At current prices)	4.6	–7.2	14.3	26.4	28.9	36.3
Increase in money supply (M3)	18.1	15.9	18.6	15.9	17.7	19.9
Foreign exchange reserves (including gold and SDRs at end of period in Rs crores)	5544	7820	8151	7687	7040	6251

SOURCE: Figures for 1988–9 are as in *Economic Survey 1989–90*, p. 1.
Figures for 1989–90 are as in the *RBI Annual Report 1989–90* pp. 1,2,25,121.   P = Provisional.
Other figures from *Economic Survey, 1988–9*, p. 2.

TABLE 2.4—*Performance Indicators for the World Economy, 1989*

Group and region	Real growth of GDP 1980–89	1989	Growth of Exports (volume) 1980–89	1989	Gross domestic investment/GDP 1980–89	1989
Industrial countries	3.0	3.6	4.8	7.6	20.9	21.5
Developing countries	4.3	3.3	6.1	8.1	24.3	24.6
Sub-Saharan Africa	1.0	3.5	0.0	10.1	16.1	15.2
East Asia	8.4	5.1	14.7	8.1	30.0	30.7
South Asia	5.5	4.8	6.1	9.6	22.3	21.4
Eastern Europe	1.4	0.0	3.8	2.0	29.4	24.8
Middle East, North Africa, and other Europe	2.9	2.5	6.4	1.4	25.9	24.1
Latin America and the Caribbean	1.6	1.5	4.9	4.4	20.1	20.6

SOURCE: *World Development Report 1990*, p. 8.

TABLE 2.5 — *Prospects for the 1990s — World Economy*

Group and region	Real GDP growth rates			Real GDP per capita growth rates		
	Trend 1965–80	Recent experience 1980–89	Forecast 1989–2000	Trend 1965–80	Recent experience 1980–89	Forecast 1989–2000
Industrial countries	3.7	3.0	3.0	2.8	2.5	2.6
Developing countries	5.9	4.3	5.1	3.4	2.3	3.2
Sub-Saharan Africa	5.2	1.0	3.7	2.0	-2.2	0.5
East Asia	7.3	8.4	6.6	4.8	6.7	5.1
China	6.4	10.1	6.8	4.1	8.7	5.4
Other	8.1	6.4	6.3	5.5	4.2	4.6
South Asia	3.6	5.5	5.1	1.2	3.2	3.2
India	3.6	5.6	5.2	1.2	3.5	3.4
Other	3.9	5.0	4.8	1.2	2.2	2.4
Eastern Europe	5.3	1.4	1.9	4.5	0.8	1.5
Middle East, North Africa, and Other Europe	6.3	2.9	4.3	3.9	0.8	2.1
Latin America and the Caribbean	6.0	1.6	4.2	3.4	-0.6	2.3

SOURCE: Ibid., p. 16.

TABLE 2.6 — *Performance Indicators for Developing Regions of the World—selected periods*

Region	Growth of real per capita GDP (per cent)		
	1965–73	1973–80	1980–89
Sub-Saharan Africa	3.2	0.1	-2.2
East Asia	5.1	4.7	6.7
South Asia	1.2	1.7	3.2
Eastern Europe	4.8	5.3	0.8
Middle East, North Africa and Other Europe	5.5	2.1	0.8
Latin America and the Caribbean	3.7	2.6	-0.6

SOURCE Ibid., p. 11.

TABLE 2.7 — *Industrial Economies* — *Economic and Financial Indicators*, December 1990
(Percentage change)

	Industrial Production		GNP/GDP		Retail Sales (volume)	
	3 months	*1 year*	*3 months*	*1 year*	*3 months*	*1 year*
Australia	+9.7	−1.5	+2.4	+0.6	−6.3	−1.6
Canada	−11.3	−4.8	−4.0	−1.0	−8.4	−4.4
France	−8.2	+0.7	−1.6	+1.8	+2.5	−0.3
Germany	+4.1	+4.0	+1.5	+4.5	+9.6	+9.4
Holland	+9.6	+4.4	+10.3	+3.4	+1.1	+5.3
Italy	−8.7	+0.4	+2.7	+1.8	+13.2	−4.2
Japan	+2.6	+7.1	+2.1	+4.7	−10.7	+4.5
Spain	−0.2	−0.4	+3.4	+3.7	+8.4	+10.2
Sweden	−1.3	−3.6	−0.6	−0.5	−8.4	−6.7
Switzerland	−9.7	+3.6	−0.4	+1.7	−14.4	−0.8
UK	−8.1	−3.8	−3.8	−1.3	−0.9	−2.6
USA	−8.5	−3.3	−1.6	+0.5	−11.0	−4.7

SOURCE: *The Economist*, 20 April 1991.

TABLE 2.8—*Industrial Economies—Economic and Financial Indicators,*
December 1990

	Unemployment Rate (percentage)		Consumer Prices	
	Latest	Year ago	3 months	1 year
Australia	9.2	6.2	+2.9	+6.0
Canada	10.5	7.2	+5.8	+5.0
France	9.2	8.9	+3.9	+3.3
Germany	6.1	7.2	+2.1	+2.9
Holland	4.9	5.3	+3.5	+2.6
Italy	9.6	10.8	+7.8	+6.5
Japan	2.0	2.1	+7.3	+3.8
Spain	15.2	15.8	+7.2	+6.5
Sweden	2.2	1.3	+7.6	+10.9
Switzerland	1.0	0.6	+7.8	+5.3
UK	7.0	5.6	+6.4	+9.3
USA	6.8	5.2	+6.6	+6.1

SOURCE *The Economist*, 9 Feb. 1991; 20 April 1991.

REFERENCES

1. *World Development Report 1990*, World Bank, Oxford University Press New York, p. 7.
2. *The Economist*, 16 March 1991, p. 71.
3. Source of Figures (SOF): *The Economist*, London, 4 May, 1991, p. 105.
4. SOF: Op.cit., 18 August 1990, *South Korea Survey*, p. 15.
5. SOF: *World Development Report 1990*, p. 11, Table on pp. 180, 181.
6. Op.cit., p. 17, World Bank study entitled 'Sub-Saharan Africa: From Crisis to Sustainable Growth!'
7. Ibid., p. 15.
8. Op.cit., B. B. Conable, President World Bank in Foreword, p. iii.
9. 'A Survey of World Trade', *The Economist*, 22 Sept. 1990, p. 5.
10. OTCA = The Ommibus Trade and Competitiveness Act 1988.

3

The Historical Perspective: Capitalism, Socialism and Mixed Economy

Government during the Sixth and Seventh Plan periods (1980–1 to 1989–90), boldly decided to break with some of the policies of the past and embarked upon a series of measures, broadly described as 'liberalization'. The new policies met with immediate success, and not only was there economic revival and stimulated industrial and infrastructural growth, but also marked success was achieved in reaching the plan targets. The overall rate of growth of GDP in real terms increased to about 5.5 per cent per annum, which was commendable.

Fiscal and economic liberalization and emphasis on competition have yielded good results, but what is necessary is not only to further extend these policies but also to effect such dimensional changes with regard to the role of the public sector and inter-sectoral allocation of resources as would stimulate growth with equity and facilitate transition towards a market economy. We propose to discuss in this and the subsequent chapter the concept of liberalization; the genesis and basic assumptions of a liberal market economy and its strength and weaknesses; and the evolution of the welfare state and mixed economy. Since we will be covering a vast canvas and traversing the history of economic thought evolved over a period of more than two centuries, our survey will necessarily be selective, focusing on major trends and leading strands of thought relevant to our central theme.

CONCEPT OF LIBERALIZATION

Liberalization implies the diminution and curtailment of governmental controls and regulation of the vast fields of the establishment, financing, and working of industrial enterprises, business decision-making, inflow of foreign investment and other capital, pricing of certain commodities, earning and spending of foreign exchange, and various other aspects and sectors of the economy. It would also include the policy of reduced state intervention and privatization of public enterprises. In regard to foreign trade, it implies a diminution in the levels of protection and a shift from quantitative restrictions to tariffs.

While the role of the public sector is discussed in a subsequent section, we may observe that the adoption in the fifties of the centralized model of planning with emphasis on heavy industry—broadly described as the Mahalanobis model—largely along the lines of planning in the Soviet Union, resulted in concentration of economic power and decision-making in the hands of the state, and the private sector was obliged to function within the parameters laid down in the Industrial Policy Resolution and the framework of economic policies formulated by government. Almost every aspect of business policy and actions was controlled, and although functioning as a mixed economy, the predominant role in the economy was assigned to the public sector, and the vast network of controls (including the MRTP Act) hampered the progress and growth of the private sector. The allocation of economic resources and their investment in various sectors of the economy was determined in accordance with the priorities laid down in successive Plans. Funds mobilized from the private industrial sector and the household sector, through heavy taxation and savings, were largely channelized into investment in the public and agricultural sectors. The state, however, through the medium of financial institutions, provided part of the funds required by the private sector to finance the development of industries.

The large quantum of investment in the public sector did not yield adequate returns; and the overall rate of growth of GDP in the economy during the first three decades of planning was about 3.5 per cent. Progress in agriculture was also tardy and, besides, the return flow of funds to the budget through taxes or savings from this sector was negligible. While small savings were scattered in the hands of a large number of farmers and others in rural areas, agricultural taxation could not be imposed owing to a strong farm lobby. It was only with the consummation of the Green Revolution in this decade in certain parts of the country that growth in agriculture gathered momentum.

During the eighties, as stated, government adopted liberalization as a conscious policy. Principally it involved dismantling licensing and other controls over industry, a degree of de-regulation with regard to cement, steel, and certain other industries, lowering the rates of taxation and rationalization of fiscal and other economic policies, and opening up various sectors of industry to the private sector, including steel and power, entry to which had previously been largely restricted to the public sector. The policy in regard to inflow of foreign capital and technology was also liberalized. Price controls were reduced, and emphasis was placed on competition and improvement in technology and quality of products to stimulate exports and enable Indian industries to face external competition in international markets. The policy of liberalization was success-ful, but certain strains developed in the economy, including inflation, budgetary deficits, a foreign exchange crunch, and internal and external debt problems, of which more later (Chapter 11).

GENESIS OF LIBERALISM: DOCTRINES OF ADAM SMITH AND RICARDO

The study of modern economics and liberalism may well begin with the doctrines of Adam Smith, whose *Wealth of Nations* was published in 1776. He emphasized a self-regulating natural order and the inevitable imperfections of human institutions. If artificial restraints were removed, the simple system of natural liberty would assert itself. Every individual seeks to promote his own good, which he knows best and should be left free to pursue; he does not intend to promote public good, but in pursuing his own welfare each individual is 'led by an invisible hand to promote an end which was no part of his intention.... By pursuing his own interest, he frequently promotes that of the society more effectually than when he really intends to promote it.'[1] The intervention of governments in human affairs generally had deleterious effects.

Adam Smith asserted that if imported goods were cheaper than those produced at home, imports should be freely allowed and restrictions on internal trade, agriculture, and industry also were harmful. If the individual was allowed the freedom to maximize his profit, benefit would accrue to society as a whole. The State should concentrate only upon defence, justice, education and certain public works and institutions. Its principal duty was to preserve free competition, as only competition promoted natural liberty and ensured that all persons in society were rewarded with the just fruits of their labour. Competition also contributed to economic growth and satisfaction of human wants of all the members of society. If state policy strove to maintain competition, monopolies would cease to exist.

Adam Smith's doctrine of economic liberalism—*laissez-faire* in effect—constitutes the basis of the economic system of capitalism and free enterprise. It enabled Britain, which was on the eve of the Industrial Revolution, to achieve industrial growth and international leadership in that age. Together with Ricardo and Mill, Adam Smith constituted the Classical School. Ricardo's principal contribution was his theory of economic rent, which survives to this day, and the law of distribution of the national product amongst workers, landowners, and capitalists in the form of wages, rent, and profit. He asserted that since the total national product was limited, if the share of one class was increased, that of others would be reduced.

SAY'S LAW AND CLASSICAL ECONOMICS

Say's Law of Markets,[2] which constitutes the core of classical economic theory, holds that 'Supply always creates its own demand' and general over-production or glut of capital goods could never occur in an economy. The process of production of commodities involves payment of remuneration to the factors of production. These factor-incomes provide the purchasing power which generates demand for the goods produced. All production will therefore be sold, and as such there cannot be surplus or over-production, or unemployment. Full employment of labour and other resources was considered to be the normal state, and even if there was any deviation, the tendency would be towards restoration of full employment. Actually, according to classical economists, interference with market forces would result in unemployment, and consequently the state should refrain from intervention in the economic field.

A. C. Pigou argued that if interference by the state or trade unions ceased, prices, wages, and interest rates would find their own level by adjusting to the changed circumstances. The existence of competition would lead to reduction in wages until it became economical for entrepreneurs to provide employment to all those who sought work. Thus the free working of the economic system without interference from the State provides the basic remedy for unemployment. Pigou was not, however, a devotee of *laissez-faire* and argued that state intervention was necessary to reduce economic inequalities and control and check monopolies.

Alfred Marshall[3] belonged to the Classical school, and was a realist. In the formulation of his theories of value and distribution he endeavoured to make them fructuous and contribute to the determination of economic policies. He believed that value was determined by both supply and demand, which could be compared to the two blades of a pair of scissors: demand depended upon marginal utility, and supply upon marginal effort and sacrifice, reflecting the cost of production. In his analysis of equilibrium between supply and demand and determination of price, he emphasized the element of time. In the longer-term the influence of supply on price was greater, while in the shorter term, demand was crucial.

Similar techniques of analysis, particularly the marginal concept, were applied to the theory of distribution. Marshall established the relationship between income, supply, and demand of the factors of production, and the price of their products. In the long-run, the earnings of the factors of production would be equal to their marginal real cost. His insistence that supplies of factors were variable, partly determined by price, imparted a dynamism to his instruments of analysis, rendering them useful for application to real world problems. The concept of consumer's surplus developed by him was useful in assessing the effects of taxes on commodities with elastic and inelastic demand, and also inspired the development of welfare economics by A.C. Pigou.

Pigou[4] was deeply concerned about the best possible allocation of scarce resources between different users in society. He refers to certain maladjustments which prevent optimum allocation of resources between different occupations, when private interest has free play. The causes are: firstly, the value of the marginal private net product (MPNP) of resources employed exceeds or is less than the value of the marginal social net product (MSNP); and secondly, in the case of certain goods and services, the ratio between the people's desire and the satisfaction resulting from the fulfilment of desire is greater or less than that in respect of other goods and services. Thus, MSNP exceeds MPNP when the utilization of resources produces not only the planned goods or services which are sold and paid for, but also generate for the community certain products and services for which there cannot be a charge. The benefits of a lighthouse, for example, may also be availed of by ships which cannot be subjected to toll tax. Pigou was of the view that it would be equitable from the standpoint of least sacrifice, to impose taxes on unduly expanded occupations, and to provide bounties out of the proceeds to occupations which are unduly contracted.

Classical economists have emphasized cost, without paying attention to the demand side. Stanley Jevons, Carl Menger, and Leon Walras, in the late nineteenth century, advanced the theory of market mechanism by synthesizing utility and cost elements. The concept of marginal utility and its role in the determination of price, in conjunction with marginal cost, marked a real advance. Walras also introduced the concept of general competitive equilibrium. He showed how the economy as a whole could be analysed. In his theory of production, Walras applied his general equilibrium analysis to the problems of pricing the factors of production. Walras, Jevons, and Pareto introduced mathematics into economics. J. S. Mill was an ardent advocate of liberty and emphasized that the state or individuals are not justified in interfering with liberty of action of any person even for his own good; that interference may be warranted only to prevent harm to others.

Enjoying both economic and political freedom in the nineteenth century, the USA prospered greatly. America was a virgin field, government intervention and controls hardly existed, and there was infinite scope for energetic hard work, innovation and enterprise; these resulted in spectacular progress and dispersed development. Jefferson[5] (1801) proclaimed that the ideal of the state was that of a wise and frugal government which would restrain people from injuring one another, but otherwise leave them free to regulate their own pursuits of industry and improvement.

WELFARE STATE OR MIXED ECONOMY: THE MIDDLE WAY

The origins of the welfare state can be traced to Count Otto von Bismarck, who introduced in West Germany in the 1890s old age compensation, and sickness and accident insurance. About twenty-five years later, Lloyd George sponsored legislation in Britain, incorporating similar social security measures. It was, however, in the post Second World War period that the Beveridge Report provided a comprehensive scheme of social security, designed to transform Britain into a welfare state. Pigou gave intellectual support to social security measures. He believed that the transfer of resources from the rich to the poor increased the sum total of human satisfaction in society, as the marginal utility of money declined with its increase and was higher in the hands of the poor than the rich. This gave impetus to the movement towards the welfare state. Welfare measures also had an automatic stabilizing effect upon the economy. Compensation during times of unemployment and depression, by increasing purchasing power, acted as a compensatory factor, reducing unemployment and stimulating economic activity.

In 1935 social security measures were initiated in the USA. The point is that the welfare state was firmly established as a model of modern capitalism. Meanwhile, with rudimentary beginnings, by the early thirties Sweden had developed perhaps the most comprehensive social security system in the world, covering persons from the cradle to the grave. Consumer and farmer co-operatives were also established to provide support to farm prices. Besides, during the depression of the thirties, Swedish budgetary policy resorted to fiscal deficits in order to sustain demand and employment. It was almost a precursor to Keynes' doctrine published in his *General Theory*[6] in 1936.

These developments are significant, in that Sweden showed a *middle way* to a world engulfed in the great depression and greatly concerned about the weaknesses of the *laissez-faire* or capitalist system based on orthodox classical doctrines, which was unable to cope with the depression and unemployment, on the one hand, and Marxist and other revolutionary forces pressing for acceptance of socialism as an economic system, offering a millenium to the people, on the other. Further, orthodox classical economics received a severe blow from the ideas of Keynes, who repudiated Say's Law which holds that production creates its own demand and that full employment equilibrium always existed in society. Classical economics would be revived again in the second half of the twentieth century but the concept of the modern economic system of mixed economy had come to stay.

Essentially a compromise between *laissez-faire* or a competitive market economy and socialism, the modern mixed economy or welfare state covers a broad spectrum, with the US capitalist system at one end and economies with a large public sector like India at the other. But the essential similarity between the USA and India is that they are both democracies, individual freedoms exist and are immensely valued by the citizens of both the countries. The mixed economy has elements of both market and command. It relies essentially on the market system for its economic functioning, but there is state intervention in varying degrees in diverse fields to regulate the growth and operations of the private sector. In several countries, particularly developing ones, besides licensing and other restrictions, government seeks to modulate business activity through the operation of fiscal and monetary measures, and allocation of funds and credit facilities through financial institutions. The people in a mixed economy have freedom of consumption and choice of occupation. Allocation of resources in the private sector, between various industries and areas, is determined largely by operation of the price mechanism, but decisions regarding investment and output are influenced by the State. The entire gamut of decisions, however, regarding investment, production, pricing, location of industry, provision of funds and credit for the *public sector*, are taken by the central planning authority and government, although the modern trend is towards maximizing the autonomy, of public enterprises, particularly in regard to their operations.

Extensive social security and welfare measures, as earlier indicated, and factory and labour legislation, constitute an essential element of policy in most mixed economies. Transfer payments, subsidized food, and essential commodities made available through the public distribution system, progressive taxation and inheritance taxes, and various measures directed towards securing greater equality in incomes and wealth are a common feature. This is particularly true in developing economies with dualistic character—a poverty-ridden rural sector, existing side by side with an affluent urban sector with pockets of poverty. The state also actively seeks to curb monopolistic tendencies and unfair trade practices. An important change in state policies and attitudes is however in evidence. While in the early decades of the post-war period, the tendency was towards nationalization of core sector industries, utilities, and essential services like banking and insurance, during the eighties the trend is towards privatization. The UK Government under Margaret Thatcher took the lead, followed by many other countries. Besides, in most mixed economies, controls are being relaxed and liberalization measures initiated. The basic trend is towards transition to market economies, although state intervention and social security measures in some degree or the other have become integral features of modern mixed economies.

THE KEYNESIAN REVOLUTION

The great depression of the 1930s provided the perfect setting for the formulation of Keynes' Theory of Employment, Interest, and Money. While there was considerable unemployment and falling incomes in a number of economies, the classicists asserted that there could not be unemployment and the operation of an economic system would automatically produce full employment. They also emphasized that savings equalled investment and equilibrium always existed in an economy at full employment level, the rate of interest acting as the equilibrating mechanism between savings and investment.

Keynes' theory propounded that an increase in income, output, and employment results in an increase in consumption, but by a lesser amount, as the *marginal propensity to consume* is less than unity (one) and declines with increasing income. In other words, part of the increased income results in savings. Despite increase in the rate of interest, increased savings might not be invested for precautionary or other motives or the desire to hold liquid money, described by Keynes as *liquidity preference*. Also, employment was determined by Effective Demand, which in turn was determined by the Aggregate Demand Function (Receipts) and Aggregate Supply Function (Costs). The point at which the two functions were equal, was the level of effective demand and the economy was in equilibrium at that level. Entrepreneurs would continue to increase employment of workers (and other resources) so long as their receipts from sale of output exceeded their costs of producing that output, but would stop further employment at the point where receipts were equal to costs. Keynes stressed that this point did not necessarily represent full employment equilibrium as was believed by the classicists. It could be, and often was, under-employment equilibrium.

He argued that savings created a gap between income and consumption, and the fact that part of the savings were not invested accounted for unemployment. Investment needed to be stepped up to fill this gap and stimulate effective demand, which would increase employment. If investment was increased, total income would increase by an identical amount because investment creates income and the extra income would be sufficient to produce additional savings, equivalent to the quantum of new investment. Savings depend upon income and liquidity preference. Investment however depends upon output as well as return on capital employed, known as *marginal efficiency of capital* and rate of interest (besides business confidence and tax policy).

Keynes disagreed with Pigou's thesis that wage-cuts would increase employment; on the contrary, he said that wage-cuts, by reducing purchasing power in the hands of labour, would aggravate shortfall in demand and further increase unemployment and unsold production. Actually, Pigou viewed wages as a part of costs, while Keynes' conception was that wages constituted incomes and purchasing power.

The crux of Keynes' thesis was that in times of depression and unemployment, it was necessary for the state to intervene and increase investment by borrowing and spending on programmes of public works. The increase in money supply would increase aggregate demand and cover the deflationary gap. This would bring about adjustment between supply and demand and restore equilibrium, so as to reduce over-production and general unemployment. He put forward his concept of functional finance and asserted that in times of depression, the state should formulate deficit budgets. While the War contributed to the propagation of Keynes' ideas by demonstrating the success of state intervention, to Simon Kuznetz goes the credit of providing the statistical underpinnings of Keynes' Theory. He showed that the enormous expenditure by the State during the War resulted in breaking the underemployment equilibrium and full utilization of installed capacity of the productive apparatus. Kuznetz not only developed the concepts of Gross National Product and National Income, but also gave statistical values to the components. He provided estimates of Gross National Product through empirical investigation, giving details of the total production of various goods and services in the public and private sectors, as also the incomes of different kinds derived from various sources. Kuznetz's work on GNP accounting—described by Samuelson[7] as 'this great invention of the twentieth century'—immensely contributed to the advancement of macroeconomics, and secured the Nobel prize for him. Although classical economics suffered a setback, Friedrich von Hayek of the Chicago monetarist school maintained that 'the price system will fulfil [its]...function only if competition prevails, that is, if the individual producer has to adapt himself to price changes and cannot control them'.[8]

DISILLUSIONMENT WITH KEYNES' THEORY AND REVIVAL OF LIBERALISM

Keynesian philosophy was essentially a policy instrument designed to check depression and unemployment. Through State intervention in the form of deficit budgets and public spending, aggregate demand was increased in order to stimulate economic activity. But during the early seventies in the USA and other countries, inflation manifested itself, and with the oil shock by the end of 1973 it amounted to 13.5 per cent per annum (1974–5). Added to this, the cost–push effect of the price–wage spiral also became evident; high wage settlements resulted in high prices, which in turn escalated the pressure for further rises in wages.

The Keynesian remedy in reverse—deflation and increasing unemployment requiring reduction in public expenditure and hike in taxes—was neither popular nor politically expedient. Besides, these measures were ineffective against the newer type of wage–price inflation. The consequence was disillusionment with the Keynesian theory. The impotence of Keynesian policy instruments to check inflation, which was also accompanied by high levels of unemployment, stagflation in short, led to the search for other remedies. Economists, particularly monetarists, argued that government regulations and intervention should be reduced to encourage market competition. Besides, Milton Friedman and other economists of the Chicago school, who were exponents of the classical competitive market, advocated strong monetarist action in the form of reduction in effective monetary resources in the economy and increasing interest rates, both of which were politically acceptable measures.

Jimmy Carter in the USA and Margaret Thatcher in the UK were receptive to the prescription, and strong monetarist measures were initiated in these countries. Interest rates were substantially increased. The combined effect of a lower level of lending and deposit-creation owing to high interest rates restricted money supply and stagnating economic activity, inflation was controlled and prices declined to within tolerable limits. Monetarism had scored and Keynesianism suffered an eclipse. The success of the programme, even though unemployment was high (to be remedied later), gave a boost to liberalism and classicism. The monetarists asserted that the progress made and prosperity achieved by various capitalist economies during periods when there was no state intervention and later despite (limited) interference, bore testimony to the soundness and success of market economy and liberalism. Milton Friedman, Hayek, and others also referred to the price society had to pay for state intervention and rejection of the market's guiding hand and central role. Government interference had resulted in curtailment of economic and political freedom and threatened to stall economic progress.

ECLIPSE OF DEMOCRATIC SOCIALISM

Democratic socialism could perhaps best be described as a utopian concept, put forward by a galaxy of thinkers, including the Fabian socialists, but lacking in real substance. As an economic system it did not take root in any country, and remained more a theoretical model, deriving inspiration from Karl Marx and as a protest against the excess of early capitalist societies.

Certain characteristics of socialism are familiar, but bear repetition, if only to highlight the structural and conceptual weakness of the system: state ownership of all or the principal means of production, maximization of social security and welfare, establishment of a classless society, and equal opportunities for all. The institution of private property is sought to be abolished, and equal distribution of the national product is emphasized. The various tasks performed automatically in a market economy by competition and price mechanism are to be executed either by a central planning agency or regional boards and managers of public enterprises. These include, *inter alia*, decision on what to produce, how to produce, and for whom to produce; fixation of prices for the myriads of commodities and services provided by the state and nationalized industries; decisions with regard to remuneration of the factors of production, allocation of resources to achieve optimum output and incomes; and determination of the consumption and occupation of millions of people, besides satisfaction of the usual collective wants.

The tasks are formidable, and liberal socialists have pleaded for decentralization and freedom of management for public enterprises. They seek to have both planning and market pricing, so that the system provides the advantages of both conscious collectivist planning and freedom. The crucial point is whether it is possible to 'reproduce the capitalist pricing process without ... capitalist institutions: private property and the material means of production, market exchanges between independent firms, actual competition, risk taking, and the profit motive'.[9] If the liberal socialist economy cannot maintain an adequate pricing system it will not succeed. As Galbraith rightly says, 'Socialism, if one considers the variety of human wants and the complexity of the capital and labour structure for satisfying them, is a theoretical (and practical) impossibility. And it is intrinsically in conflict with liberty.'[10]

The alternative would be to introduce central planning and pricing by the planning authority and social security services. The state has also to determine fiscal and other economic policies, provide efficient economic management and, above all, operate public undertakings and collective farms at a high level of efficiency to provide goods, services, and food to the people, and to generate surpluses to plough back for growth. But if extensive and all-embracing centralized planning has to be introduced, all the citizens are to be servants of the state and decisions are taken by centralized authority and managers of public enterprises, would it be possible to retain the democratic character of socialism? Would it not inevitably lead to authoritarianism and suppression of personal liberty and initiative? Besides, even if under authoritarian socialism (in effect communism) in the Soviet Union and other countries, government has not been able to operate public undertakings, state departments and collective farms efficiently and effectively, would it be possible to achieve high levels of efficiency under a democratic set up?

The Labour Government in Great Britian nationalized a number of large-scale industries and utilities, but as is now well known, the operational efficiency attained was low, and return on investment meagre. In India and a number of other countries which have developed a sizeable public sector, occupying the key sectors of the economy, the results have also not been satisfactory. Many of the enterprises are in the red, while the return on capital employed is poor, certainly less than most comparable enterprises in the private sector. There is perceptible change and instead of nationalization, Great Britain and a number of European countries and Japan are engaged in privatization of industry.

LIBERALISM AND MARXISM:
WAS MILL A BETTER PROPHET THAN MARX?

Two centuries constitute a small period in the life of humanity, as aeons of time—unreckoned by man—have elapsed since the origin of the world. But the last 200 years constitute an eventful period. It has witnessed the rise and fall of totalitarian communism and democratic socialism, both deriving inspiration from Marxism. Writing in 1848 on the question whether capitalism or socialism would be the ultimate form of human society, John Stuart Mill said that this would 'depend mainly on one consideration, viz. which of the two systems is consistent with the greatest amount of human liberty and spontaneity'.[11] Mill also emphasized that freedom was indivisible and political liberty could not exist without economic freedom. Mill was assailed by doubts whether under communism, any haven would be left for individuality of character, or any scope for intellectual diversity and stimulating collision of thoughts and ideas, from which emanates mental and moral progress. He had forebodings that public opinion might become a tyrannical yoke; and the surveillance of an individual by the state (each by all) and the individual's absolute dependence on the latter would grind down all individuals into a dull uniformity of thought and action, and their liberty might be jeopardized. How prophetic!

Karl Marx (1818–83) was a great thinker and revolutionary who founded and provided leadership to a political movement and the ideological underpinnings to the philosophy of socialism. Marx's critique included a severe indictment of capitalism on a number of grounds:

1. that unequal distribution of power emanating from the ownership of property existed in capitalist society;

2. there was unequal distribution of income, and the workers,

who earned surplus value were deprived of it by capitalists and paid only the marginal wage, barely sufficient for subsistence;

3. recurring crises, depression, falling wages, unemployment and increasing 'immiserization' of the working classes were inevitable in the economic set up of capitalism, and these factors would sound its death-knell. Monopoly, increasing concentration of economic power and wealth in the hands of the capitalists, and exploitation of workers earning bare subsistence, inbuilt in the system, would lead to social polarization and revolt of the proletariat against the bourgeoisie and the establishment of the socialist (communist) state.

Marx's prophesies, however, did not materialize. The enormous productive power of capitalism, reinforced by advancing technologies, resulted in workers obtaining an increasing share of the national product, which together with welfare measures, brought about considerable improvement in their living standards. Besides, with the growth of large corporations, trade union strength and bargaining power (in the nature of countervailing power), also increased in proportion. The macroeconomic policies of governments contributed to warding off great depressions, crises, and unemployment. The 'ever-increasing misery' of the working classes, visualized by Marx did not come about, and the advanced industrial economies were insulated against the revolution he forecasted. In countries like the Soviet Union and China where revolution did occur, the revolt was against feudalism in the context of war and inner conflicts bordering on anarchy, and not against capitalism.

Besides, in a communist society, the state did not wither away, nor did it act as a benevolent arbiter of authority. On the contrary, government assumed centralized power and command—both political and economic—and individual liberty was suppressed. In the economic sphere also, the communist state, with its command economy, complete ownership of the means of production, collectivized farms, and centralized planning, accompanied by centrally determined allocation of resources and pricing, failed to attain the high levels of growth, production, and incomes earlier envisaged. The teeming millions of workers, who were all employed by the state were able only to achieve standards of living which were a fraction of the standards of affluence enjoyed by people in the West and Japan. The contrast was nowhere greater than in the two Germanies.

The picture that emerges today is that the communist system in the Soviet Union and Eastern Europe lies in a shambles while capitalism, based upon liberal market economy with varying degrees of state intervention, and emphasis upon personal liberty, fundamental rights, and upholding of human values, has flourished in the USA, Western Europe and most free democracies of the world. Mill proved to be a better prophet than Marx!

REFERENCES

1. Adam Smith, *The Wealth of Nations* (1776), ed. W. R. Scott, 1925, vol. ii, p. 206.
2. J. B. Say, *Traite d'Economie Politique*, cited in Alexander Gray, *The Development of Economic Doctrine*, Longmans Green, London, 1948, p. 267.
3. Alfred Marshall, *Principles of Economics*, 8 edn., Macmillan, London, 1947, pp. 124, 323 *et seq.* and 504 *et seq.*
4. A. C. Pigou, *Public Finance*, 3rd edn., Macmillan, London, 1956, p. 94.
5. Thomas Jefferson (1801) in first inaugural address quoted by Milton and Rose Friedman, *Free to Choose*, Secker & Warburg, London, 1980, p. 4.
6. J. M. Keynes, *General Theory of Employment, Interest and Money*, Macmillan, London, 1936.
7. Paul A. Samuelson and W. D. Nordhaus, *Economics*, McGraw Hill Int. ed., Singapore, 1985, p. 102.
8. Friedrich von Hayek, *The Road to Serfdom*, University of Chicago Press, Chicago, 1944, p. 49.
9. George N. Halm, *Economic Systems*, Oxford & IBH Pub. Co., Calcutta, 1960, p. 182.
10. J. K. Galbraith, *A History of Economics*, Hamish Hamilton, London, 1987, p. 190.
11. John Stuart Mill, *Principles of Political Economy*, 1852, Book II, Ch. 1, Sec. 3 (also ed. J.M.Robson, Toronto University Press, Toronto, 1965, p. 208).

4

Basic Assumptions of Liberal Economy: An Analysis

We now propose to examine, from a theoretical and analytical point of view, the basic assumptions of a liberal or free market economy; the extent to which these assumptions reflect actual conditions in real life; and the emergence of the mixed economy. The free market economy, as we will see, must be distinguished from present-day capitalist society and the system of *laissez-faire*.

In the case of both the *laissez-faire* and free market economies, it is assumed that there is no government interference. Yet basic differences exist: the free market economy is an abstract system and not an economic system prevalent in the real world. It is actually an ideal system (Halm), which constitutes the basis of capitalist models. It shows how the capitalist system would work, provided the assumptions upon which the system rests exist in their pure form. The *laissez-faire* (hands off) economy is a real world model, but in its pure form, has not existed anywhere (except to a large extent in Britain in the nineteenth century).

Let us now analyse the basic assumptions[1] of a liberal or free market economy:

1. It is a free society in which complete political and economic freedoms exist, and there is no coercion on the part of authority in any manner unless somebody impinges upon the rights of others.

2. The free market economy is completely free from state interference and is not controlled, regulated, or planned by government. Government, of course, performs its basic functions of providing good administration, maintaining law and order, defence preparedness, and foreign relations, ensuring the proper functioning of the economic system, and satisfaction of collective wants in general. But it does not issue directives as to what is to be produced, how and where people are to work, where factories are

to be located, and for whom production is to take place; and above all, it does not itself engage in productive activity, establish or take over industrial enterprises, or compete with private industry.

3. There are no monopolies in any form, and competition is assumed to be free, perfect, and pure. Free and perfect competition implies a market situation in which there are a large number of buyers and sellers of homogeneous commodities, competing with one another, and no firm has power by itself to influence the market price. Hence, under conditions of equilibrium, prices would tend to equal marginal cost on the supply side and marginal utility on the demand side.

4. The ownership of property and means of production are vested in private hands; and the factors of production, such as land and capital are privately owned. There is complete mobility of the factors of production, which can easily be transferred from one industry to another, while labour is free to work where it chooses and for the wage it is able to obtain.

5. The citizens in a free market economy have complete freedom with regard to: (a) what they choose to consume, thereby determining the consumption pattern in the economy; (b) selection of occupation or profession for earning their livelihood; (c) disposal of their income and its allocation between present and future consumption; in other words, the quantum of savings they retain by sacrificing present consumption; and (d) the mode and nature of investment of their savings. Thus savings and investment are determined by the households themselves without any external influence.

6. Finally, it is assumed that in a free market economy, income is derived in monetary form, by the factors of production—land, labour and capital—by sale of their goods and services; and in the shape of profits earned by operating industries privately owned by them.

BASIC ASSUMPTIONS

Let us now consider how far the assumptions of the abstract model of a free market economy are actually found in the modern capitalist system. The latter, however, is clearly distinguishable from the *laissez-faire* system, as in most economies of the free world, state intervention (besides satisfying collective wants) does take place in some degree or the other.

During the last fifty years, even in the USA, the bastion of capitalism, the role of government in the economy has been expanding. It actually began during the great depression of the 1930s in international trade, and was extended to the domestic field. Depression was regarded as the failure of the liberal market economy and led to the proliferation of governmental intervention in many directions, including transfer of power from local and state governments to the federal government. Transfer payments directed at provision of social security, as also intertwined with egalitarian objectives, increased; while policies ostensibly designed to regulate operations of industry and improvements, promote education, protect the consumer, avoid unemployment, and check cyclical fluctuations in the economy, resulted in extension of the scope and field of government intervention. There has hardly been any movement in the reverse direction. Milton Friedman[2] believes that 'the limitations imposed on our economic freedom threaten to bring two centuries of economic progress to an end. Intervention... has greatly limited our human freedom.'

What is true of the US economy is more starkly evident in the case of other capitalist systems. In Britain, for instance, the Labour Government introduced various socialist measures within the democratic framework, including nationalization (and re-nationalization) of various utilities, core sector and other large-scale industries. State controls and regulations expanded, and the powers of trade unions increased. Government sought to provide maximum social security, but results have not proved satisfactory. When the National Health Service encountered difficulties, people increasingly turned to private medical services. Unemployment and inflation graphs soared. The operation and profitability of public enterprises was unsatisfactory. Economically, Britain lagged behind other European countries. Dissatisfaction with the Labour government grew in intensity, and in 1979 Margaret Thatcher was re-elected with a majority. Thatcher turned the tide, gave great impetus to privatization of industry, reduced state intervention and controls, and checked the power of trade unions. The economy made a miraculous recovery, of which more later.[3] In Sweden also, similar difficulties as in Britain surfaced. Inflation and high levels of unemployment, dissatisfaction with high taxes and social security programmes manifested themselves. The tide turned and there was a change of government. It is clear therefore that capitalism does not exist anywhere in the world in its pure *laissez-faire* form, and most countries have mixed economies in which both the private and public sectors (of varying magnitudes) coexist, and there is state intervention to a limited or extensive degree.

In any society, the optimum allocation of scarce economic resources is of vital importance, both from the point of view of growth and equity. Society must determine three fundamental economic problems which are, however, interdependent: (1) what goods should be produced and in what quantities; (2) how should the commodities be produced; and (3) for whom the goods should be produced. While in a centrally planned economy, the central planning authority, in consultation with government, takes these vital decisions, in a market economy these matters are decided largely by free economic forces, that is, by a system of markets, prices, incentives, and profits. Firms produce goods which yield the maximum profits to them; they employ the best techniques available in order to produce goods at the lowest cost; and the production of commodities meant for consumption by the people is determined by the decision of the consumers, casting their dollar ballots on how they propose to spend their wages, profits, and incomes. Most capitalist economies in the West do not have centralized planning, although in France indicative planning has been in existence for many years. The allocation of scarce economic resources, however, particularly in the case of public sector investment, may not be entirely left to market forces, and the authorities may also interfere with other economic processes. The degree and dimension of state intervention is indeterminate, depending as it does upon the discretion of the authorities.

Political liberty is the *sine qua non* of true democracy and most economies of the West are largely based upon adult franchise, with an actively functioning sovereign parliament representing the will of the people, and an independent judiciary upholding the rule of law. But in certain developing countries,[4] dictatorship may replace democracy, leading to negation or dilution of political liberty. Inevitably, economic freedoms also suffer erosion, although basically the capitalist system may be maintained. The process of determining the allocation of resources (other than public sector investment), pricing commodities, remunerating the factors of production, and other vital issues are largely determined by market forces. Government, however, quite often seeks to influence decisions indirectly through fiscal and monetary policies, tariffs, and other economic measures, as necessary. Direct state intervention is also possible and does sometimes occur in accordance with the exigencies of the situation. Actually, capitalism manifests itself in a diluted form, and most countries have developed a welfare state. The objective of government action is usually the promotion of public interest and the welfare of society.

What about other assumptions? Individuals in real market economies are free to choose their occupations, but in actuality, occupational choice is conditioned by education, training, innate ability, and general market conditions. Education and training positively tend to secure equality of opportunity and consequently equality of incomes. But if there is depression in the economy and widespread unemployment is prevalent, jobs may not be available for all those willing to work. In that event, both mobility and the freedom to choose occupations is limited. Individuals have the freedom in a capitalist society to save and invest according to their choice. But escalation in taxes reduces post-tax incomes, and the marginal propensity to consume remaining constant, the quantum of savings is reduced. Besides, taxes may be kept high and provision made in tax laws to allow tax rebates on investment in life insurance policies, national savings certificates, public provident and mutual funds, or new company shares. Overtly, the individual is still free to modulate his savings and investment at will, but actually there is an inbuilt compulsion to save and invest in approved channels if tax allowances are to be claimed. Essentially, however, individuals have the freedom to determine the quantum of savings and investment of funds.

The capitalist system has been subjected to the criticism that unemployment is often high, particularly in times of depression. Productive resources may be wasted and opportunities for employment and growth of national income may remain below their full potential. However, with the advent of Keynes' theory and functional finance, counter-cyclical measures in a depression are generally initiated, quite often with success. Even otherwise, in most countries, active efforts are made by governments to stimulate employment, alleviate poverty and to provide compensation or relief under social security schemes. One of the assumptions of capitalism was that free or perfect competition exists in society. However, in actual practice, owing to the induction of technology and establishment of large corporations, monopolistic tendencies tend to constrict competition. Besides, thanks to the profit motive, owners of capital and means of production try to establish monopolies to maximize their gains. The state in a number of countries has been intervening to curb monopolies and such other devices for reducing competition. Anti-trust laws have been promulgated and sometimes monopolistic combines broken up.

The growth of the public sector in a number of countries, including Britain, France, Italy, and a great many developing countries, has resulted in the state not only engaging in industrial activity but also in competing with the private sector, to the detriment of the latter. The state has also in certain countries (for instance, India), been determining prices of certain goods produced by the private sector. Administered prices have sometimes resulted in distortions in supply and demand, and also in retarding the growth of industries.[5] Pricing of commodities is best left to the operation of the market mechanism.

The ownership of property and means of production in capitalist societies is largely in private hands, leading to a degree of concentration of economic power and inequality in incomes. A consequence of this could be that the choice of consumption in the case of the underprivileged is curtailed to that extent. However, there are many countervailing factors to dilute the effect of such concentration in modern societies. Of this more later.[6]

This critical analysis of the assumptions of the concept of a free market economy shows that in the real world, while some of the assumptions do not exist, others are found in diluted form or conditioned by other factors. Yet it is undeniable that capitalism, in the shape of the mixed economy with free markets, not only survives but flourishes both in the West and in developing economies with democratic regimes.

Shift Towards Liberalization

There has been a great revival of liberalism and classical economics; besides, the US administration under Ronald Reagan and the British Government under Margaret Thatcher implemented a series of measures, including sizeable reduction in tax levels, rationalization of social security programmes, and reduced state intervention, which marked a real shift in policies towards liberalization. The wheel has turned full circle, and in the UK, other Western countries, and Japan, privatization of government-owned industries and enterprises is being effected in place of nationalization and expansion of the public sector, which during the post-war period was regarded as an important component of progressive government policy.

The failure of centralized planning, not only in the Soviet Union, but in other countries also which adopted it, to sufficiently accelerate growth and stimulate production and incomes, the inability of the public sector to attain the requisite levels of operational efficiency and generate surpluses, and the healthy effect in capitalist economies of measures involving reduction in controls and taxes, have all tended to buttress the demand for extended liberalization and transition towards a market economy, with minimal controls, taxes, and state intervention. This has been reinforced by the assertions of distinguished libertarians[7] like Milton Friedman and Hayek that political and economic freedoms are like Siamese twins, one cannot exist without the other; and that government governs best which governs least. But then this is precisely what Adam Smith, Ricardo, and Mill insisted upon two centuries ago. We have come back after traversing the wide expanse of economic history to the point where we started. The assumptions of liberalism may only partially exist, but the doctrine of the free market economy and Adam Smith's theory of the 'invisible hand' are sound, and capitalism based upon this philosophy is as vibrant as ever. While other economic systems are withering away—to use Marxist phraseology—transition to a market economy, privatization, and liberalization are on the upswing.

REFERENCES

1. George N. Halm, *Economic System*s, Oxford & I.B.H. Pub. Co., Calcutta, 1960, p. 22.
2. Milton and Rose Friedman, *Free to Choose*, Secker & Warburg, London, 1980, p. 64.
3. *Vide* ch. 7.
4. Bangladesh in the recent past, for instance.
5. The Fertilizer Industry; and the Cement Industry before decontrol in India.
6. *Vide* ch. 16.
7. Libertarians = economists who lay stress upon the central role of personal freedom in economic affairs.

5

Challenges and Strategies for Developing Economies in the Nineties

CHALLENGES OF THE NINETIES

The challenges facing the nation during the ensuing decade, which is a precursor to the twenty-first century, are basically to increase, through planned economic development, the prosperity of the people, effect an improvement in the standards of living, reduce unemployment, and to alleviate poverty in the country. The basic necessities of life, such as food, clothing, shelter, elementary education, and health services have to be provided. While pursuing the directive principles laid down in the Constitution, conditions have to be created in which every person has the opportunity to develop to his fullest potential. In this context restructuring the educational system assumes great importance.

The dimensions and parameters of a strategy of development are determined by the challenges confronting the nation and the objectives that are to be achieved. Broadly, the backward and traditional mould of the economy has to be transformed into a modern and forward-looking society, and the institutional framework, economic, social and political, has to be strengthened. The economy must move into a higher orbit of growth-rate and transcend the stage of self-sustaining growth. The strident advances in science and technology—which are engines of growth—have to be harnessed for modernization of industry, agriculture, and defence. Capital has to be productively used and installed capacity fully utilized to increase production. Efficient implementation of plan projects needs to be ensured through effective supervision, and public expenditure rendered more fructuous. District level planning, monitoring, and decentralization have to be effected in order to ensure that the benefits of welfare measures reach the target groups in full. While backward areas have to be developed, regional imbalances reduced, and the social and economic services and public distribution system made more efficient, it is imperative to control population growth so that the fruits of development are not neutralized by increase in numbers.

The NIEs of South-East Asia, particularly South Korea, Singapore, Hong Kong, and Taiwan—the Asian tigers—as also Thailand and Malaysia, have demonstrated that developing economies have enormous potential for growth. With the induction of foreign investment capital and modern technology, and with liberalized policies in a competitive environment and stimulated exports, economies can be dynamized, and a sustained rate of growth between 10 to 12 per cent per annum in real terms achieved, leading to a diminution in the gap between the developed and developing countries. Stating that structural reforms have to be co-ordinated and appropriately sequenced to maintain macroeconomic and fiscal balance, and that management of such reforms will prove a challenging task, the World Bank in its 1991 Country Memorandum for India presented at the Aid India Consortium[1] went on to say: 'India has the industrial and human resource base to match the growth performance of the successful East Asian countries. Tapping this potential requires both stabilization and fundamental reforms that, among other things, redefine the role of the state…India needs sustained faster growth at or above the 5.3 per cent per annum rate of 1980s.' One of the basic challenges facing the country is to emulate these achievements and strengthen the country's industrial and agricultural base and technological capabilities, so as to accelerate the momentum of growth, while ensuring allocative efficiency, economic stability (control of inflation), and distributive justice.

Dynamic as is the modern world, the nature of the problems and challenges facing a nation keep on changing, and hence flexibility in planning, policy framework, and instrumentalities for its implementation are imperative. Modification in the strategy of growth may be necessitated by internal and external developments, such as an increase in the prices of essential imports like oil, effect of protectionism abroad on exports, or availability of external credits. Changes in the level of incomes, prices, and availability of goods and services may also necessitate modification in the allocation of resources. A consensus is now developing that the economy must grow rapidly, even if this involves taking some hard decisions and modification of age-old policies. We shall now address ourselves to the evolution of new strategies of growth to enable the country to face the challenges of the nineties.

'STRATEGY' DEFINED

Clausewitz on War[2] defines 'Strategy' as 'the employment of the battle as the means towards the attainment of the object of the War'. Strategy determines the plan and 'links together the series of acts' (chain of actions) which lead to the final decision. Strategy must deploy forces according to plan, but effect modifications in the general scheme in response to the exigencies of the situation. Genius lies not so much in the invention of new modes of action, as in the 'exact fulfilment of silent suppositions, the noiseless harmony of the whole action', which manifests itself in the final result. Applied to the economic sphere, 'Strategy' has parallel implications. Battles have to be won in various fields to achieve the ultimate objective of economic growth and human welfare. Strategy incorporates the whole gamut of economic planning, management, and implementation; it links together the series of acts that constitute the entire development process; and it covers the set of fiscal, industrial, and other economic policies directed to achieve the planned objectives. It provides for coordinated progress on all fronts, and for flexibility that facilitates modification in plans and the policy framework from time to time, as necessitated by developing situations (oil price rise or drought, for instance). The success of the strategy would be judged by the final denouement, the extent to which the targets and goals have been attained.

The achievement of a higher growth-rate in the eighties is creditable, but this has been accompanied by a decline in the balance of payments position and foreign exchange reserves, and a rise in internal borrowings and external indebtedness; besides, the level of investment has been sustained through a cumulative rate of inflation of about seven to eight per cent. Inflation is the most insidious and regressive form of taxation and adversely affects the weakest sections of society. We shall address these and other problems in the course of evolving the new strategy.

INTER-SECTORAL MISMATCH BETWEEN PRIVATE SAVINGS
AND PUBLIC DEMAND FOR INVESTMENT

While stepping up the domestic savings rate from 10 per cent of GDP in the early fifties to above 21 per cent in 1985–6 has been a commendable performance, savings have stagnated during the last four years in the region of 21 to 22 per cent. Actually, the bulk of the increase in savings has taken place in the household sector. As Sukhamoy Chakravarty[3] said, 'This has involved an inter-sectoral mismatch between the increase in savings and the increase in demand for investment. The public sector, whose savings have not increased proportionately, has been obliged to rely, in growing measure, on borrowing from households. This is the crux of the problem of plan financing.' It has resulted in a vicious circle of heavy borrowings, escalating interest burden, and further borrowings to meet the interest and other liabilities, largely on account of public sector consumption.

Prof. Chakravarty raised a fundamental issue, central to the Indian fiscal policy framework, which needs to be addressed. It has been established that, (a) the investment in public enterprises does not yield adequate surpluses and revenues; (b) the proliferation of activities by the public sector and the continual escalation in non-plan expenditure have necessitated transfer of considerable funds from private savings, but the outlays have not yielded commensurate returns, nor has there been efficient utilization of money invested. Actually, part of the money has not reached the target groups and there have been wastages and leakages; and, (c) the level of efficiency in the private sector and the return on capital employed are normally higher than in the public sector, as also the quantum of capital investment required for generating employment per head is lower in the former.

Any calculus of cost-benefit analysis, in the context of the above, would suggest a dimensional change in the pattern of sectoral allocation of resources in the economy between the public and private sectors. The public sector outlays—both plan and non-plan—need to be drastically curtailed, which postulates a containment of its role (discussed in the next section) and an enlargement of the role of the private sector in the country's industrial and infrastructural development. The sector that generates savings and has the capacity to utilize such savings more efficiently and economically, should be allowed to retain the bulk of the savings for purposeful investment. The state should act only as an adviser and guide to the private sector, even as the allocation of investment resources is largely influenced by market forces, which in any case cannot for long be ignored by the state or the private sector.

The fundamental question of inter-sectoral mismatch of savings and demand for investment thus reinforces our central thesis that the evolution of a new strategy of growth for the nineties is imperative to,

(a) step up the rate of growth in the economy;

(b) reduce the incremental capital–output ratio;

(c) resolve the problem of inter-sectoral mismatch between private savings and demand for investment, applying some restraint upon the ever-increasing public sector borrowing and the consequent interest burden, and reducing budgetary imbalances;

(d) effect a dimensional change in the role of the public and private sectors in the development of the economy; and

(e) reduce the role of government agencies in centralized decision-making, and allow market forces to play their natural role—subject to such checks as are necessary—in the allocation of resources and the pattern of investment. Actually, the trend towards placing greater emphasis on market incentives and substituting indirect policy instruments for direct physical controls has commenced, although it is yet to gather momentum.

The new strategy must impart momentum to the processes of growth; exploit the ever-widening impulses that are generated in the economy as a consequence of the modified policy framework, patterns of investment and production, and induction of science and technology; and achieve accelerated growth which alone can provide the wherewithal for improved welfare and better standards of living for the people.

ROLE OF THE PUBLIC SECTOR IN THE TRANSITIONAL AND TAKE-OFF STAGES OF GROWTH

The economy is basically sound and poised for growth; what is needed is a thrust and momentum. In order to accelerate the rate of growth, one of the imperatives is to redefine the role of the public sector. Essentially, the public sector should largely concentrate on infrastructural development like power, oil, transport, communications and other utilities, and industrial fields which the private sector is not able to develop. The burden of development of the rest of the industrial economy should devolve on the private sector. The basic thinking behind the new strategy is to improve the overall efficiency and productivity of investment, achieve better utilization of resources, and plough back surpluses to generate further growth.

During the early fifties, when plans were formulated, emphasis was placed on two key aspects: capital formation and implementation within the framework of a mixed economy in which the public sector was to occupy a dominant position. P. N. Dhar has said,[4] 'The Keynesian analysis of the determinants of the level of activity as extended by Harrod–Domar models...laid heavy emphasis on increase in capital stock as the key element for economic growth.... The plans were implemented in the framework of a mixed economy with an increasing role for the public sector and a state-regulated private sector.' Under the policy framework, as determined, the public sector was to occupy the 'commanding heights in the economy' and new investment in basic and core sector industries was to be made largely in the public sector. Increased allocation of resources to the public sector *vis-à-vis* the private sector was intended to give it a greater share in the capital stock in the community. Greater regulation and control over private sector industries was to be exercised to ensure that the growth of the private sector was within the parameters and in accordance with the objectives defined in the Plan. Emphasis was also laid upon infrastructural development, but the power, communication, and rail transport sectors were to be developed by the public sector. The constituent elements of the strategy for rural development included, *inter alia*, stimulating agricultural growth through improved supply of inputs and better availability of rural credit, effecting structural changes in the socio-economic framework and institutions in the rural areas, and building large and medium irrigation projects by the state.

When a policy decision was taken that the public sector would occupy the 'commanding heights in the economy', it was envisaged that it would tackle critical infrastructural and unexploited areas of development which the private sector was hesitant to enter, and provide the thrust to the country's efforts towards technological self-reliance. Besides, there were also certain socio-economic objectives to be fulfilled during the last two decades. But conditions have now changed and the economic setting is different.

The private sector has developed immense capabilities, technical and managerial, to build and operate industries which the public sector had in the past pioneered. Besides, speaking objectively, the average efficiency of private sector enterprises is on the whole greater than that of public sector and joint sector projects. This is partly attributable to the profit motive on the one hand and lack of autonomy in public enterprises on the other. However, there is mismanagement also in some areas in the private sector, as is evident from the sizeable number of sick units. However that may be, it cannot be gainsaid that the overall operational efficiency and return on capital employed in public sector units are disappointing and have a decelerating effect upon the economy as a whole.

While formulating schemes to finance the Seventh Plan, credit was taken for flow of sizeable resources to be generated by public enterprises, but unfortunately the financial results, operational efficiency, and resources generated have not lived up to expectations. They have failed to augment the revenues of the state and provide resources for further development in fresh fields. The joint sector concept was developed and implemented to provide an amalgam of private sector managerial efficiency with public sector financial participation and a certain degree of monitoring. Empirical evidence shows that while certain large joint sector projects in Gujarat, Maharashtra, and the South have performed well, there are a number of medium-sized projects where the results have been disappointing or which are suffering from sickness or potential sickness. The inevitable conclusion is that although in large projects, financial participation by the public sector may facilitate financing of the project, dual management does not provide the answer to the problem of achieving optimum productivity and operational efficiency.

The state, as we have seen, was expected to ensure the growth of infrastructure, without which the superstructure of economic development is not feasible. Power, transport, communications, coal, oil, fertilizers, and irrigation works and dams are all essential for growth. But unfortunately, the public sector in India failed to develop infrastructure adequately,[5] with consequent deleterious effect upon growth.

We now approach a crucial question. What about the public

sector, built up over the past few decades with huge investment? The production covers a vast medley of goods and commodities, ranging from steel, cement, coal, and oil to heavy engineering, electricals and chemicals, machine tools, telecommunication equipment, and textiles, paper, and watches to gold, diamonds, bread, and shoes. Many of these units were incorporated in the public sector, while others, through nationalization or take-over of sick industries, as considered expedient, were acquired from time to time. The committee of senior secretaries of the government in 1990–1 appointed to review the public sector and improve its performance, is reported to have taken a decision that some chronically loss-making concerns should either be closed down or disposed of. The decision is rational and praiseworthy.

There is no doubt that privatization of certain of the units is an appropriate remedy, but the dilemma may be that units which are losing heavily and are over-burdened with surplus labour, may not find buyers, while government may be disinclined to part with units which are performing well. Besides, the feasibility of giving shares to workers or to the public would be limited to profit-making companies. One point should be clear. According to Oskar Lange,[6] nationalization was not a policy for the timid; this, ironically, also applies to privatization. Assuming that government has the boldness to take drastic decisions—and intractable problems call for tough resolutions—a high-powered committee may draw up a list of industries which government would like to retain and the balance privatized. In the eventuality of some of the loss-making units proving to be unsaleable, they may either be closed down or leased out. The scheme outlined above seems to be the only practicable way of avoiding the drain of resources by losing concerns and low productivity units. Besides, as in the UK, the proceeds of privatization of industries would contribute towards balancing the budget, reducing the heavy burden of accumulated debts and losses incurred by inefficient industries. The financial institutions are more or less controlled by the state and act under the direction of the ministry of finance. This is a sector which has functioned efficiently. As the country progresses towards a market economy, part of the shares may be offered to the public, and the institutions made wholly autonomous.

The real issue today is in regard to the extent to which the public sector should participate in industrial development activities. The truth is that there is general disillusionment all over the world, and even in communist countries, about the benefits accruing to the economy from investment in the public sector, and this is attributable to the generally inefficient performance of public enterprises. Basically, the allocation of resources in the community, after providing for the requirements of the public sector for its traditional functions, as well as defence production and development of nuclear energy, space resarch, and allied activities, should be left to the operation of market forces. There should be free competition in production, free choice in consumption, and the principles of social market economy should be allowed to operate. The financial institutions may discourage investment in the production of commodities which have low priority or where outlays would be infructuous. Otherwise, the entire field of industrial activity should be assigned to the private sector for development.

Limits to State Intervention

Empirical evidence of growth experience the world over during the second half of the twentieth century suggests the necessity of a reappraisal of the role of the state and the market. Basically, the countries where state intervention had been kept to a minimum like West Germany, Japan, and the USA achieved higher rates of growth than countries like the UK (till the seventies), Eastern Europe and the Soviet Union. In the developing world too, NIEs like South Korea, Taiwan, Singapore and Hong Kong performed better than China, Brazil, Ghana and Indonesia. India's performance improved in the eighties with liberalization; and China also forged ahead when it moved towards a more market-oriented system. The *World Development Report 1991*[7] advises that state intervention should take place only in areas where the markets cannot function effectively; conversely, governments should not undertake work in areas and sectors in which markets and the private sector are able to function efficiently (*vide* chapter 22). The state should also encourage domestic and international competition.

These conclusions reached by the World Bank on the basis of its extensive analysis and study of trends in development broadly confirm our assessment of the role of the public sector. It is felt that the return in money terms on investment in the public sector, as also on the basis of cost-benefit analysis, is inadequate, and a consensus is developing that further investment in this sector should be severely limited. Several countries are resorting to privatization of public enterprises to increase operational efficiency in a competitive environment to generate surpluses for growth and buttress public revenue.

REFERENCES

1. World Bank, 'Country Economic Memorandum for India presented at Aid India Consortium meeting in Paris in Sept. 1991', *The Economic Times*, Calcutta, 7 October 1991.
2. *Clausewitz on War*, ed. Anatol Rapoport, Penguin Books, Harmondsworth, 1968, p. 241.
3. Sukhamoy Chakravarty, *Development Planning, the Indian Experience*, OUP, Delhi, 1987, p. 83.
4. P. N. Dhar 'Past Performance and Current Issues' in *The Indian Economy*, ed. R.E.B. Lucas and G. F. Papanek, OUP, Delhi, 1988, pp. 4, 6.
5. *Vide* ch. 7, section on Infrastructure.
6. Oscar Lange and F.M. Taylor, *On the Economic Theory of Socialism*, University of Minnesota Press, Minneapolis, 1956, p. 125.
7. *World Development Report, 1991*, World Bank/OUP, New York, p. 9.

6

Elements of Growth: Crucial Role of Capital Formation

Traditional society is characterized by low per capita income, high consumption and a low level of savings and investment. Capital assets in real terms, such as plant and machinery and equipment, are inadequate; science and technology and their application to the processes of production, barely exist. Above all, the economic, social and legal institutional framework is not developed. Without education and work-experience, skilled workers are not available. Besides, feudal elements may be so powerful that the gains of development are almost entirely appropriated by them, with the consequence that there is hardly any motivation for the vast number of people to take the initiative and stimulate growth and incomes.

Development of underdeveloped economies implies transformation of the entire economic and social structure of society and modernization of the institutional framework. D. Goulet[1] emphasizes three basic components of development: freedom, life-sustenance, and self-esteem. The people must have political and economic freedom. They should be free from want, ignorance, and squalor, for it is obvious that unless a person has access, in an adequate measure, to the basic necessities of life such as food, clothing, housing, education, and health services, he will virtually be a prisoner on the margin of subsistence with no education and no skills. Only if the means of subsistence are available can a person develop his self-esteem, higher values, and culture. With education and development of technical skills, there is progressive improvement in standards of living and material wealth. As incomes increase, the proportion of income absorbed by consumption declines and savings can be made, making investment possible. In order to reach the take-off stage or stage of self-sustaining growth, the economy must increase savings and investment from 3 to 5 per cent to 12 to 15 per cent of GDP.

CRITICAL INPUTS FOR DEVELOPMENT

Capital and technology are the principal missing components of growth in underdeveloped economies. But what may be as important as capital and know-how, is the need to overcome certain inherent deficiencies: political and economic instability, lack of competent organs of public administration and infrastructure, poor literacy and inadequate trained manpower, dearth of entrepreneurial and management skills, and motivation. Effective government, education, and social justice emerge as critically important factors for development. It is clear that in order to efficiently use real capital assets and productive capital imported from abroad or developed indigenously a conducive environment is necessary, as also the creation of economic and social overheads, and the institutional framework that is a necessary accompaniment. It is true that technicians may also be invited from the machinery suppliers and persons may be sent abroad for acquisition of technical skills, but the prerequisites of development indicated above are imperative for the initiation and progress of developmental schemes in society in order to achieve comprehensive growth.

Arthur Lewis, Nurkse, Schumpeter, Libenstein and various other leading growth economists have propounded seminal propositions on the elements necessary for stimulating growth, such as massive investment by entrepreneurs creating recurring waves of industrial progress necessary to break the underdevelopment equilibrium, the critical minimum effort necessary, and other factors. It would be useful for readers to familiarize themselves with some of the principal theories and propositions, and we shall now deal with them.

W. ARTHUR LEWIS' ANALYSIS OF CAUSES OF GROWTH

Let us now consider the constituent elements of a development strategy. The obvious beginning of such a study would be to project Sir W. Arthur Lewis' basic propositions about the causes of growth which, despite the passage of some eventful decades of development of underdeveloped economies, remain as relevant and valid as when propounded. Lewis identifies three principal causes of growth, which are usually coexistent: (a) capital formation which involves per capita increase in capital and other resources; (b) increase in knowledge and its application to the processess of production; and (c) 'the effort to economize, either by reducing the cost of any given product, or by increasing the yield from any given input of effort or of other resources. This effort to economize shows itself in various ways; in experimentation, or risk-taking; in mobility, occupational or geographical; and in specialization, to mention only its chief manifestations.'[2] Lewis distinguishes between economic and other institutions and policies which are favourable to growth and those inimical to it, and emphasizes the need to create a new legislative and administrative framework more suitable for economic growth. He suggests that a part of the state's revenues should be used to finance productive enterprises through government financial institutions, such as Development Banks. These words are prophetic. Most developing countries have established such Banks and they have played a catalytic role in financing new industrial enterprises and expansion of existing ones.

A government's decision to absorb a large percentage of profits in taxes has momentous consequences. It may sharply inhibit growth both by removing the incentive to invest, and also by depriving firms of the finance for new investment. It has taken economists and administrators more than thirty years to imbibe this simple message. After experimenting with high taxes—the maximum marginal rate of personal taxation at times exceeding 97 per cent in certain countries, both developing and developed—the world trend today is towards low taxes.

It was increasingly felt that leaving the allocation of scarce economic resources in developing economies in the initial stages of growth simply to the market mechanism is fraught with danger of misallocation of resources and distortion in development. Part of the resources may gravitate towards production of consumer goods for the élite, which may offer attractive returns, while the infrastructure and basic industries, usually capital intensive, may be starved of funds. The provision at least of the basic amenities of life like food, clothing, shelter, health services, and the rudiments of education is imperative in society. The logical answer appears to be that planning of some kind is necessary, *inter alia* to identify, mobilize and stimulate generation of resources, both physical and financial, and to effect their allocation according to predetermined priorities and to ensure that they are used efficiently and economically.

MISSING ELEMENTS IN PLANS: GALBRAITH'S PROPOSITION

J. K. Galbraith[3] is of the view that modern development plans are usually investment plans, reflecting decisions on the best employment of scarce capital resources. The principal objective is to accomplish an adequate rate of economic growth. The various segments of the plan have to be matched and phased. Efforts are directed at mobilization of capital and investment resources to finance the plan from internal and external resources. He emphasizes that, besides the usual formulation of the plan, there are three further and often missing elements of a good plan. The plan should incorporate a strategy for the economy to progress. Priority should be accorded to certain infrastructural matters which are vital, such as a highly efficient transport system, low cost supply of steel and reliable sources of power. These are of basic importance for industrialization. Similarly, water, fertilizers, and improved seeds can revolutionize agriculture. Other elements are also important, but priorities have to be determined.

Besides physical targets, attention must be given at any stage of development to managerial performance, labour productivity, costs and returns. Targets should be fixed for achievement in these spheres too. Modern planning must incorporate a theory of consumption. Besides deciding how much should be withheld from present consumption, it is also necessary to determine in the plan the overall consumption pattern in the economy. For a developing country, principal attention should be given to wage-good items of mass consumption. Modernization and upgradation of technology to increase production, reduce costs, and maintain international competitive ability are indispensable. Induction of the latest technology is of even greater significance for a developing country, which must export, remain competitive, and earn foreign exchange to pay for developmental imports in an adverse, protectionist economic environment.

BREAKING THE UNDERDEVELOPMENT EQUILIBRIUM

Economic growth, particularly in the early stages of development, is a function of capital formation. The importance of accumulation of capital as the leading factor for economic growth has been recognized by all. Ragnar Nurkse believes that the dichotomy between demand and supply is also applicable to the forces that account for accumulation of capital. The well-known vicious circle of poverty, to which is attributable the persistence of underdevelopment of economies, he defines as 'a circular constellation of forces tending to act and react upon one another in such a way as to keep a poor country in a state of poverty'.[4] While the supply of capital depends upon the ability and willingness to save, the demand for capital is determined by the inducement to invest: and there is a circular relationship on both sides of the problem of capital formation. On the supply side, the small capacity to save, resulting from the low level of real income, is a reflection of low productivity, consequent upon paucity of capital, which is due to the small capacity to save. On the demand side, the inducement to invest is low because of the restricted purchasing power of the people, consequent upon low real incomes, which again is due to low productivity—a result of the small amount of capital used in production. This may be caused partly by the small inducement to invest. The low level of real income, reflecting low productivity, is a point that is common to both circles, and the economy is in a state of underdevelopment equilibrium.

In order to break the vicious circle of poverty, it is necessary that a large number of entrepreneurs invest in a number of industries; and there is a substantial volume of investment in the economy, so that incomes and demand for products increase all round. According to Joseph Schumpeter's *Theory of Economic Development*[5] (regarded in the West as a theory of business cycles), rapid growth is engineered by investment of various entrepreneurs creating recurrent waves of industrial progress. He emphasizes the simultaneous action of a large number of industrialists making investments, producing new commodities, making innovations and combining the factors of production in diverse ways. Investment in a variety of industries, supported by new technologies and innovations, increases incomes and productivity, and has a multiplier effect upon other industries; and the initial investment promotes a wave of new applications of capital over a wide field of diverse industries. Schumpeter[6] refers to long waves in economic activity, each of which consists of an industrial revolution which is periodically reshaped by introducing new methods of production. These waves result each time in an avalanche of consumer goods that permanently deepens and widens the stream of real income, although initially disruption, losses and unemployment may occur. While investment by an entrepreneur in an industry may face difficulty, in that there may not be sufficient demand for its products, a wave of capital investment in a large number of diverse industries would tend to increase the momentum of industrial growth, because the amount paid out to various factors of production would provide the necessary demand for the products of those industries.

STATE INTERVENTION IN EARLY STAGES

It may be necessary, in the early stages of development till such time as indigenous entrepreneurship has not developed, for the state to undertake substantial investment in a large number of industries, with the aim of providing the impetus and base for industrial progress. The importance of maximizing the marginal savings ratio, which is a crucial determinant of growth, can hardly be overemphasized. Out of every increment of income, the proportion of savings should be increased to the maximum extent possible. In the early period of industrialization, if savings are insufficient, taxation may have to be used as an instrument for compulsory savings, but as development proceeds, the importance of incentives for voluntary savings increases, for two reasons in particular: taxation beyond certain levels becomes self-defeating and counterproductive; and secondly, if money is transferred from private savings to public consumption, it is a loss to the community. Hence, for development purposes, there should be a judicious mixture of various instruments of resource-mobilization, particularly taxation and borrowings. Besides, a policy and institutional framework of incentives for private savings and investment, and for provision of capital and loans to entrepreneurs for the establishment of new industries and expansion and modernization of existing enterprises, are necessary for development. The development banks have to function almost as a reservoir through which the savings collected by the state are made available for capital outlay throughout the economy.

In the early stages of development, underdeveloped economies generally need both private and public saving and investment. Individual countries necessarily must work out their own policy mix in accordance with their distinctive needs, opportunities, and environment. It may however be emphasized that once an economy reaches the transitional or take-off stage, the quantum of private savings and foreign aid as available should normally be sufficient for accelerating economic growth; and the dependence of the economy upon public saving and investment should be limited to provision of infrastructure, defence, and nuclear energy and research, besides collective wants.

ROSTOW'S STAGES OF ECONOMIC GROWTH

W. W. Rostow, in his *The Stages of Economic Growth*,[7] seeks to identify five stages of development, and to classify societies in accordance with those stages: traditional, transitional, take-off, maturity and high mass consumption. Rostow says that take-off is the great watershed in the life of modern societies; it is the stage during which the obstacles and resistance to steady growth are finally overcome and the forces of growth acquire momentum and become dominant. Infrastructure is built up and technological progress permeates industry and agriculture. The rate of effective savings and investment rises from about 5 per cent to about 10 per cent or more to ensure self-sustaining growth. Defining take-off, he says,[8] 'first, it is the period in the life of an economy when, for the first time, one or more modern industrial sectors take hold, with high rates of growth, bringing in not merely new production functions but backward and lateral spreading effects on a substantial scale; second, for a take-off to be said to have occurred, the economy must demonstrate the capacity to exploit the forward linkages as well, so that new leading sectors emerge as the older ones decelerate'.

The economy should also have the capability of successfully coping with the structural crisis arising out of the initial surge of growth and to induct advanced technologies which accelerate and sustain growth. The take-off may cover a period of about two decades. Instead of spreading investment thinly over vast sectors of the economy, it is necessary in the interest of growth to channelize and concentrate resources upon selected modern industrial sectors with high rates of growth, and to induct and apply modern and sophisticated technology. Upon the appropriate selection of leading industrial sectors, and intensive application of inputs to areas with potential for high agricultural growth, as also the appropriateness of the technology adopted, would depend the successful growth of the economy. As these sectors grow, not only will they impart momentum to growth, but also transmit it to other sectors of the economy. As the older sectors decelerate, new leading sectors must take over. The development of modern and sunrise industries with high technology should be accorded priority. Factors of production—men, materials and resources—need to be transferred from the less to the more efficient sectors, and as the experience of Japan indicates, such transfer facilities accelerate the growth of the economy.

Take-off may be followed by the stage of maturity, about sixty years after take-off begins (forty years after the end of take-off). In this period, society effectively applies the most modern technology to the bulk of its resources. New leading sectors accelerate, while the older ones decelerate. According to Rostow, the steel industry is one of the symbols of maturity. Rostow has indicated the tentative approximate dates of Take-off and Technological Maturity in respect of certain leading countries:

TABLE 6.1—*Dates of Take-off and Technological Maturity*

Country	Take-off	Technological Maturity
Great Britain	1783–1802	1850
USA	1843–1860	1900
Germany	1850–1873	1910
France	1830–1860	1910
Sweden	1868–1890	1930
Japan	1878–1900	1940
Russia	1890–1914	1950
Canada	1896–1914	1950
China	1952–	—
India	1952–	—

SOURCE W. W. Rostow, *The Stages of Economic Growth*, pp. 38, 39.

During maturity, nations have to decide between various political and socio-economic alternatives: should wealth be channelized towards high mass consumption, the evolution of a welfare state, or for imperialist objectives? Most countries will reach the high mass-consumption stage, whatever be the balance of choices. We are not particularly concerned with this stage here.

Despite severe criticism by S. Kuznets and others—that the demarcation between the transitional stage and take-off, and between take-off and maturity, is blurred, and empirical and quantitative evidence is not available—Rostow's thesis has commanded world-wide attention because of three factors. He has provided useful insight, analysis and description of the development process; he has identified key growth variables during various stages of development; and his identification of the take-off stage and the determinants and prerequisites for take-off provide valuable assistance in the formulation of a policy framework for growth in developing countries.

KEYNESIAN THEORY OF EMPLOYMENT AND DEVELOPING ECONOMIES

The Keynesian Theory of Employment and Incomes was formulated as an anti-cyclical measure with reference to the need to increase effective demand in the context of depression in developed economies in order to maintain full employment. V.K.R.V. Rao examined the applicability of Keynes' multiplier theory to underdeveloped economies and concluded that it was not appropriate for the purpose. In developed economies, during periods of recession, certain resources or factors of production are under-employed; government, through budget deficits, would be able to increase real output and real savings. It is true that in underdeveloped economies, surplus labour exists, but other complementary factors like capital equipment, raw materials, and skilled workers are not available, and output in the consumer goods industries cannot be easily increased.

The consequence is that an increase in investment initially brings about a rise in incomes and employment. But even though the marginal propensity to consume is high, the multiplier principle does not operate and the secondary, tertiary and other increases in output, incomes and employment do not take place. The consumption goods industries are not able to respond to the stimulus of increased government spending (deficit financing). As Dr Rao says,[10] 'the primary increase in investment and, therefore, increase in income and employment leads to a secondary and a tertiary increase in income, but not to any noticeable increase in either output or employment either in the agricultural sector or the non-agricultural sector. The multiplier principle, therefore, works with reference to money income but not with reference either to real income or employment.'[6] Such deficit financing would lead to inflation. However, if investment has taken place and there are unabsorbed resources and unutilized capacity already built up, and real income is rising, inflation may not occur. Limited deficit financing could be used as an instrument for stimulating economic growth. This however constitutes a different category and is considered later.[9]

CRITICAL MINIMUM EFFORT THESIS: LIBENSTEIN

Harvey Libenstein says that underdeveloped economies are characterized by the existence of a vicious circle of poverty and a state of low income equilibrium; in order to break the vicious circle and take the economy into a higher income level equilibrium, a certain 'critical minimum effort' is necessary. If the capital accumulation is of a sufficient magnitude to ensure that the income-raising factors are stimulated beyond the maximum of income-depressing factors, the critical minimum effort would be reached and the economy would progress on the road towards sustained development. Transition from the state of backwardness to a more developed one with steady secular growth postulates that the economy should receive a stimulus to growth greater than that of a 'certain critical minimum size'. The quantum of investment representing the critical minimum effort required must be large enough to reduce or overcome indivisibilities and diseconomies of scale in the economy, counter other factors, such as population explosion, which tend to depress development, and to generate sufficient momentum in the system so that the growth-stimulating factors continue to be operative. The investment must also be concentrated among a few industries of an optimum size rather than be spread over a large number of small units; and it should be made in a sizeable 'lump', and not in the form of marginal or small increments made by various individuals whose decisions are un-correlated.

It would appear from this thesis that in the early stages it may be necessary for the state to intervene and to make sizeable investment, say in accordance with a central plan for development.[11]

IMPORTANCE OF HIGHER PRODUCTIVITY

With an advance in the process of industrialization, structural changes in the economy take place. While the share of agriculture in GDP is high in the early stages, as industrialization proceeds the contribution of agriculture in GDP declines, and the share of industry and services correspondingly increases. Two broad categories of studies of economic growth have been undertaken. Colin Clark in 1940 and Simon Kuznets during the period 1950 to 1970 undertook studies to analyse standard patterns of growth in various economic sectors, and in respect of different types of manufacturing activity. Another type of study was undertaken to account for the different sources of economic growth and to identify the contribution of increase in productivity through intensive use of factor inputs, as distinguished from their extensive application.

Studies have recently (1986) been made to integrate the two methodologies within a single framework. The growth of industrial economies, rapid and sustained over a period of time, takes place both through extensive use of factor inputs and intensive utilization of factors of production. In the earlier stages of development, there is rapid growth with accumulation of capital and employment of an increasingly large labour force in industry. Both internal and external factors of production are mobilized, but as industrialization progresses, the extensive use of factor inputs slows down, and limitations of inflow of foreign aid also begin to manifest themselves. Naturally, in such a situation, increase in the efficient use of available economic resources becomes critical to accelerating the pace of development.

According to the *World Development Report 1987*,[12] total factor productivity is computed after subtracting the contribution attributable to growth in the use of labour, land, and capital from GDP growth. Japan and Korea achieved high GDP growth-rates both by extensive growth of factor inputs and by realizing sizeable increase in productivity of various factors of production. Brazil and Venezuela, however, achieved a high GDP growth rate mainly through extensive growth of factor inputs. These studies relate to the period 1960–75. In the case of Argentina and Columbia, factor inputs grew at about the same rate, but the GDP growth in Columbia was about two per cent higher than that of Argentina. This was a consequence of higher productivity norms achieved by Columbia.

These studies highlight the importance of increasing productivity of the factor inputs in the context of scarce economic resources. With every plan and rising industrialization, an increasing quantum of resources have to be garnered in order to sustain the rate of growth. Naturally, the pressure on resources will be correspondingly lower if better utilization of the input factors such as capital, labour, and land (for agriculture in particular) yielded better output, with the same factor inputs through increase in productivity. This would also lower the capital–output ratio. It must be realized that despite the passage of time and progress, the interaction of technological change, specialization, and trade constitute the essence of advance in industrialization. The function of technology in stimulating the rate of growth of GDP is discussed in greater detail in ch. 13. Government, *inter alia*, has particular responsibility on two broad fronts. It must ensure that transport, communication and power are available in adequate measure. Government should encourage development, and the projected supply of infrastructural inputs should be large enough to cope with the increased requirements of developing industry and agriculture. Secondly, the institutional framework, social, legal, administrative and even political, must be such that it is conducive to the creation of an environment and climate which encourages investment, and causes the factors of production to respond to the incentives that are provided. It may be observed in this context that at one time the licensing policy in India had become so restrictive and short-sighted that industries whose production exceeded the installed capacities were threatened with penalties; in another country, an entrepreneur who achieved high utilization of machinery would have been rewarded. Fortunately, the conditions are entirely different now, and industries are permitted to achieve production upto a certain specified percentage above the installed capacity.

Ursula K. Hicks has touched upon a vital point which has often been ignored and leads to a considerable wastage of resources. A strategy for development has two distinct aspects: on the one hand, the construction of new works and induction of new technologies for producing goods and services are vital; on the other, the maintenance and improvement of existing works and services are equally important. The latter aspect is often neglected, leading to deterioration in equipment. The salaries of civil servants and teachers fall into arrears; serious imbalances and consequent political and social discontent occur. The Central Government must obviate such a situation; it has not only to provide the physical infrastructure for full capacity utilization and establishment of new industrial complexes but also to ensure that the resources are put to optimum use for the good of the entire economy.

SAVINGS

In India, success achieved in the Sixth and Seventh Plans is partly attributable to sizeable additional resource-mobilization effected, often in excess of targets during the plan periods. A structural change in the economy has taken place, in that the ratio of savings to GDP increased from about 13.6 per cent in 1964–5 to about 21 per cent in 1988–9,[13] besides the potential for further increase in the savings rate to about 23 to 24 per cent by the year 2000. The importance of the high savings rate in the economy lies in its having enabled the country to achieve increased capital formation of about 23.9 per cent in 1988–9 as compared to 17.1 per cent in 1969–70. Almost 90 per cent of this investment has been financed from internal resources, reflecting the degree of self-reliance achieved. In this context it may be observed that if the inflow of foreign equity capital, borrowings, and aid can be maintained at the level of 2.9 per cent of GDP in 1990–1, it would provide the foundation for the achievement of a higher growth-rate during the Eighth and Ninth Plan periods. This postulates that the Incremental Capital Output Ratio (ICOR) is brought down from about 4.3 to less than 4.0 during the course of the Eighth and Ninth Plan periods (1990–2000), of which more later.[14]

An analysis of the composition of gross savings shows that the bulk of the increase in savings was accounted for by the household sector. Between 1969–70 and 1988–9, household savings increased from about 12.1 per cent to 17.1 per cent of GDP, while public savings declined from 2.8 to 2.0 per cent in the respective years. Corporate savings moved between about 1.5 and 2.1 per cent of GDP.

The factors that have contributed to the remarkable upsurge in private household savings are:

- High interest rates on medium- and long-term savings instruments.

- Provision for deduction from total income of savings in specified instruments under the Income-tax law.

- Widespread expansion and penetration of the banking system deep into the rural areas, as a consequence of nationalization of banking in 1969.

- Sizeable mobilization of savings by institutions like the Unit Trust and Mutual Funds, Life Insurance Corporation and others.

- Increase in the quantum of funds raised by means of the capital market through debentures and equities.

Public savings have fallen short of targets. The erosion in public savings is attributable to the sizeable growth in total expenditure. Additional revenue mobilization during the Sixth and Seventh Plan periods has been in excess of targets. Yet there has been an excess of current expenditure over current income, resulting in a negative balance on current revenue account of 0.4 per cent of GDP in 1985–6. Actually it should be possible to increase the rate of public sector savings by a qualitative increase in the operational efficiency of public enterprises and a quantum jump in the resources generated by them. According to the Long-term Fiscal Policy, the internal extra-budgetary resources of public enterprises should improve from 2.9 per cent in 1985–6 to 4.1 per cent in 1989–90.

According to the Fiscal policy document, it was necessary to improve the built-in revenue-raising capacity of the tax system so that the automatic growth in revenue improves. Another priority is to reduce the non-plan expenditure. Both these exercises are vital if the Balance from current revenues (BCR) is to be increased to a positive figure. The Policy envisaged that public savings should increase from 2.5 per cent of GDP in 1985–6 to 4.3 per cent in 1989–90. This was to be achieved by converting the Balance from current revenues of −0.4 per cent in 1985–6 to a positive 0.2 per cent of GDP in 1989–90. The considerable amount of additional resource mobilization undertaken by government during the last two decades often exceeded targets. Tax revenues have been buoyant; voluntary compliance with taxes has increased with reduction in tax rates and punitive measures adopted to counter tax evasion. Despite controversies, it is undeniable that reduction in tax rates and other measures have brought about a positive increase in revenues. All these factors should have resulted in an increase in public savings, but escalation in non-plan expenditure exceeded the growth of revenue, resulting in deficits.

There is widespread recognition of the need to control administrative and non-plan expenditure. That is no easy task because of various commitments of government, particularly in regard to writing off part of farmers' loans, rationalizing pensions and other payments, and sizeable increase in allocation of funds for increased employment and rural development. Interest payments and subsidies need to be controlled. The difficulties in reducing internal and external indebtedness and subsidies have been analysed subsequently.[15] Drawings of the public sector upon the financial savings of the household sector should be limited. This is only possible if the inter-sectoral mismatch between private savings and public demand for investment is reduced. Basically, the role of the public sector has to be limited as a measure to reduce its financial requirements, and allow funds to be more productively utilized by the private sector which generates them.

Private savings are buoyant and if the existing savings policy formulated by government during the Seventh Plan period continues, not only would this buoyancy be maintained, but could be further stimulated. There is however a dark cloud on the horizon. The Chelliah Committee (1986–7) surprisingly made negative suggestions with regard to penalizing savings which mature and may be used for personal consumption. Savings are partly intended for personal consumption at a future date and if withdrawals for personal use are taxable, and incentives for savings are weakened, the total volume of small savings would decline. It is imperative therefore that the existing savings schemes and tax incentives in respect of savings are not tampered with; actually, such incentive schemes should be extended to stimulate savings. Savings schemes, however, should be properly framed so that they are productive and do not involve excessive loss of revenue. In this context, hundred per cent tax exemption under the section 80 CCA deposit scheme is causing considerable loss of revenue to the government without commensurate benefit. Such exemption should be withdrawn and tax rates lowered.

The new strategy for growth needs to concentrate on the following aspects for increasing the ratio of savings to GDP in the economy:

1. There must be an increase in user charges, as has also been emphasized by the World Bank. Betterment levies, charges for irrigation facilities and various inputs supplied to the prosperous farmer should be adequately raised. User charges yield double efficiency gains: firstly, the supply of public services and goods is allocated efficiently; and secondly, the need for distortion in taxes is avoided by their use. Subsidies tend to become indiscriminate; actually they should be targeted to groups who really need them. For instance, there is no equitable justification for making fertilizer and food subsidies available to the affluent farmer and consumer.

2. Government's current expenditure needs to be drastically reduced; it is vital that a high-powered official committee examines ministerial expenditure carefully and takes remedial action.

3. Increase in operational efficiency and generation of surpluses by public enterprises is vital to a resurgence in growth of public savings.

4. Land revenue should be increased on larger holdings and be made progressive.

5. If agricultural incomes cannot be taxed through income-tax and wealth-tax, indirect taxes on both agricultural inputs and the commodities consumed in the rural areas should be raised.

6. The tax base should be widened and a large number of self-employed persons who do not pay taxes should be brought within the tax net. A scheme should be devised for rewarding the survey teams who bring new assessees into the tax fold. The rewards should be linked to the quantum of tax realized from such assessees. Administration needs to be tightened and, after drawing up lists of traders and businessmen in each market, in the urban areas in particular, the tax net should be extended to cover them.

7. We shall deal later with tax reform for increasing buoyancy and elasticity of revenues, and raising the overall ratio of tax to GDP.[16]

8. It is common knowledge that a very substantial amount of black money is circulating in the economy. In the interest of national development, some equitable scheme should be devised for mobilization of funds from this vast reservoir, of which more later.[17]

9. The capital markets have undergone a structural transformation and mobilization of funds in the form of new capital issues of the corporate sector have substantially increased over the past few

years. The consents granted during 1988–9 and 1989–90 by the Controller of Capital Issues (CCI) for raising capital are considerably higher than in earlier years, of which more later.[18]

Assistance sanctioned and disbursed by Financial Institutions are indicated in the following Tables:

TABLE 6.2— *Overall Assistance by Institutions*

Assistance	1988–89	1989–90	(Rupees, crores) Increase
Sanctioned	13760	15572	13.2 per cent
Disbursed	8486	9341	10.1 „ „

SOURCE *RBI Annual Report 1989–90*, p. 109.

This is an indication that on the whole the investment climate and the tempo of investment were maintained during the year 1989–90. The overall buoyancy in capital markets, as reflected in the sizeable increase in funds raised, bears eloquent testimony that there is considerable scope for additional mobilization of savings through the capital markets. The investment habit is increasing in urban areas, and tremendous scope exists for its further spread. The rural areas remain almost unexplored and efforts in this direction are likely to be promising.

10. The sustained institutional intervention in the capital market in the form of investment of sizeable funds mobilized by UTI, LIC and other corporations and mutual funds, a satisfactory monsoon in 1989–90, and encouraging corporate performance, have stimulated investment activity and the share markets have improved substantially in 1988–9 and 1989–90, after a period of sluggishness in 1987–8. Buoyant conditions have prevailed in the markets. According to the Reserve Bank, an analysis of the financial results of 337 companies for 1987–8, published in 1988–9, showed that the value of production rose by 9.4 per cent as compared to 7.3 per cent in the previous year. The extension of the policy of liberalization of industrial policy should stimulate new investment.

Factors favourable to a higher savings and growth rate include better infrastructure, greater capacity utilization in the public sector, and an improved policy environment for industrial development. The constraining factors include recurring losses by many public sector enterprises, inadequate return on capital employed, and sizeable increase in government expenditure.

There is considerable scope for mobilization of private savings in rural areas; large amounts have been invested in the rural sector during the successive plans, but the resultant incomes have not been adequately taxed. Savings find their way into investment in gold and. silver and other unproductive assets. Instruments for attracting the savings of farmers and others should be devised and intensively promoted. Banking in rural areas should be further extended and efforts made to realize the considerable potential that exists in regard to mobilization of rural savings which would substantially increase savings in the country as a whole.

TABLE 6.3 — *Gross Domestic Saving and Domestic Capital Formation*
(As percentage of GDP at current market prices)

Year	House-hold Sector	Private Corporate Sector	Public Sector	Total	Gross Domestic Capital Formation
1950–51	7.5	0.9	1.8	10.2	10.0
1954–55	8.1	1.2	1.6	10.9	11.0
1959–60	9.7	1.3	1.7	12.6	14.3
1964–65	8.4	1.7	3.5	13.6	16.2
1969–70	12.1	1.5	2.8	16.4	17.1
1974–75	12.4	2.1	3.8	18.3	19.2
1979–80	16.2	2.2	4.6	23.0	23.5
1980–81	17.4	2.1	3.6	23.0	24.7
New Series					
1980–81	16.1	1.7	3.4	21.2	22.7
1981–82	15.0	1.6	4.6	21.1	22.8
1982–83	13.5	1.6	4.4	19.5	21.0
1983–84	15.1	1.5	3.3	19.9	21.1
1984–85	15.1	1.7	2.8	19.6	21.0
1985–86	15.7	2.1	3.2	21.0	23.4
1986–87	17.2	1.7	2.7	21.6	23.4
1987–88	16.6	1.7	1.9	20.2	22.1
1988–89	17.1	2.1	2.0	21.1	23.9
1989–90	17.8	2.1	1.7	21.7	24.1

SOURCE *Economic Survey 1988–89*, Government of India, S 10 & S 11. Figures for 1988–9 and 1989–90 are from *Economic Survey, 1990–91*, S9. Ratios of Individual Sectors may not add up to the total because the figures have been rounded up.

CAPITAL–OUTPUT RATIO

The other important aspect, besides stimulating savings, is to reduce the incremental capital–output ratio (ICOR) from 4.3:1 to about 4:1. Since there is considerable unutilized capacity in both the public and private sectors, higher productivity can be achieved through increased utilization of existing plant, given better availability of infrastructure. The capital–output ratio increased from 3.5 during the period 1951–2 to 1959–60, to 5.5 for the period 1970–1 to 1979–80. It subsequently declined to 4.45 during the period 1980–1 to 1983–4. K. N. Raj has partly attributed the increase in the capital–output ratio to high cost of infrastructure in developing countries. This is in line with Arthur Lewis' view that infrastructural capital costs tend to be very high in periods of urbanization.

It has been observed both in India and other developing countries that as industrialization of the economy progresses, the quantum of investment in the energy sector is considerable. The rising cost of capital equipment the world over, together with increase in maintenance costs and at times the indifferent quality of physical resources, all tend to increase the capital–output ratio in the energy sector. Besides, there is the factor of increasing energy intensity in agriculture, comprising electricity consumed directly in farming, diesel oil for running pump-sets and tractors, and inputs such as oil-based chemicals and fertilizers. Sukhamoy Chakravarty noted that capital (fixed and working) directly needed by agriculture has increased, while a change in the elements constituting the inter-industry matrix has taken place. Consequently, 'the economy now has to devote a larger percentage of total investment to maintain the same rate of growth in the final consumption of agricultural produce than in the fifties and the early sixties, when agricultural expansion largely took the form of an increase in the area cultivated'.[19] Besides, with industrialization, costs of production have increased instead of coming down. Actually, with an increase in the average size of industry and volume of output, economies of scale should have eventuated and the unit cost of production fallen, but this has not occurred. This is another factor that has increased the capital–output ratio.

As noted earlier, the economy has moved from an average growth rate of about 3.5 per cent per annum to about 5.5 per cent per annum at constant factor price during the last decade. During the first four years of the Seventh Plan period also, the average rate of growth has been about 5.9 per cent, which is encouraging. In order to improve the incremental capital–output ratio, the following measures may be suggested:

1. Priorities in regard to allocation of resources have to be determined, and it has to be ensured that they are utilized efficiently and in accordance with predetermined priorities. Fiscal policies and planning need to be rationalized. They involve formulating a phased investment programme, projecting current spending needs, and assessing revenue availability and borrowing requirements for about five years in the context of a consistent macroeconomic framework. Pragmatic budgeting, efficient implementation, and effective monitoring are necessary if the quality of spending and utilization of funds are to be improved.

2. The productivity of existing capital stock and labour has to be raised. Increased infrastructural availability and proper maintenance programmes and incentives are necessary to ensure that full utilization of installed capacity of plant and machinery, and other capital stocks and factors of production, is achieved, to realize optimum levels of productivity.

3. The expenditure of the modern state covers a broad spectrum comprising plan and non-plan expenditure, both by way of revenue and capital. What is necessary is to improve the quality of public spending. High public spending and deficits need to be reduced by curtailing current and non-plan expenditure and non-productive investment. Leakage and wastage in expenditure have to be brought down to a minimum through efficient and continuous monitoring. Zero-based budgeting should be intensified. Strict control by financial advisers to the ministries is necessary to ensure that wasteful expenditure is controlled.

4. Modernization and technological upgradation of existing plant and induction of state of the art technology are necessary, so that economies of scale are realized, cost per unit of production is reduced, and industry remains competitive. The demand base for a number of commodities can be widened only by reducing the unit cost of production.

5. It is observed that even though planning has attained high levels of sophistication, implementation is weak and uncoordinated, with considerable leakage of funds, and ineffective monitoring. It appears that one of the remedies for inefficient implementation is

decentralization. More and more functions which can be transferred to local governments, should be delegated to them. The people in rural areas should be involved in, say building roads, irrigation, water supply, sanitation, transport, health and educational services. Since the benefit would accrue to the rural economy, there would be improvement in the quality of public services. District monitoring committees should be constituted under the aegis of the district collector to check wastage and leakage, and to ensure that funds are properly spent to yield optimum results.

6. The potential for increase in agricultural production in the country is vast; the strategies formulated by government are commendable (*vide* ch. 9). What is needed is effective implementation and efficient functioning of the institutional framework. This would enable the achievement of the targeted growth rate of 4 per cent in agriculture (Seventh Plan). The growth rate could be further accelerated to about 4.5 per cent in the late nineties, provided the structural institutional changes, partially implemented, are further stimulated. The Green Revolution needs to be extended to other states, particularly Bihar, Tamil Nadu and Uttar Pradesh.

7. In order to alleviate poverty and supplement the incomes of farmers and landless labour in rural areas, non-agricultural activities in the rural sector should be encouraged. Government should provide an institutional framework for identifying cottage industries and trades, formulating schemes, creating infrastructural facilities, supplying finance and offering guidance for the development of such activities. The beneficial effects would be inestimable.

8. Employment and incomes have to be created in areas where the economy has a comparative advantage. Domestic structural adjustments, as necessary, may be made to ensure that exports are stimulated.

9. Considering that the plant–load factor is extremely low in certain regions, and even the average of 56 per cent is comparatively low, there is enormous scope for increasing the output of power even with the existing plants. As for new plants in the project stage, state of the art technology needs to be inducted. Transmission losses have to be reduced and maintenance of plants improved. All these factors would not only reduce the capital–

output ratio in the energy sector, but improved infrastructural availability would contribute to more effective utilization of industrial capacity, reduction in loss of production, increase in irrigation capacity, and a sizeable decline in ICOR.

10. Delays in completion of projects, particularly capital-intensive plants, have resulted in increasing the capital–output ratio. Delays in completion in the context of inflationary increase in the costs of plant and machinery all over the world have led to over-capitalization. Costs of construction, due to inadequate monitoring and wastages, have also been high, particularly in the case of large irrigation and power projects, steel and heavy engineering plants. The cumulative effect of all these and other factors, such as determination and location of plants on grounds other than economic, technology, and poor quality of equipment has been to increase the capital–output ratio. Efficiency of investment needs to be greatly improved.

Reduction in ICOR is imperative if the ambitious growth-rate targets for the nineties are to be achieved. Considering that, (a) there is great scope for reduction in non-plan expenditure, (b) utilization of installed capacity of plant and machinery is inadequate and considerable scope for increasing production and productivity with the existing equipment exists, (c) technological upgradation and modernization would also assist in increasing productivity of capital and other factors of production, and (d) with effective monitoring and performance audit (and perhaps *panchayati raj* and devolution of funds), leakage and wastage of money could be reduced, it is reasonable to conclude that ICOR can be brought down to below 4:1 within the nineties.

HARROD–DOMAR MODEL

The formulation of developmental plans postulates certain basic decisions about the dimension and parameters of growth. The growth rate is usually determined on the basis of the objectives of planned economic development and the feasibility of achieving the requisite rate of growth. The planners have to formulate estimates about the quantum of investment for achieving the growth rate, taking into account, *inter alia*, the national income, the savings rate in the economy, and the capital–output ratio. The growth model which broadly constituted the basis of long-term planning in India is the well-known Harrod–Domar Model. The term capital–output ratio may be amplified prior to discussing the Model.

As George Rosen[20] says, 'the capital–output ratio may be defined as the relationship of investment in a given economy or industry for a given time period to the output of that economy or industry for a similar time period'. The capital investment required to obtain a particular amount of output is estimated. Generally the reference is to incremental capital–output ratio (ICOR), which indicates the amount of additional or incremental net output obtained from the investment of a given amount of capital during a particular period during which capital formation takes place.

According to Harrod and Domar, the most crucial determinants of growth are capital accumulation and investment. Investment has a dual role: It creates income and employment on the one hand; and on the other, it augments the capital stock in the community and increases its productive capacity. They thus emphasize both aspects of the investment process: income generation which represents the demand side and productive capacity creation or accretion to capital stock, which represents the supply side.

Harrod and Domar emphasize that if the economy is to move along a path of equilibrium, real income and output must grow at a rate proportional to that at which the productive capacity in the economy, in the form of capital stock, is increasing. If adequate income is not created and effective demand does not exist at a sufficiently high level, there would be excess or idle capacity. As a consequence, investment outlays, incomes, and employment will be reduced. The equlibrium path of continuous growth of the economy would not be maintained. As Prof. Alak Ghosh expounds, 'the maintenance of a full employment equilibrium level of income, or even a smooth uninterrupted growth in real national income, requires that the volume of spending, resulting from effective demand, generated by investment, must be sufficient to absorb the increased output, resulting from additional productive capacity, made possible by investment'.[21]

In order to maintain full employment it is essential that the volume of investment must steadily increase, so that it enables continuous matching between growth in real national income and expansion of the productive capacity of the stock of capital. This means that in a growing economy, new capital formation must continuously take place.

The Harrod version of the Model may be explained in its simplest form. Assuming that:

Y_t = National Income during a particular period;

S_t = National Saving during a particular period;

g = Rate of Economic Growth;

$\frac{1}{c}$ = The reciprocal of Capital–Output Ratio;

dY = Income Generation;

the rate of growth is determined by the following formula:

$$g = \frac{S_t}{Y_t} \times \frac{I}{c}.$$

Assuming that the planners opt for a growth rate of 6 per cent with ICOR 4:1, the ratio of Investment to National Income could be worked out as follows:

$$g = s \times \frac{1}{ICOR}.$$

Now $\frac{S_t}{Y_t} = s = \frac{I_t}{Y_t}$ (since Savings S = Investment I; and

$$s = \frac{S_t}{Y_t}, \text{ that is, the ratio of savings to national income)}$$

$$\frac{6}{100} = \frac{S_t}{Y_t} \times \frac{1}{4}$$

$$\frac{6}{100} \times \frac{4}{1} = \frac{S_t}{Y_t} = s$$

$$s = \frac{24}{100}.$$

The rate of investment or savings has to be about 24 per cent.

Now,

$$g = \frac{S_t}{Y_t} \times \frac{1}{c} \quad \text{as above.}$$

$$c = \frac{I_t}{d_t}$$

$$= \frac{I_t}{Y_{t+1} - Y_t}$$

$$\frac{1}{c} = \frac{Y_{t+1} - Y_t}{I_t}.$$

Hence,

$$g = \frac{S_t}{Y_t} \times \frac{Y_{t+1} - Y_t}{I_t}$$

$$g = \frac{S_t}{Y_t} \times \frac{dY}{I_t}$$

$$g = \frac{s}{c}$$

or,

$$g = \frac{Y_{t+1} - Y_t}{Y_t}$$

$$g = \frac{dY}{Y_t}.$$

The Harrod–Domar Model may be used to explain the capacity-creation and income-generation aspects. Over a particular period of time, assuming a constant savings ratio s, and capital output ratio c, the productive stock of capital will increase by

$$\frac{s}{c} \times Y_t.$$

Now income generation is equal to $dY = Y_t - Y_{t-1}$,

$$dY = \frac{s}{c} \times Y_t$$

$$\frac{dY}{Y_t} = \frac{s}{c}.$$

$$\text{Hence } g = \frac{S_t}{Y_t} \times \frac{1}{c}.$$

The above formulation shows that income-generation between two periods represented by $dY = Y_t - Y_{t-1}$ is equal to expansion of productive capacity of capital stock, represented by $\frac{s}{c} \times Y_t$, and these represent the state of Long-run equilibrium.

DOMAR MODEL

According to Domar's Model also, Investment has a dual role: on the one hand it generates income, and on the other it increases productive capacity. In order to maintain full employment equilibrium level of income, investment should increase at such rate that increase in income or demand (aggregate demand) is equal to the rate of growth in productive capacity (aggregate supply).

According to Domar, the net potential social average productivity of investment is indicated by O ($= dY/I$) and I.O is the total net potential increase in output and is known as the sigma effect. This represents the supply side of the system.

On the demand side, investment increases income via the multiplier effect, that is, through the multiplier $\frac{1}{a}$.

Assuming that:
annual increase in income is denoted by   dY
increase in investment   dI
propensity to save   a (alpha) $= dS/dY$,

increase in income will be equal to the multiplier (1/a) times the increase in investment, that is

$$dY = dI . \frac{1}{a}.$$

To maintain full employment the equilibrium level of income, aggregate demand should equal aggregate supply. This gives the fundamental equation

$$dI. \frac{1}{a} = I. \sigma$$

Dividing both sides by I and multiplying by a, we get

$$\frac{dI. \frac{1}{a}. a}{I} = \frac{I \sigma a}{I}$$

$$\frac{dI}{I} = a \sigma$$

This corresponds to Harrod's formula

$$\frac{dY}{Y} = s. \frac{1}{c} = g.$$

It would appear from the equation that to maintain full employment, the rate of growth of investment dI/I must be equal to the rate of growth in productive capacity $a \sigma$.

The Harrod–Domar Model was originally evolved in relation to a developed economy, intended to obviate the possible effects of secular stagnation. The Model has been subjected to criticism, yet growth equations using it have proved to be most useful as a component of macroeconomic planning in underdeveloped countries.

REFERENCES

1. D. Goulet, *The Cruel Choice: A New Concept on the Theory of Development*, Atheneum, New York, 1971.
2. W. Arthur Lewis, *The Theory of Economic Growth*, George Allen & Unwin Ltd., London, 1957, p. 11.
3. J. K. Galbraith, *Economic Development in Perspective*, USIS, Delhi, p. 31.
4. Ragnar Nurkse, *Problems of Capital Formation in Underdeveloped Countries*, Basil.Blackwell, Oxford, 1955, p. 4.
5. J. A. Schumpeter, *The Theory of Economic Development*, Harvard University Press, Cambridge, Mass., 1934, pp. 63–6.

6. J. A. Schumpeter, *Capitalism, Socialism and Democracy*, George Allen & Unwin Ltd., London, 1943, p. 68.
7. W. W. Rostow, *The Stages of Economic Growth*, CUP, Cambridge, 1960.
8. W. W. Rostow, *The Economics of Take-Off into Sustained Growth*, Macmillan & Co. Ltd., London, 1963, pp. xviii, xix.
9. *Vide* ch. 8.
10. V.K.R.V. Rao, 'Investment, Income and the Multiplier in an Underdeveloped Economy' in *The Economics of Underdevelopment*, ed. A. N. Agarwala and S. P. Singh, OUP, Bombay, 1958, p. 211.
11. Also *vide* App. I.
12. *World Development Report 1987*, World Bank/OUP, New York, pp. 52, 53.
13. SOF: *Vide* Table 6.3 attached.
14. *Vide* next section.
15. *Vide* chs. 11 and 15.
16. *Vide* chs. 15 to 18.
17. *Vide* ch. 17.
18. *Vide* ch. 7.
19. Sukhamoy Chakravarty, *Development Planning*, OUP, Delhi, 1987, p. 56.
20. George Rosen, *Industrial Change in India*, 1959, p. 37.
21. Alak Ghosh, *New Horizons in Planning*, The World Press Private Ltd., Calcutta, 1982, p. 44.

7

New Initiatives for Growth

Government should take new initiatives to promote accelerated growth and inflow of sophisticated technology. Liberalization, dismantling the network of controls, and reduction in taxes and interest rates would stimulate savings, investment and incomes, which in turn would provide the wherewithal for further capital formation and generation of incomes, thereby setting in motion a process of continuing growth. A directional change in the economy is therefore necessary. Given the severe constraint on resources for public investment, the thrust for development has to be provided by the private sector. The strategy should be two-pronged: to create an environment in which the corporate sector is able to mobilize capital from the capital market for expansion through public issues, and to leave a larger residue of funds with the corporations out of profits to plough back into business. Lower interest rates would reduce costs of production.

The objective of economic policy is to achieve prosperity for the people and alleviate poverty. The most effective method for accelerating economic growth is competition. In the words of Dr Ludwig Erhard, the architect of German reconstruction, 'only by competition can an economy expand to serve all people, especially in their capacity as consumers, and dissolve all advantages that do not result directly from higher performance. Free competition thus leads to progress and profits for the whole social order.'[1] The framework of economic policies should be liberalized and the vast network of economic controls progressively dismantled. Planning should aim at generating broadly based mass purchasing power, and taking ever-widening circles of the people above the poverty line and into higher orbits of prosperity.

Increased productivity and efficiency in the utilization of resources need to be realized, together with modification in the scheme of allocation of scarce means and resources, and the pattern of investment and production. The faster rate of growth of less capital intensive industries in response to a modified pattern of domestic demand and export growth needs to be sustained. Improvement in infrastructure is necessary for better utilization of installed capacity. The basic remedy is control of expenditure, continuous monitoring, and effective implementation of plan projects and public enterprises, and productive use of capital. All this needs efficient financial control and good house-keeping by government at a macro level.

The new strategy must aim at accelerating the momentum of growth, while ensuring that viability in the external balance of payments is maintained; that inflation is controlled; and that the environment and natural resources are protected. This postulates that efficiency and quality of production are improved, so that industry becomes competitive and exports are stimulated. Increased foreign exchange earnings would facilitate an increasing volume of imports of capital goods, raw materials, and maintenance goods, which would sustain a faster rate of growth of industry.

The policy framework for development of industry needs to be modified. The new strategy should adopt a balanced approach in regard to allocation of resources for the development of heavy and light industry. While strategic, basic, core, and infrastructural industries have necessarily to be developed, the growth of other industries should be governed by the logic of expanding demand through agricultural growth and export increase, and emergence of comparative cost advantage. Efficiency has to be increased. This postulates the operation of the price mechanism and adequate provision for incentives.

COMPETITION AND MARKET ECONOMY

Free competition and a market economy confer a dual benefit on the economy: on the one hand, it increases efficiency and maximizes productivity among producers, while on the other, it ensures that the gains of the increased productivity reach the vast majority of the people. The West German government in the post-war period wisely acted on the principle that competition would maximize investment and productivity, resulting in efficient allocation of economic resources, and lead to economic development and its attendant prosperity and high levels of employment and standards of living for the people. This doctrine applied to India would imply that, while some degree of planning in a mixed developing economy like ours is necessary for the proper allocation and utilization of scarce means and resources, the regulations and controls binding private enterprises should not be so great as to stifle initiative and enterprise, and thereby hamper economic growth. The benefits of higher production and productivity should percolate to all strata of society; and as the purchasing power in the hands of people grows, so do their living standards improve. In order to meet the increased demand emanating from the higher purchasing power with the people, the production of essential commodities, wage goods and items of mass consumption must be substantially increased, and should be available to the people at large at reasonable prices. Competition and a free market economy would ensure that the benefits also accrue to the consumer.

The World Development Report 1991[2] states:

> Competitive markets are the best way yet found for efficiently organizing the production and distribution of goods and services. Domestic and external competition provides the incentives that unleash entrepreneurship and technological progress. But markets cannot operate in a vacuum—they require a legal and regulatory framework that only governments can provide.... That is why governments must, for example, invest in infrastructure and provide essential services to the poor.... A consensus is gradually forming in favor of a 'market-friendly' approach to development.

L. K. Jha emphasizes certain measures for stimulating growth and improving living standards. There shoud be decentralization of authority to levels at which new opportunities can be perceived and new initiatives taken, while eliminating controls and regulations which have outlived their utility. Greater reliance should be placed on incentives and promotional measures, so that both the public and private sectors improve their performance and a new momentum is imparted to growth. Besides, the availability of wage goods must be maximized and the generation of new job opportunities stimulated; 'They will sustain each other, strengthen the resource base, provide a measure of immunity from inflation, and contribute to a perceptible improvement in the living standards of the people'.[3] Relief in personal taxes in line with the world trend would provide the household sector with a greater quantum of disposable income, stimulating demand for goods and services, while higher savings would expand the scope for investment. With effective mobilization of savings, there should be an upsurge in economic activity, production and employment.

INFLOW OF FOREIGN CAPITAL

The new strategy must concentrate upon increasing the quantum of foreign investment capital, borrowing in foreign countries and making active efforts at securing higher levels of foreign aid. The basic idea is that greater investment and a larger plan are possible if the private sector is encouraged to garner resources on a higher scale, and foreign investment capital flows into the country together with a greater volume of modern technology. Efforts should therefore be made to garner a larger quantum of foreign aid from friendly prosperous countries like the UK, Japan, West Germany, Italy, France, and Canada. (Positive self-reliance does not mean starving ourselves of investible resources, as may be available.) The net inflow of external assistance amounted to Rs 3955 crores in 1989–90 as against Rs 3645 crores in 1988–9, principally due to a larger quantum of aid from Japan and IBRD. This bears evidence that the potential of greater assistance does exist, provided a degree of finesse is exercised to secure it.

The aid giving countries should also take cognizance of the progress made by the Indian economy, and the potential of aid in stimulating growth. As Gopi Arora, then Finance Secretary, pointed out at the Aid India Consortium Meeting in June 1989, 'it is far wiser to increase concessional external assistance, both multilateral and bilateral, when production and development strategies show every promise of fulfilment, than to try and put together a package when things appear to go wrong. This way the cost is much less and the rewards much greater.'[4] Though development outlays have been financed predominantly by domestic savings, there can be little doubt that external assistance continues to be the important supplement for achieving economic growth and social justice.

Interest rates are comparatively low in certain countries, although they have been raised during the last twelve months. Corporate bond yields, according to *The Economist*,[5] are: Japan 7.85 per cent, West Germany 9.00 per cent, Holland 9.94 per cent, Switzerland 7.22 per cent, France 10.80 per cent, and the USA 9.53 per cent. There is enormous scope for raising funds by government itself, and various financial institutions and banks from the international money markets in these countries, some of which are flush with funds. The institutions may float medium-term bonds, guaranteed by the Government of India. If large companies like TISCO, Hindalco, and Century are able to raise money in the international markets, they should be freely permitted to do so. More corporate entities should be encouraged to obtain equity and borrow from the International Finance Corporation, an affiliate of the World Bank.

Certain institutions like the IDBI, ICICI, and UTI have raised some money in international markets, but the quantum of funds mobilized is miniscule in magnitude in relation to the potential. Japan, West Germany, Switzerland, and the Netherlands provide scope for borrowing cheaply, and full advantage needs to be taken of this source of finance, which has vast potential. It is, however, necessary that borrowing in foreign capital markets is productively utilized so that it becomes self-financing, and repayment of interest and capital are made from surpluses generated by such utilization. Since repayment would also have to be in foreign exchange, such funds must be largely invested in export-oriented, productive concerns. A separate cell should be constituted in the Ministry of Finance to guide and monitor both the raising of money in foreign capital markets and its proper utilization, repayment, and servicing.

There is obviously tremendous scope for improving the level of foreign investment in India. Reorientation of policy to attract direct foreign investment could increase such investment in the first stage from $200 million to $1000 million per year and thereafter to $2000 million annually. The inflow of foreign investment in South Asian countries, particularly Thailand, Singapore, and Taiwan, is considerably higher. On the basis of the present GDP, $2000 million may amount to about 1 per cent. As we have indicated above, such increase could fill the vital gap both in regard to foreign exchange resources and financing of plans. The country has achieved great success in financing ninety per cent of the plans from internal resources. Self-reliance is no doubt desirable, but if growth and welfare can be accelerated by stepping up the components of foreign aid and capital, we are of the distinct opinion that sentimental considerations should not be allowed to act as a constraint. The investment climate must be improved, as must the policy framework, and propitious conditions created for inflow of foreign investment capital.

PERSPECTIVES FOR INDUSTRIAL GROWTH

The country has taken tremendous strides in industrial development during the last four decades. A solid foundation has been built in the fields of basic and core sector industries like steel, cement, heavy engineering and electricals, fertilizers and petrochemicals, and infrastructural industries like oil, power, coal, railway equipment, as also the manufacture of tanks, aircraft, advanced defence equipment, and nuclear energy. Besides, the manufacturing capacities cover a broad spectrum ranging from synthetic and natural fibres, chemicals and automobiles to sophisticated equipment like radars, electronic goods, and telecommunication equipment. The industrial base is widely diversified and fundamentally strong, and is conducive to the building of a superstructure of highly sophisticated capital goods, atomic and defence equipment, and various sunrise industries, with the capacity to absorb the latest technologies and scientific advances for growth and modernization. However, the rate of industrial growth, particularly during the earlier planning period, has been chequered, owing to certain decisions like too great an emphasis on heavy engineering and capital intensive goods. Excessive licensing and controls, and infrastructural shortage and bottlenecks acted as a brake and slowed down the momentum of industrial development.

TABLE 7.1—*Annual Growth Rates in Major Sectors of Industry*

Year	Mining	Manufacturing	Electricity	General
(Weights)	(11.46)	(77.11)	(11.43)	(100.00)
1981–82	17.7	7.9	10.2	9.3
1982–83	12.4	1.4	5.7	3.2
1983–84	11.7	5.7	7.6	6.7
1984–85	8.8	8.0	12.0	8.6
1985–86	4.2	9.7	8.5	8.7
1986–87	6.2	9.3	10.3	9.1
1987–88	3.8	7.9	7.6	7.3
1988–89 (Estimated)	7.9	8.9	9.6	8.8

SOURCE *Economic Survey 1989–90*, GOI, Delhi, p. 50.

It would be seen that during the year 1986–7, the Manufacturing sector with 77 per cent weightage grew by 9.3 per cent as against the Seventh Plan target of 8 per cent. The Mining and Electricity sectors fell short of targets of 13 per cent and 12.1 per cent, growing only by 6.2 per cent and 10.3 per cent. The stimulated growth during 1988–9 at 7.9 per cent, 8.9 per cent and 9.6 per cent in the Mining, Manufacturing and Electricity sectors needs to be maintained in future years.

The overall industrial and infrastructural growth in 1988–9, after the drought year 1987–8, bears evidence to the resilience and strength of the Indian economy; the recuperation has been swift and impressive. As we have already seen, the impact of drought in 1987–8 was also much less than in the earlier drought year 1979–80. This was attributable to improved performance in the infrastucture, particularly growth of coal and oil-based generation of power and better availability of imported industrial inputs. Liberalization of trade and industrial policies also contributed.

LIBERALIZATION AND DISMANTLING OF CONTROLS

Government's policy of liberalization and economic reform has stimulated industrial growth and needs to be pursued with vigour. Since resources for development are scarce and limited, the achievement of accelerated growth postulates greater efficiency in the use of capital and other factors of production. Productivity of both capital and labour has to be stimulated. Bold and new strategies, innovative to a degree, are necessary to accelerate the tempo of industrial development. The macroeconomic framework of industrial policies, in which state intervention and regulations constitute dominant instrumentalities for determining the allocation and utilization of resources, needs to be radically modified and market forces and incentives allowed to play their legitimate role in modulating the nature and direction of industrial development. Government has taken initiative in this direction and greater reliance is being placed on indirect policy instruments instead of direct physical controls. Government, in pursuance of its liberalization policy, has emphasized modernization and technological upgradation in industry, increased productivity, and reduction in costs of production with a view to increasing competitiveness of products and stimulating their export. Indian industries are being exposed to a certain amount of external competition.

Government's liberalization policies have attracted widespread attention and have been commended by the World Bank and other international agencies. The World Bank has highlighted in its Development Report for 1988,[6] the economic progress and policy reforms in India and China. The GDP in China increased from an average of 5.4 per cent during the period 1973 to 1980, to 10.3 per cent between 1980 and 1987, and touched 12.7 per cent in 1985, which is highly commendable. The population is rising at 1.6 per cent per annum—a moderate growth—and the per capita income has grown rapidly. The rise in China's growth rate is largely attributable to extensive domestic reforms and efficient economic management. Transition is taking place from the macroeconomic framework of a centrally planned economy to that in which market forces would be increasingly operative. A dimensional change in the relative roles of public and private sectors is gradually being effected in India. Given the resource constraints in regard to expansion of the public sector, the private sector in the Seventh Plan has been assigned a larger role in accelerating industrial development. Greater opportunities have been afforded to the private sector for development of sunrise and technologically sophisticated industries like electronics and telecommunications, oil refineries, petrochemicals, oil exploration, and steel. Earlier, entry of the private sector into most of these sectors was restricted.

The significant point is that inevitably the process of liberalization is slow and halting. Decision-making in government takes its own time, and a policy matter has to pass through many tiers of authority before a decision is taken. Meanwhile, it takes about two to four years from the conception of a project to its consummation. Owing to inflationary increase in the costs of capital goods, there is escalation in project costs; besides, many hurdles have to be crossed before a plant is established and commissioned. The whole system of industrial licensing and controls is cumbersome and time-consuming. If the momentum of industrial growth is to be accelerated and we are to catch up with countries like Korea, Singapore, Taiwan, Japan, and Western democracies, there is no alternative to removing the network of industrial licensing and controls, and adopt a simple system in which entrepreneurs would be guided by market forces and conditions in regard to establishing an industry, and sectoral allocations of resources in regard to private industrial investment would be influenced by government with fiscal, financial, and institutional instruments.

We would suggest that no licence should be necessary for setting up an industrial project if foreign exchange is not required. An industrial bureau should be set up to provide in-depth studies of demand and supply of commodities, as projected over the next five to ten years, for the guidance of entrepreneurs. Since most medium- and large-scale projects require finance, and often equity, from financial institutions, over-investment in any industry would automatically be discouraged and finance refused by institutions which have adequate financial and technical infrastructure and expertise for the appraisal of new projects. If the advice of industrial bureaus and institutions are discouraging, few entrepreneurs would take the risk of setting up industries where either over-investment has occurred or the prospects are gloomy. Checks and balances against over-investment in any particular industry or misdirected investment in general, should be inbuilt in the policy framework and system for institutional finance; if necessary, the market research wing of central financial institutions should be strengthened.

Shankar Acharya,[7] Advisor in the Government, expressed the view that:

licensed private sector units suffer from all the ills of industrial licensing which have been repeatedly underlined by official and unofficial reviews, including pervasive corruption, costly delays, uneconomic investments, political interference, fragmentation of undertakings into uneconomic scale units, barriers to entry and expansion and heavy administrative costs. And those medium and large-scale units may well have the greatest potential for efficient growth.

It is thus essential that the network of controls and regulations is dismantled, and a socio-economic and legal framework in which industries can be set up is expeditiously created.

Besides industrial licencing, there are various other spheres of economic activity in which government intervention and regulations have become almost a way of life, such as imports and exports, foreign exchange, capital issues, regulations for small and medium industries, extensive labour and factory legislation, company law, and others. Due to shortage of foreign exchange, certain restrictions are necessary; but a substantial part of the restrictive legislation is dispensable. Reduced legislation and regulations would be of advantage to industry and trade, and conducive to economic growth. Single window clearance should be provided for all sanctions required to set up an industry. Preferably, financial institutions should also be associated with the department or agency — like the Secretariat of Industrial Approvals — which grants government approval for the project, so that the financial requirements of the project are also provided simultaneously with other approvals.

The basic objective of introducing the MRTP in the sixties was to reduce concentration of economic power, but now the position has changed. The number of large and medium houses, competing with each other, has increased. Besides, thanks to the nationalization of commercial banks and the enormous powers of financial institutions, the public sector's economic power as compared to MRTP companies is vast. Currently, the exposure of Indian industry to imports has also reduced their economic power. In view of these developments, there is now no rationale for continuing the MRTP provisions in law. The MRTP Act, by providing constraints on industrial development, has slowed down the industrial progress of the country. The MRTP law unfortunately impinges most heavily upon large-scale industry, which has the financial strength and managerial capacity to undertake large projects, secure economies of scale, undertake research and development, and induct sophisticated technology. Here again, what is needed is a bold decision to abolish the MRTP Act, or place it in a state of suspended animation in the interests of accelerating industrial growth. Closer collaboration between government and industry, and greater official support to industry as in Japan would facilitate establishment of industries and expansion of existing units, of which more later. The productivity of existing capital stock and labour has to be raised. Proper maintenance programmes and increased infrastructural availability are necessary to ensure that full utilization of installed capacity of plant and machinery and other factors of production is achieved so as to realize optimum levels of productivity.

SHIFT TOWARDS INDICATIVE PLANNING

The Planning Commission needs to transcend its old mores of thinking and formulating plans. Planning should be indicative and flexible, and not doctrinaire; otherwise it is likely to be self-defeating and counter-productive. The Planning Commission should draw on the vast reservoir of experience of FICCI and Assocham in formulating development plans. The corporate sector should also be freely permitted to develop infrastructure, basic and core industries. The artificial sectoral restrictions and barriers laid down in the Industrial Policy Resolution need to be lowered, and even abolished. Increased growth should emanate not so much from increase in public investment as from an expansion of private industrial activity. Efficiency and technological change have to become the prime movers and engines of growth.

The private sector, constituted of a large number of entrepreneurs and corporate promoters, investors and innovators, whose ranks are being continually reinforced as the impulses of industrial development, generated by technological and other advances, spread in wider circles, has immense potential. Reinforced with 'miniaturized technology', the medium- and small-scale industries afford a large field for industrial growth and stimulated employment as ancillaries to large-scale industries. Low taxes, dismantling of the complex network of controls and regulations, and reduced interest rates would provide stimulants for accelerated growth.

STATE OF THE ART TECHNOLOGY

Britain under Margaret Thatcher achieved almost an 'economic miracle' between 1984 and 1987. In particular, when the British economy grew as fast as Japan and achieved three times the growth-rate of West Germany and France.

TABLE 7.2 — *Economic Indicators for the UK*

	1984 (*Annual basis*)	1987 (*Annual basis*)
	Percentage	
Industrial production	(−) 1.8	4.9
GNP in real terms	2.6	5.3
Retail Sales	3.9	8.8
Unemployment	12.9	9.2
Inflation	6.2	3.8

SOURCE Compiled from various issues of *The Economist*, London, in 1984 and 1987.

The growth was facilitated by reducing inflation, closing uneconomic factories, making companies competitive, and reducing the powers of trade unions. Above all, an increasing number of British companies were now operating with state of the art technology, comparable to that of their foreign competitors. The importance of science and technology, and incorporation of the latest advances in developing both the infrastructure and the industrial framework conducive to accelerating the momentum of growth, can hardly be over-emphasized, and we propose to further discuss the subject in a separate chapter.

A dimensional change is necessary in regard to management–labour relations in public sector enterprises. With labour participation in management and such other socio-political measures as may be necessary, consciousness should be instilled in labour that public enterprises belong to the nation and they have a stake in the well-being of the concerned unit. The management must also actively endeavour to alleviate the grievances of labour, so as to ensure smooth industrial relations, leading to improved productivity. Increase in wages and bonus should be linked to productivity wherever possible, and suitable schemes framed for the purpose. The twin principles of 'hire and fire' and reward for good work should be introduced in some of the undertakings on a pilot project basis. If the scheme proves successful in securing a higher level of efficiency, it should be extended to other units. The public sector is afflicted with militant trade union leadership, low levels of productivity, high wage-levels, and general lack of discipline. It is necessary that government does not allow trade union leaders to jeopardize the investment of the people in the public sector.

As regards management–labour relations in the private sector also, the problems are more or less similar. Frequent strikes and go-slow tactics and non-co-operation in improving norms of work calculated to increase productivity adversely impinge upon production. Militant trade unionism, sometimes with outside leadership, and a multiplicity of trade unions, internecine rivalry and infighting, are some of the problems afflicting industry. On political considerations labour laws have given enormous rights to labour, without the creation of a socio-economic framework and environment in which labour is induced to conscientiously discharge its obligations to industry and the country. Management equally has the reciprocal responsibility of ensuring that the legitimate interests of labour are protected. TISCO is a sterling example in the corporate sector, where both management and labour have developed excellent understanding and co-operation, thereby enabling utilization of over 100 per cent plant capacity. The instance of Japan may be cited where labour seeks to achieve optimum production, and even when workers protest by symbolically wearing protest badges, they continue to work and maintain production. Government must evolve an equitable policy package for improving industrial relations. With optimum production as the objective, labour should be induced to follow improved norms of work which lead to higher productivity, and as a corollary, improved wages.

The high overall level of interest rates in the economy needs to be revised downwards. Government, which was borrowing at about 5 per cent against long- and medium-term securities, is at present paying about 11 per cent, which is prohibitive. Lower interest rates are necessary to reduce the high interest burden on the revenue budget. The commercial bank lending rates at 18 per cent and more are also exorbitant and contribute to raising the unit cost of production and perpetuation of a high-cost economy to the detriment of exports, although direct bank lending rates for export production are on a concessional basis. A word of caution is, however, necessary. Reduction in interest rates on small saving instruments and long-term bank deposits, as also dilution of tax concessions linked to such savings, may adversely affect household savings. What is necessary is to reduce the spread between the bank lending and borrowing rates through increased operational efficiency and reduced working cost of the banks. Besides, the inflation rate has to be kept down at about 5 per cent if a reduction is to be effected in interest rates.

Increase in operational efficiency of public enterprises should be achieved, *inter alia*, through greater autonomy, techno-economic surveys, effective budgeting and monitoring, productivity-linked wages system, and improved technology. Tax reform and stepping up incentives for stimulating capital formation and providing a boost to industrial expansion are dealt with in subsequent chapters.

It is obvious that if the public sector cannot expand in a big way, the private sector has to shoulder the burden of development and it must take giant strides in regard to industrial development if the momentum of growth is to be accelerated.

Inevitably, therefore, the capital market has to be stimulated, for only a buoyant market can facilitate the mobilization of large amounts of equity and debenture capital. Besides fiscal and other incentives for promoting capital formation, government has increased the limits of tax-free dividends and Unit incomes. Capital gains on shares held for more than a year are exempt upto 60 per cent of profits, besides the initial exemption of Rs 10,000, increased to Rs 15000 in the 1991–2 Budget.

What is of greater importance is that Unit Trust, LIC, and other institutions and mutual funds are flush with funds, and their sustained investment on a large scale has revived the capital markets and triggered a boom since October 1988. The fundamental factors are also favourable to a rise in share prices in that, with a good monsoon, both agricultural and industrial production are expanding, corporate results and dividends are encouraging, and the economy on the whole is in good shape and resurgent.

TABLE 7.3 — *Consents granted by the C.C.I. to Government and Private Sector Companies*

Capital Issues	(excluding Bonus Shares) in crore rupees
1986–87	5579
1987–88	5278
1988–89	8072
1989–90	11705

SOURCE *RBI Annual Report 1989–90*, p. 112; *1987–88*, p. 55; Controller of Capital Issues.

The prevalent buoyancy in the capital market has enabled several companies to raise considerable amounts of capital, and it is envisaged that it may be possible to raise about Rs 12,500 crores a year in 1991–2 and subsequent years. Government has established the Securities and Exchange Board of India (SEBI) to ensure that the stock exchange and capital markets function in a disciplined manner. The Board seeks to maintain and accelerate the momentum of growth of capital markets, financial institutions, and intermediaries, while ensuring that the interests of investors and the general public are protected.

While on the one hand, the policy of liberalization and dismantling of the network of controls should be further pursued, interest rates and taxes on corporate and personal incomes need to be reduced further in line with the world trend, so as to maintain a healthy investment climate, conducive to capital formation and inflow of foreign investment capital with modern technology. Increased capacity utilization in both the public and private sectors and improvement in the operational efficiency of public enterprises would all contribute to an upsurge in industrial production. Increase in the productivity of scarce resources and factors of production is vitally necessary to reduce the unit cost of industry, increase competitiveness both in the internal and international markets, and reduce the capital–output ratio.

ACTIVE GOVERNMENT SUPPORT TO INDUSTRY: SCENARIO IN JAPAN

The Japanese economy in the decade after 1955 achieved high growth rates in the region of 8 to 12 per cent per annum in real terms which, by any standards, was a signal performance. The oil crisis of 1973 and severe global recession brought on a slump in 1974, but the subsequent recovery was swift, and since then, except during the second oil shock in 1979, the economy has achieved a steady rate of expansion of over 5 per cent, which again is remarkable for a developed industrial economy. The average growth-rates for the period 1965 to 1989 for certain leading economies are indicated in Table 7.4. These high rates of growth enabled Japan to almost close the gap in relation to national and per capita incomes between itself and Western industrial democracies.

The Japanese progress was largely attributable to certain factors, which bear analysis:

1. Almost half the rapid growth of 10 per cent in the post-war period was due to technological innovation, of which more later (*vide* ch. 14).

2. The savings and investment rates were high, almost double the rates in the USA (*vide* Table 7.4).

With among the highest savings and investment rates in the world, coupled with a high debt–equity ratio, the economy during the period 1955 to 1972 gathered and maintained a vigorous momentum of growth. Capitalization was at a high level, and risk capital was available in adequate measure.

3. There was a remarkable upsurge of national feeling and

consciousness that the national goal of surpassing the West had to be realized at all costs; this manifested itself in a work-ethos of unsurpassed dedication and commitment by government, management, workers, and the general public.

4. Herman Kahn[8] states that the achievement of rapid economic growth by Japan was, *inter alia*, attributable to excellent management of the economy and cooperation of labour; this resulted in a controlled and, to some degree, a collectivist (Japan Inc.) economy, but still competitive and market-oriented capitalism.

The important point, besides the high debt–equity ratio permitted, is that entrepreneurial risk-taking in Japan touched high levels in establishing new industries. This helped the Japanese economy to achieve high rates of growth, and at the same time also to cover losses occurring in other concerns. A large Japanese firm in financial difficulties would almost certainly be assisted by the government, by arranging for a merger or through additional loans from banks. In any case, employees, stock-holders, debtors, and other individuals involved would be almost certain of being looked after. Thus one of the reasons that many large modern Japanese firms can afford to operate in a seemingly risky way is that they know their government and society stand behind them and that they will not be mercilessly driven to the wall.[8] This tacit support of the government enabled industry to enter new technologically advanced areas and take risks which industrialists in other countries would probably avoid.

TABLE 7.4—*Real GDP Growth, Investment and Inflation 1965–89 (Average)—Selected countries* (Percentage change over previous year)

	GDP		Investment		Inflation	
	1965–80	1980–9	1965–80	1980–9	1965–80	1980–9
Japan	6.6	4.0	6.9	5.7	7.6	1.3
USA	2.7	3.3	2.8	4.7	6.5	4.0
West Germany	3.3	1.9	1.7	1.9	5.2	2.7
France	3.8	2.1	3.8	1.8	8.6	6.5
UK	2.9	2.6	1.3	6.9	10.7	6.1

SOURCE: Compiled from *World Development Report 1991*, World Bank/OUP, New York, Tables pp. 204, 207, 219.

TABLE 7.5 — *Ratio of Savings to GNP (%) for Japan*

1957–61	33.4
1964–68	36.4
1971–74	38.7
1976–80*	34.0

SOURCE *OECD Economic Survey*, Japan, July 1976,
p. 46.
* Estimates.

Besides indicative planning, there is close liaison between industry and government, and the various official departments make strenuous efforts to ensure that all possible facilities are provided for establishment of new industries in the shortest possible time, that adequate finance is available for industry, and in times of crisis government renders every possible help to industry to tide over the difficulties. Another important factor is that in the second and third stages of industrialization in Japan, the government has concentrated on the development of modern and sunrise industries, and insisted that industry fall in line with government policy. Companies have to release men, materials, and resources for more efficient enterprises. It is this transfer of factors from less efficient to more efficient sectors that facilitates rapid economic growth.

This shows how necessary it is that there should be almost continuous dialogue between government and industry in developing economies. Joint consultative committees for industries should be established, while those existing should be rendered more effective and purposeful. In the case of sick industries, timely assistance on the requisite scale at the stage of incipient sickness could pre-empt deterioration and bring about a revival.

It has been observed that financial institutions and banks in India often tend to be fair weather friends to industry. Once an industry runs into serious difficulties, the supply of timely and adequate finance dries up. The BIFR (and IRBI earlier)[9] have been established to assist in the revival of sick industry and effect their reconstruction, but it appears that BIFR has not been armed with sufficient powers to implement its schemes. The Board should be empowered to direct institutions and banks to provide the necessary funds for reconstruction and implement the schemes devised by the BIFR. The Reserve Bank should modify its norms and in the case of a sick industry, saddled with heavy losses, permit write-off of accumulated interest due, where necessary. At present, generally, only funding is permitted and this is often a serious hurdle in the reconstruction or amalgamation of sick industry. If an industry fails to revive, even the principal provided by the financial institutions is lost.

Active support by government, institutions and banks to industries at all stages of development is imperative; it would be an important factor in enabling Indian industry to venture in high technology and risk-prone areas, and to expand and modernize.

TABLE 7.6 — *Trends in Production of Infrastructure Industries*

Industry	Unit	Weight	April–March		
			1987–88	1988–89	1989–90
Electricity	Million KWH	11.43	201894 (+7.6)	221125 (+9.5)	244971 (+10.8)
Coal	Million Tonnes	6.61	179.74 (+8.5)	194.57 (+8.3)	200.85 (+3.2)
Seleable Steel	Thousand Tonnes	5.21	8588.0 (+4.5)	9206.0 (+7.2)	9028.7 (−1.9)
Crude Petroleum	–do–	2.41	30357 (−0.4)	32040 (+5.5)	34076 (+6.4)
Petroleum Refinery Products	–do–	1.52	44407 (+2.7)	45384 (+2.2)	48300 (+6.4)
Cement	–do–	1.60	39550 (+8.1)	44295 (+12.0)	45603 (+3.0)
Composite Index of Infrastructure Production (1980–81 = 100)		28.77	178.6 (+6.0)	193.2 (+8.2)	205.1 (+6.2)

NOTE Figures in brackets indicate percentage variations over the corresponding figures of the previous year.

SOURCE *RBI Annual Report 1989–90*, p. 25.

INFRASTRUCTURE

One of the major causes of under-utilization of capacity in industry and consequent loss of production, incomes, and revenues is shortage of power. The estimated deficiency of power availability increased from 7.9 per cent in 1985–6 to about 10.9 per cent in 1987–8. That power shortage increased despite considerable increase in additional capacity and plant–load factor, bears evidence of the tremendous increase in demand for power that comes with rapid industrial development. The availability of power, coal, transport, and communications must always remain way ahead of the progressive demands of growing industry. One of the principal criticisms of the public sector is that while it engaged in diverse industrial activities, it has failed to perform its basic duty of ensuring that the infrastructure keeps pace with estimates of future demand.

Improved plant–load factor (PLF) of electricity generating units from about 56 to 65 per cent would sizeably augment infrastructural availability and remove production bottlenecks. Efforts should be made to increase the PLF in the eastern region from a low of about 23 to 39 per cent to about 50 per cent. With increase in capacity utilization, better maintenance and reduction in transmission and generation losses, the total availability of power would greatly increase, requiring minimal additional investment. The establishment of a high-powered national techno-economic Power Board, with the specific objective of increasing the PLF in existing plants all over the country, would provide the requisite thrust to the exercise undertaken by government in this direction. If a private sector captive power unit of an aluminium plant in U.P. can achieve a PLF of above 80 per cent, it is certainly possible to sizeably increase the PLF all over the country from the present low levels, provided determined efforts are made to remove the operational constraints, and check the activities which cause losses in generation and distribution.

Entrepreneurs in underdeveloped countries often face difficulty in building up industrial complexes because of insufficient infrastructural facilities in the districts in which their projects are located. There are various backward areas in which adequate power, transport, communications, housing, and other social overhead facilities may not be adequately available. Building roads, railway sidings, housing, even captive power plants, all increase the cost of the project; and interest charges enter the cost of production. Actually, it is one of the principal functions of the state to build the infrastructure. The concept of growth centres is well-conceived, but here again in implementation, the various infrastructural facilities fall short of requirements.

Production of crude petroleum, which grew at a remarkable pace during the eighties, almost reached a plateau of around 30,000 tonnes during the years 1984–5 to 1987–8, and increased by about 5.5 per cent during 1988–9, and by 6.4 per cent in 1989–90 to 34,000 tonnes.[10] There was also improved capacity utilization of refineries. The imperative need to increase production of oil at the present juncture can hardly be over-emphasized. With the international prices of crude oil at above $25 a barrel, thanks to the Gulf crisis, and the precarious balance of payments position, the country is in the throes of an oil crisis, the ramifications of which extend to various industries with petro-products as their inputs, and adversely affect production and profitability. Scope for reduction in consumption of oil and allied products does exist, and government is making active efforts in this direction. The effective solution, however, to this lies in fruitful investment in oil exploration and increased production. It is learnt that the ONGC has decided to raise annual production from Bombay offshore oil-fields from 22 million tonnes to 30 million tonnes[11] by the end of Eighth Plan through investment of Rs 10,000 crores. It is also proposed to implement the gas flaring reduction project, for which finance is being sought from the World Bank.

Liberalization has an important role to play in regard to increase in the production of cement and fertilizers. The cement industry was in bad shape with inadequate return on capital employed, outdated technology, and many of the industrial units incurring losses. Investment was not forthcoming due to price controls. During the decade of the seventies, production increased by only 5.5 million tonnes. Partial decontrol (later full decontrol) had a catalytic effect, and production soared from about 20 million tonnes in 1980–1 to about 45.6 million tonnes in 1989–90. At this level of production, there appears to be an equilibrium between demand and supply. The fertilizer industry would also be able to increase production sizeably if price controls are removed. Modification in norms has subdued its growth, which is likely to lead to larger fertilizer imports and the consequent loss of foreign exchange.

Production of coal has been increasing by more than 8 per cent per annum during the years 1986–7 to 1988–9,[12] but the rate of growth was lower at 3.2 per cent in 1989–90. However, the principal complaint of business against the coal industry is in regard to the quality of coal, which adversely affects the quantum and quality of production of steel, cement, power, and other user industries. Nationalization has caused the price of coal to escalate very considerably, and this has enhanced costs of production all round in the industrial sector. The demand for coal is greater than supply, with a gap of about 12.5 million tonnes. Import of about 4.5 million tonnes of coking coal would partially cover the demand. The heavy losses incurred by the coal industry, which is almost entirely in the public sector, despite periodical price increases, calls for an in-depth study to determine whether partial or full privatization would assist in reducing the burden of these losses on the public exchequer.

The steel industry recorded a setback in production of (−)1.9 per cent in 1989–90 from a 7.2 per cent increase in 1988–9, and 4.5 per cent rise in 1987–8.[13] The shortfall in production occurred due to shortage of coking coal and power. The Durgapur Plant of SAIL and Indian Iron recorded lower production levels. There is a sharp difference between capacity utilization in the public and private sectors: in the SAIL plants of about 76 per cent; TISCO about 105 per cent. This has a corresponding impact upon profitability. Here too demand is likely to exceed overall supply. The importance of import substitution for the country at this juncture can hardly be over-emphasized; and the steel industry needs to produce flat products and sophisticated grades of alloy and special steels in sizeable volume in order to obviate imports of these categories of products which involve foreign exchange. Besides, the industry should also expand its volume of exports.

The development of exports would necessitate quality control and competitive prices. Production would have to be maximized and regularity in export supplies ensured; a general toning up of the industry would in the long run benefit the producing units. The best solution for stimulating production and efficiency in the industry is price decontrol; besides, there should be no restrictions, as in the past, on the entry of new producing units. Government has liberalized its policy and many sponge iron projects are under construction and on the drawing boards. Integrated steel plants, right from the mining of ore to the production of saleable steel and steel products, should be permitted. The modernization of older steel plants, like Indian Iron, has become imperative, and the schemes should be implemented expeditiously.

While there has been criticism of government's earlier policy of concentrating investment on heavy industry, in fairness it must be recognized that the steel and heavy electrical plants built up pursuant to this policy have laid firm foundations for India's industrial development and its defence requirements. Jawaharlal Nehru was the architect of modern India, and his foresight and vision in regard to the country's future goal of building up a highly sophisticated and industrialized Indian economy immensely contributed to the country's industrialization and progress. That there have been shortcomings in implementation in the form of considerable cost and time overruns in the public sector steel plants, and policy constraints on the entry of new firms in the industry restricted its progress, is true, but on the whole, the structural framework and sinews of the country's industrial growth are strong. The country's economy has great resilience, and despite temporary setbacks and short-term crises, there can be little doubt that it will eventually resume its path of steady growth.

REFERENCES

1. Ludwig Erhard, *Prosperity through Competition*, Thames & Hudson, London, 1958, Preface.
2. *World Development Report 1991*, World Bank/OUP, New York, p. 1.
3. L. K. Jha *Economic Strategy for the 80*s, Allied Publishers Private Ltd., Delhi, p. 152.
4. Gopi Arora, Speech reported in the *Economic Times*, Calcutta, 20 June 1989, p. 1.
5. *The Economist*, London, 2 Dec. 1990, p. 120.
6. *World Development Report 1988*, World Bank/OUP, New York, p. 24.
7. Shankar Acharya, 'Towards Reform of Industrial Policy', in *Seventh Plan Perspectives*, ed. M. S. Adiseshiah, Lancer International, Delhi, 1985, p. 147.
8. Herman Kahn *The Emerging Japanese Super-State*, Penguin Books, Harmondsworth, 1973, pp. 123, 250.
9. BIFR = Board of Industrial and Financial Reconstruction.
   IRBI = Industrial Reconstruction Bank of India.
10. SOF: *RBI Annual Report 1989–90*, p. 25.
11. SOF: Report in *Financial Express*, 9 Nov. 1990.
12. SOF: *RBI Annual Report 1989–90*, pp. 25, 26; *vide* Table 7.6.
13. SOF: *vide* Table 7.6.

8

Control of Inflation: Friedman's Monetarist Approach versus Supply Side Factors

Inflation is a global phenomenon; with the second oil shock in late 1979, it engulfed most developing and industrial countries. However, since 1980, inflation recorded a decline. This was partly attributable to a substantial fall in oil prices, and lower international commodity prices. Budgetary deficits had also been reduced in major industrial economies. The fiscal deficit as a percentage of GNP declined from 5.4 per cent in 1983 to 4.6 per cent in 1986 in the seven major industrial countries. Average inflation, as measured by the GDP deflator, came down from 9.3 per cent in 1980 to 3.4 per cent in 1986.[1] It is evident that inflation had been controlled in most OECD countries. The average inflation rate in the developing economies also declined from about 16 per cent in 1980 to about 8 per cent in 1986. A distinction, of particular relevance to developing economies, is generally made between a 'functional rise' in prices and an inflationary increase. A moderate rise of about 4 to 5 per cent per annum is considered to be in the nature of a functional rise, necessary to channelize productive resources for investment in the expanding sectors of the economy. This is confirmed by W. W. Rostow's[2] empirical studies: according to him inflation contributed to several take-offs. During the late 1790s in Britain, in the 1850s in the USA, and in 1970s in Japan, capital formation was assisted by price inflation, which resulted in resources moving away from consumption to profits.

Before discussing the current economic situation in the country after the third oil shock in 1990, we would like to trace the basic causes for the inflationary build-up in the economy during the Seventh Plan period, despite reduction in buffer food stocks and imports of essential commodities to reduce pressure on prices. Because of government's successful economic management, despite drought during 1987–8, prices increased only by 10.6 per cent, whereas they had risen by 21.4 per cent in 1979–80, which was also a year of drought. Besides, past experience shows that prices increased sharply after the drought during the first quarter of the following year. During the first quarter of 1988–9 prices rose only by 2.3 per cent which was the lowest first quarter increase in the eighties. The buffer stock of food-grains and timely imports of pulses, a developed public distribution system and restricted growth of M3 money supply, during 1987–8 at 15.3 per cent, enabled the economy to successfully cope with the drought and keep inflation within manageable proportions. Due to high budgetary deficits, the increase in money supply ranged during the Seventh Plan period between 15.3 and 19.9 per cent, leading to excess liquidity in the economy. Besides, there was the overhang of liquidity from earlier years. The fiscal imbalance has been compounded by a chronic shortfall in the production and supply of certain commodities like pulses, oilseeds, and edible oils. Although domestic supplies were buttressed through imports, foreign exchange constraints also acted as a restraining factor. Increase in administered prices of commodities and services like steel, coal, petroleum, and railway freight year after year have added to cost–push inflation, and since these are basic commodities and services, the price rise enters into the cost of production of a wide range of other goods and products, leading to a spill-over of cost-push increases to various sectors of the economy. These price increases, particularly during periods of high inflation, far exceeded the functional price rise conducive to accelerating the momentum of growth.

IMPACT OF THE UNION BUDGET 1990–91

The Union Budget 1990–1 has had an inflationary impact. The budgetary deficit of Rs 7,602 crores has increased owing, *inter alia*, to higher write-off of farmers' loans than Rs 1,000 crores provided and larger incidence of dearness allowance to employees than the token provision of Rs 100 crores, resulting from inability of the ministries to cut expenditure in order to absorb the additional instalments of dearness allowance as envisaged in the Budget speech. But of even greater relevance is the cost–push effect of the increase in the prices of diesel, petrol and tyres, railway freight, telecommunication charges, and other levies. The costs of transport and other service industries have risen. The hike in the administered prices of some commodities or others has almost become an annual feature of pre-budget or budgetary exercises, and there is no denying its widespread inflationary impact. The scope for buttressing stocks of sensitive items through imports is restricted by limitations of foreign exchange. If inflation is to be controlled, the authorities will need to impose fiscal self-discipline, restrict budgetary deficits, and control excess liquidity in the economy. On the supply side, the availability of essential commodities has to be augmented and the public distribution system strengthened. Inflation is not only the most regressive form of taxation, but the resources available for investment and development are also reduced by its impact upon the government budget.

The then Finance Minister stated that the deficit on revenue account in the 1991 Budget was attributable to certain compulsions inherent in the present situation. The Budget had to bear the pressure of a higher defence allocation and an increased share of rural sector outlay, which had been stepped up from 44 per cent to 49 per cent. The earlier growth model was being restructured with greater emphasis on employment generation.[3] Government wanted horizontal growth of the national economy, covering all segments of the people. The Finance Ministry would exercise monthly checks to ensure that government's expenditure remained under control, and revenue collections transcended Budget estimates for 1990–1. Government expected the corporate sector to respond to the reduction in the basic corporate tax rate from 50 per cent to 40 per cent[4], and the generation of increased production and revenues leading to lower budgetary deficits.

In view of the sizeable budgetary deficits, and continuous increase in money supply largely to finance government's overspending, drastic measures are imperative so that inflation does not get out of control. Certain measures of control necessary are:

1. A two-pronged approach is necessary to contain inflationary pressures: the aggregate money supply and consequent upsurge in demand should be reduced, and aggregate real output increased.

2. There has been an increase in money supply by about 18 per cent in 1988–9 and about 20 per cent in 1989–90, while real

output (GDP) increased by 10.6 per cent and 4.5 per cent in the respective years. The basic point that needs to be emphasized is that the Reserve Bank should limit expansion of currency on government account to the extent that the money stock is either equal to the growth of real output, or marginally higher. If under special circumstances there is expansion of currency, there should be mechanism for automatic extinction of such money by suitable surplus budgeting or open-market operations. Fiscal policy has a crucial role to play by cushioning the monetary impact of government's operations. Greater reliance on surpluses generated by the budget and public sector undertakings, and correspondingly diminished recourse to borrowings to finance plans is imperative to check inflation.

3. Both household and public savings should be increased substantially. Various measures to achieve this have been suggested earlier. It is necessary, however, to emphasize in this context that expenditure financed by deficits creates high-powered money, which has a multiplier effect in the economy with consequent inflationary rise in prices. The concept of safe limit to deficit financing should be borne in mind. According to the World Bank report,[5] 'excessive fiscal deficit and the resulting financing requirements of the public sector have often been at the root of macroeconomic imbalances'. Where larger deficit financing becomes necessary, the extra money created should be liquidated or mopped up within a certain period of time.

4. High excise duties and wage payments contribute to cost–push inflation, particularly on account of the cascading effect of excise duty, customs duty, and sales taxes on raw materials and intermediate goods. Although MODVAT helps in reducing this effect, it is desirable to keep these duties within reasonable limits. Wage increase must be linked with productivity. Additional resource mobilization should concentrate on obtaining greater revenues and savings from the rural areas, where considerable scope exists. Increasing the ratio of taxation to GDP and taxing rural incomes will be discussed later.

5. The parallel economy, that has developed on account of generation and circulation of black money, should be controlled. An enlightened taxation policy and reasonable tax rates, besides rationalization and simplification of the income-tax law and efficient administration, as also improvement in the sales tax

structure in various states, would encourage voluntary compliance and reduce creation of black money. Use of such money for hoarding or creating artificial scarcities should be firmly dealt with.

6. The quality of public spending must improve, and government's non-plan and unproductive expenditure be drastically curtailed. Wastage and leakage of funds has to be checked, and productivity of capital stimulated. Monitoring project and plan expenditure is necessary to ensure that they yield adequate returns and production is maximized. This would reduce the inflationary potential in the economy.

7. Increase in production of foodgrains and other agricultural commodities and industrial goods and services is necessary to augment supplies and check prices. Higher production balances the effect of increased money supply.

8. The public distribution system should be widened to cover more commodities of mass consumption, and its systemic efficiency should be increased. It is an important instrument for keeping inflation under control.

9. Where endemic shortage exists, as in the case of pulses and edible oils, there is no alternative but to maintain adequate imports till production rises to meet the demand—which keeps on rising with growth in population.

10. The manufactured products component in the aggregate supply should be substantially augmented to control prices. Infrastructural and other bottlenecks which lead to under-utilization of installed capacities operate as constraints to realization of optimum production, and the consequent loss in supply of goods adds to the inflationary potential. Improvement in power supply through increased plant–load factor and removal of other infrastructural constraints in this context would go a long way in increasing production and meeting the challenge of inflation.

MONETARIST APPROACH

Milton Friedman,[6] on the basis of extensive empirical studies, argues that equilibrium between the quantity of money and aggregate output is necessary if inflation is to be controlled. He is categoric that 'Inflation is a monetary phenomenon arising from a more rapid increase in the quantity of money than in output; there is only one cure for inflation: a slower rate of increase in the quantity of money', which modern governments can regulate. It takes a number of years for inflation to develop; naturally, the cure for inflation also takes time, and unpleasant side effects of the remedies for inflation cannot be avoided.

It is stated that on an average over the past century in the USA, UK, and other Western countries, increased monetary growth took six to nine months in working its way and producing increased economic growth and employment. It takes between twelve to eighteen months in manifesting itself in the form of price increase and inflation.

JAPAN: A CASE STUDY

Taking the case of Japan as a case study, Friedman says that the quantity of money in Japan continuously increased in 1971 and by mid-1973 it was increasing at over 25 per cent a year. It took about a year for the higher money supply to have an impact on prices, and inflation rose to about 26 per cent in 1974–5. Japan changed its policy framework and monetary growth was reduced from about 25 per cent a year to between 10 to 15 per cent per annum over a period of five years. Inflation started declining within 18 months after monetary growth had been checked, and a period of about 30 months elapsed before inflation declined to a single digit figure. Inflation was constant for about two years and then it started declining towards zero in response to further reduction in growth of money supply. A figure, presented by the Japanese Economic Planning Agency, is illustrative of Friedman's thesis.

Owing to the high rate of growth of GDP in Japan, increase in monetary growth of between 10 to 15 per cent would be conducive to stable prices. The corresponding rate of growth in money supply for the USA would be 3 to 5 per cent. Friedman's thesis that prices rise if the increase in money supply is not matched by output, is a basic proposition, the validity of which is scarcely in doubt. But his assertion that the behaviour of money is the senior partner; of output, the junior partner, may be questionable. In India, since the population is vast, adequate supply of goods and commodities of mass consumption, both of agricultural and industrial origin, is necessary to balance monetary expansion and hold inflation in check. Actually, a study of increase in money supply, agricultural and industrial production and prices over the past few years shows that the periods of high price rise above 20 per cent per annum in 1973–5 and 1979–80 more or less coincided with shortfall in agricultural and industrial production. A. P. Thirlwall regards the debate between monetarists and structuralists to be inconclusive. He says, 'Inflation has probably been a combination of both demand and supply factors; all inflations other than hyperinflations, usually are'![7]

POLITICS, ECONOMIC PERFORMANCE, AND INFLATION: THE LATIN AMERICAN EXPERIENCE

It is instructive to examine the Latin American experience of the impact of political and economic reforms introduced by governments in order to promote populist policies and redistributive programmes, and assist the rural poor and the urban working class. The World Bank[8] has cited the cases of Brazil and Peru during the period 1985–6 and Chile during 1970–3. Macroeconomic expansion, with the objective of promoting employment and raising real wages, initially increased GDP and real wages in Chile and Peru. But eventually, foreign exchange reserves were well-nigh exhausted, and recourse taken to foreign borrowings and devaluation of currencies. Inflation in Brazil increased by 400 per cent, and also flared up in other Latin American countries. Ultimately, the programmes collapsed, investments were reduced, capital outflows increased, and real wages declined. The target groups, instead of being benefited, actually suffered. Besides, there was erosion in the credibility of government, accompanied by loss of investors' confidence.

The important point is that unless production and productivity are stimulated, any expenditure out of created money or even borrowed money (beyond limits) for social welfare programmes can only lead to an upsurge in inflation. If it is allowed to grow, it ultimately leads to sharp erosion in the value of the currency and hyper-inflation, which completely undermines the stability of the economy. Internal and external indebtedness increase and the country tends to be enmeshed in a debt trap. At that stage, it becomes difficult to check inflation, even through adjustment programmes like restructuring of fiscal policy, control of expenditure, and currency reform. The policy environment needs to be changed, which is more easily said than done.

THE GULF CRISIS AND THE OIL SHOCK

The price situation during 1990–1 was fragile and latent inflationary forces were exerting their pressure. The situation was serious enough and then came the oil shock, like a bolt from the blue, which added a new dimension to the inflationary situation in the country and compounded its difficulties. While the impact of the Gulf crisis upon the Indian economy has been considered in detail in Chapter 11, it may be mentioned here that the increase in prices and shortages of diesel, petrol, and other oil products have set off a chain reaction in price hikes, which are manifesting themselves in almost all sectors of the economy. The Wholesale Price Index (WPI) had come down on a point to point basis from 10.6 per cent in 1987–8—drought year—to 5.7 per cent in 1988–9. But despite good agricultural and industrial production during the last two years, the WPI escalated to 9.1 per cent in 1989–90. Since then prices, including those of food articles, have continued to rise, and it is certain that 1990–1 will end with double digit inflation, maybe around 12 to 14 per cent. Prof. B. B. Bhattacharya[9] of the Institute of Economic Growth attributed the rise in prices of food articles to a quantum jump in the procurement prices of wheat, rice and oilseeds, and opined that government would have to resist populist demands of this nature if inflation was to be checked.

In the context of the Gulf crisis, it has become imperative that government addresses itself to the relevant macroeconomic variables: deficit financing and non-plan expenditure, interest charges and subsidies have to be controlled, so that budgetary deficits and growth in money supply are restrained; and investment is matched by resource mobilization in the form of taxation, borrowings, and surpluses of public enterprises. On the supply side, adequate availability of goods either through production or imports has to be ensured. Money invested in projects and enterprises, and development expenditure incurred, must yield goods and services commensurate with the investment.

With the increase in prices of petroleum products and its attendant downstream effects upon the costs and prices of a number of commodities, an inflation psychosis appears to be developing, and in anticipation of two digit inflation, price increases are occurring. The climate of shortages, although in the incipient stage, is rapidly setting in owing to scarcity in the energy sector, particularly of diesel and coal, the foreign exchange crunch leading to constraint in imports and the chronic infrastructural deficiencies—which the public sector has not been able to overcome despite four decades of planned development. Domestic oil production has to be increased almost on war-footing and efforts made to reduce infrastructural constraints. There is enormous potential for stepping up power generation through greater capacity utilization of existing plants, provided intensive efforts are made on a micro basis to resolve the problems of each individual unit. The overall plant–load factor (including reduction in transmission losses) can be doubled in Eastern India and increased by about one-third in the other parts of the country. Scope for increase in coal, cement, steel, and fertilizer production is also considerable, provided determined efforts are made.

Nature has been kind in that the monsoon has been satisfactory for the third successive year and foodgrains production should reach its targets. That inflation is rising despite good agricultural production, bears evidence to the seriousness of the problem. Co-ordinated efforts by government, the corporate sector, and the public at large, are necessary to check the inflation psychosis, apply restraints and implement supply and demand management measures to overcome the crisis. Government must also avoid increasing administered prices at this juncture, although pressures to do so are bound to mount (IAC has already asked for further fare rise, perhaps for the third time in 1991). The factors of production must be fully and efficiently utilized so as to achieve optimum productivity and maximum production. The entire macroeconomic policy framework should be such that adequate equilibrium is maintained over a period between money supply and aggregate output; and fiscal and other economic policies should be so attuned as to have an anti-inflationary bias.

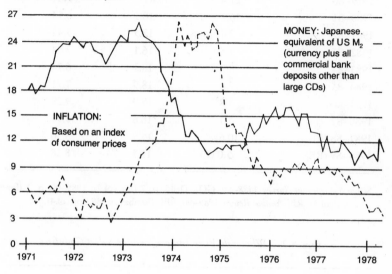

INFLATION FOLLOWS MONEY :
THE CASE OF JAPAN

Percent increase from
same month of previous year.

MONEY: Japanese.
equivalent of US M₂
(currency plus all
commercial bank
deposits other than
large CDs)

INFLATION:
Based on an index
of consumer prices

Source: Japanese Economic Planning Agency from Milton and Rose
Friedman, *Free to Choose*, Secker and Warburg, London. 1980

TABLE 8.1— *Wholesale Prices, M₃ and Deficit as Proportion of GDP*

Year	Percentage Increase over previous year Wholesale Price Index (on Point to Point basis)	M₃	Gross Fiscal Deficit as Percentage of GDP at Current Market Prices
1979–80	21.4	17.7	N A
1980–81	16.7	18.1	6.54
1981–82	2.4	12.5	5.44
1982–83	7.3	16.1	7.04
1983–84	8.2	18.1	6.74
1984–85	7.6	18.9	7.71
1985–86	3.8	15.9	9.29
1986–87	5.3	18.6	9.50
1987–88 (P)	10.6	15.9	8.50
1988–89 (RE)	5.0 (P)	17.7	8.18

SOURCE *Economic Survey 1988–89*, GOI, Delhi, p. 2 (for col.2); 1989–90, p. 1 (for col.3); *RBI Annual Report 1989–90*, RBI, Bombay, p. 86 (for col.4).

TABLE 8.2— *Wholesale Price Indices for Five Select Countries*

Year	India	USA	UK	Japan	W.Germany
				(Base 1980 = 100)	
1981	112.2	109.1	109.6	101.4	107.8
1982	115.0	111.3	118.0	103.2	114.2
1983	124.0	112.7	124.4	100.9	115.8
1984	134.6	115.4	132.1	100.7	119.2
1985	142.4	114.9	139.4	99.5	122.1
1986	150.0	111.5	145.7	90.4	119.0
1987	159.1	114.5	151.3	87.0	116.0
1988	172.3	119.0	160.0	86.2	117.5
1989					
Jan.	176.4	122.8	166.1	86.1	119.9
Feb.	177.0	123.4	167.4	86.4	120.1

Year	India	USA	UK	(Base 1980 = 100) Japan	W.Germany
March	178.9	124.2	168.2	86.6	120.5
April	101.8	125.1	171.2	88.1	121.1
May	184.5	125.9	172.2	88.7	121.2
June	186.2	125.6	172.9	89.3	121.1
July	188.0(P)	125.5	173.0	89.3	121.2
Aug.	189.7(P)	124.8	173.2	89.3	121.4
Sept.	192.3(P)	125.1	174.6	89.6	121.6

(P) — provisional

SOURCE *The Economic Times*, Calcutta, 11 Jan. 1990.

REFERENCES

1. SOF: *World Development Report 1987*, World Bank/OUP, New York, p. 16. (also *vide* Fig. 2.2.)
2. W. W. Rostow, *The Stages of Economic Growth*, CUP, Cambridge, 1960, p. 48.
3. *Vide* ch. 23.
4. The actual Corporate tax rate, including surcharge, for public companies is 46 per cent; this, however, has been increased to 51.75 per cent in the Union Budget 1991–2.
5. *World Development Report 1988*, World Bank/OUP, New York, p. 52.
6. Milton and Rose Friedman, *Free to Choose*, Secker & Warburg, London, 1980, pp. 281, 282.
7. A. P. Thirlwall *Growth and Development*, 3 ed., *ELBS*, Macmillan, London, 1986, p. 287.
8. *World Development Report 1990*, World Bank/OUP, New York, p. 12.
9. B. B. Bhattacharya, *The Economic Times*, Calcutta (PTI Report), 20 Nov. 1990.

9

Agricultural Breakthrough: Social Welfare, Justice, and Equity

The importance of agriculture in India lies in the dependence of over seventy per cent of the population upon it for their livelihood, and its accounting for about 32 per cent of gross domestic product (1988). W. W. Rostow says that agriculture has three principal roles in facilitating a transition from traditional society to a successful take-off. Agriculture must supply in adequate measure food for subsistence, not only of the rural population, but also for growing numbers of people in urban areas in the context of increasing urbanization. It must augment supplies of food and other commodities for export in order to generate foreign exchange for import of plant and machinery and technical know-how for industrial development. This occurred in the USA, Canada, Russia, and elsewhere. Agriculture also provides the demand for agro-based industrial products, such as farm machinery, fertilizers, diesel pumps, pesticides, and other inputs produced by the modern industrial sectors. 'An environment of rising real incomes in agriculture, rooted in increased productivity, may be an important stimulus to new modern industrial sectors essential to take-off.'[1]

Agriculture needs to generate surpluses for growth of modern industry, as in the late nineteenth and early twentieth centuries in Japan, Russia, and elsewhere. Japan during its early period of growth between 1870 and 1920, financed its industrial development by extracting surpluses from agriculture through a stiff land tax. A part of the increase in land incomes arising from growth in productivity was siphoned off and channelized into building up industrial complexes by the government. An increase in agricultural productivity thus constitutes a concomitant of industrial growth.

Greater purchasing power in the hands of farmers generates demand for wage-goods and other consumer items. Farm prosperity in India resulted in a large spurt in demand for bicycles, batteries, watches, transistors, fans, sewing machines, artificial silk cloth, and various other consumer goods, besides, of course, food and cloth. The industries manufacturing such goods experienced a spurt in demand which stimulated their production.

AGRICULTURAL BACKWARDNESS IN DEVELOPING COUNTRIES: CAUSES AND CURE

Various factors are responsible for low level of productivity and incomes in the agricultural sector in developing economies:

Systemic and institutional factors

Exploitative zamindari and similar land-tenure systems resulted in a major share of the income of tenant cultivators being appropriated by the landlord, leading to impoverishment of the farmer and absence of incentive to increase productivity. The subdivision and fragmentation of land gave rise to small and scattered uneconomic holdings, which were not conducive to the induction of modern technology or mechanization, and obsolete traditional methods of farming continued to dominate the agricultural landscape.

Technical and Economic Factors

Decline in farm productivity was largely attributable to outdated techniques and implements, and lack of investible capital and funds for procurement of adequate inputs like high quality seeds, fertilizers, pesticides, electric pumps, and for building minor irrigation works and channels. Overcropping of fields and inadequate manuring to replenish the productive capacity of land also compounded the difficulties. In the absence of transport, marketing, and warehousing facilities, the Indian agriculturist was long exploited by middlemen and money-lenders, who were able to appropriate much of his legitimate earnings, leaving him with bare subsistence. Lack of education and modern skills, and non-availability of credit at reasonable cost, perpetuated his poverty and indebtedness. However, during the last two decades, conditions have considerably changed for the better, particularly in areas where the Green Revolution has occurred.

ROLE OF MODERN TECHNOLOGY

The success of the Green Revolution in effecting a transformation in agriculture, increasing the prosperity of farmers, and stimulating the general development of the rural sector in states affected by it has provided a clear pointer to the importance of induction of modern technology for improvement and progress in agriculture. As Hans P. Binswanger of the World Bank and Joachim von Braun say, 'Green revolution technology reduced poverty in the favourably endowed regions where it could be adopted (M. Hossain, 1988), and commercialization did the same in areas with known or hidden potential.... The developing countries and the donor community have undertaken research and launched projects to replicate green revolution success in such low potential areas as the Sahel, the semi-arid zones in India, and the humid tropics of Africa.'[2] Actually, the scope for adoption of the methods of the Green Revolution in India and raising productivity is vast; only some regions in the country have so far adopted them. An important aspect of application of technology and modern management methods to agriculture is to adapt the various techniques to the basic conditions and institutional framework existing in India, such as small and fragmented landholding, basic shortage of capital and excess supply of labour, climatic and soil conditions, backwardness and the general apathy of farmers to change and the acceptance of innovative techniques.

The results of research in the universities and agricultural institutes in the country need to be carried to the farmers, and extension services have an important role to play in this. Establishment of demonstration farms in every tahsil is the ideal method for transmitting the message to the farmer regarding effectiveness of modern technology and methods. Inclination to accept innovation grows when its beneficial effects are actually perceived.

The district authorities should be given the responsibility of seeing that proper cooperative societies and rural banks—where they do not exist—are established to ensure that, (a) adequate and timely supply of necesary inputs, like high quality seeds, fertilizers, diesel pumps, and pesticides, is available, (b) the prices of inputs are reasonable and bear a rational proportion to the price of agricultural produce, (c) cheap credit is made available at the appropriate time, (d) economic marketing and warehousing of produce are facilitated and, (e) particularly in areas where the monsoon is insufficient, easy access to irrigation facilities and water is possible. These cooperatives should be managed by the farmers or their representatives, and the district authorities should provide overall supervision. Intervention should occur only when efficient functioning is disrupted. With state help, cooperatives could also acquire mechanized equipment and tractors for use by the farmers, as and when requisitioned.

With nationalization of banks, priority sector lending, and establishment of regional rural banks, availability of credit to farmers has improved, but only a part of the problem has been solved. The farmer needs short-term credit to finance his agricultural operations and if timely state or bank credit is not available, he has to take recourse to the traditional money-lender, who charges exorbitant rates of interest.

The building of the agricultural infrastructure in the form of large irrigation works, dams and hydroelectric power stations, tanks, electric tubewells and wells, canals, channels, warehousing and storage facilities, and thermal power works constitute the principal duties of the state and central government. The allocation in plan outlays for agriculture and rural development is considerable, and the funds should be properly utilized to develop a rural infrastructure of a lasting kind, which would facilitate increase in agricultural productivity, and enable the small farmers in particular, who have a paucity of resources, to increase yields from their farms. The basic problem is to ensure proper monitoring so that wastages and leakages do not occur, money reaches the target groups, and the scheduled creation of assets occurs. Decentralization of powers and machinery for implementation is imperative.

Necessary changes in the institutional framework should be effected to ensure that the land tenure system secures to the farmer who tills the land the greater part of the income, and the landlord does not appropriate the bulk of it. This would provide the requisite incentive to the farmers to invest their own funds in developing the fields, adequately manuring them, and putting in the best inputs available. What is needed is security of tenure and fair rents. With effective land ceiling, the surplus can be distributed amongst the small and marginal farmers, who would then become peasant proprietors. The state also owns large tracts of land, which are basically of low quality and need greater effort and inputs to cultivate. Parts of such land which are cultivable should be identified and distributed among farmers, who should be given special assistance to raise crops on them. This would benefit both the farmers and augment overall production.

The general insurance corporation needs to be activized to extend the crop insurance scheme to the entire country. The progress made in this direction is tardy, and has hardly touched the fringe of the problem. Since profitability in this line of insurance is not likely to be high—and for some time losses may be incurred—the corporation, which is almost a state monopoly despite four subsidiary companies operating, should be asked to substantially extend its coverage of areas and crops. Alternatively, a separate corporation may be set up to provide crop insurance coverage.

AGRICULTURAL BREAKTHROUGH

The current Indian strategy for the agricultural sector may now be discussed. While the monsoon during the current year should contribute to increasing the momentum of agricultural growth, government's strategy of concentrated action in selected thrust districts in 14 states should enable the achievement of the food-grains target of about 175 million tonnes in 1990–1. The framework of agricultural policy in the last decade included additions to irrigated areas, emphasis on medium and minor irrigation projects, increased supply and consumption of fertilizers, pesticides and high yielding varieties of seeds, besides institutional provision of rural credit and remunerative price support. These have paid dividends in the form of the spread of the Green Revolution. The Mid-term Appraisal of the Seventh Five Year Plan has attributed the decline in agricultural production during the first three years to a deceleration in consumption of fertilizers and high yielding varieties of seeds and non-accretion to irrigated areas. These trends need to be reversed if agricultural production is to be stimulated.

The country has achieved remarkable success in agriculture in certain parts of the country. The rate of growth of agricultural production, which was stagnating in the seventies at the rate of 2 per cent per annum, has increased to about 2.7 per cent in the eighties. The area covered by irrigation in the country has increased from about 24 per cent of cropped area in 1970–1 to about 33 per cent in 1987–8, thereby reducing the vulnerability of agriculture to fluctuations in rainfall. The Green Revolution enabled the country to increase foodgrain production from 108 million tonnes in 1970–1 to 170 million tonnes in 1988–9. Large-scale imports of foodgrains are no longer necessary, and the foodgrain stocks built up were most useful during the drought period in 1987–8.

There are, however, certain aspects of agricultural development that detract from the fine performance otherwise. The production of pulses and oilseeds has lagged behind demand with the consequence that there are recurring shortages of these commodities, necessitating imports, and high prices which affect the consumer. Besides, the upsurge in agricultural production has been uneven. There are vast differences between the yields in say Punjab, Haryana, and Maharashtra and those in Bihar, Tamil Nadu, and Uttar Pradesh. The imbalance in regard to the production of wheat and rice needs to be corrected by increasing the output of rice, besides, of course, pulses and oilseeds. The agricultural policy framework should provide for a more scientifically-oriented approach to agriculture and linked to industry. New approaches offered by genetic engineering, bio-technology, and tissue culture should be adopted. The research in dry-land farming should be intensified and it is also necessary to check deterioration in soil, water, and other resources through conservation and environmental protection measures. Imparting momentum to the co-operative movement would be of great assistance to the farmers themselves. Development of poultry farming and animal husbandry would boost rural incomes.

The introduction of the Service Area Approach (SAP) in order to make rural lending more productive has considerable potential. Branches of banks in rural areas will be required to prepare credit plans, and these integrated with block and district level plans. The crucial and pragmatic feature of the SAP is that a block level bankers' committee are to co-ordinate the activities so that the credit is supported by necessary infrastructural facilities and non-credit inputs such as fertilizers, pesticides, seeds, pump-sets, and others. This approach would also forge a better link between bank credit and production, productivity and income levels. The scheme is highly commendable, and properly implemented, the integrated approach could provide the requisite breakthrough in boosting agricultural production and reversing the trend of declining production.

A dimensional change in the prospects of agriculture and the social environment has been effected in areas like Punjab, Haryana, and Western U.P., where the Green Revolution has occurred. With better quality seeds and other inputs, there has been a transformation in productivity, incomes, and living standards of the farmers. The change in outlook and funds position has resulted in improvement in absorption of modern technology and a degree of mechanization which further enhance productivity. Marketing, storage, and credit facilities have also improved. Thus, a cycle of high productivity and fixed and working capital, better quality and increased volume of inputs, technology and skills, and improved infrastructure, resulting in higher productivity, has been set in motion, leading to rising prosperity.

The growth in agricultural production during 1989–90 amounted to 1.5 per cent as compared to 20.8 per cent in 1988–9. Production of foodgrains during 1989–90 is estimated at 173 M.T. Together with an upsurge in industrial production and value addition in the services sector, it is estimated that the overall growth rate during the Seventh Plan period would be about 5.6 per cent: the contribution of agriculture, with the benefit of good monsoons in 1988–9, 1989–90, and 1990–1 is most heartening. Although the measures adopted during the last decade and outlined above are to be commended, they have not been uniformly implemented throughout the country. Concerted action is necessary to ensure that implementation is more effective in areas of low productivity. Supporting channels as adjuncts to irrigation canals need to be built all over the country to ensure effective utilization of water for irrigation and avoid wastage. Besides remunerative prices, changes in technology and adequate marketing arrangements are necessary. Improvement in the yields in the states where the Green Revolution has not been fully consummated should give a further boost to overall agricultural production during the nineties.

SOCIAL WELFARE, JUSTICE, AND EQUITY

The problem of rural development and social welfare is both

multidimensional and of vast magnitude. Besides structural and systemic backwardness, poverty, unemployment, illiteracy, lack of the basic necessities of life like food, clothing, and shelter, constitute various facets of this problem. The difficulties are compounded by the increase in population by about 2.1 per cent per annum, which is expected to reach about 100 crores by the end of the century. In the early stages of planning, reliance for redistribution was placed on the so-called 'trickle-down strategy' based on the assumption that the consumption levels of the poor would improve as the end-product of the process of accumulation and development. But as planning proceeded, it became clear that growth in GDP does not automatically resolve these problems, and the trickle down strategy is inadequate to ensure that the gains of development adequately percolate to the lowest strata of society. Government therefore decided to provide incomes, employment, and the basic necessities of life through direct schemes for poverty alleviation, rural development, and employment creation. Despite the steadily rising population, success has been achieved in reducing the incidence of poverty, as is indicated by the following table:

TABLE 9.1—*Population Below Poverty Line*

Percentage of population below poverty line	1977–78	1983–84 (Provisional data)
Rural	51.2	40.4
Urban	38.2	28.1
TOTAL	48.3	37.4

SOURCE: Seventh Plan, Planning Commission, Delhi, 1985, p. 4.

The decline in poverty has been possible on account of various factors, including increase in agricultural production, higher rate of economic growth, and escalating Plan allocations to social welfare measures.

The outlay on various anti-poverty programmes increased from Rs 1222 crores in 1985–6 to Rs 1504 crores in 1986–7, as is shown in the Table below:

TABLE 9.2— *Welfare Programmes* (Rupees millions)

Programme	1985–86 Revised Estimate	1986–87 Budget
Integrated Rural Development Program (IRDP)	2,785.7	4,274.0
National Rural Employment Program (NREP)	3,372.1	4,426.5
Rural Landless Employment Guarantee Programme (RLEGP)	6,063.4	6,336.5
TOTAL	12,221.2	15,037.0

SOURCE *The Indian Economy*, ed. REB Lucas and G.F.Papanek, OUP, Delhi, 1988, p. 117 (Table).

The Minimum needs programme has also been formulated with the objective of improving the standards of living in the rural areas and providing education and better health services. The targets laid down in the Sixth Plan with regard to elementary education and provision of primary and subsidiary health centres have been exceeded. Drinking water supplies have now been provided to most villages. Provision of house sites to 5.4 million poor families in rural areas and financial assistance for construction of houses to 1.9 million families have been made.[3] It must, however, be said that although the various targets determined for the coverage of poor families under the IRDP and NREP schemes were fulfilled, there have been several weaknesses and lacunae in their implementation. Part of the finance allocated has not reached the target groups, thereby reducing the effectiveness of the schemes to alleviate poverty and increase employment.

Government has also built up, in consonance with the programmes, diverse organizational and administrative structures. As the Seventh Plan states, there is now an elaborate 'Development bureaucracy' administering the various schemes. What is necessary is to rationalize the whole structure, reduce duplication, and bring about horizontal co-ordination at the district level. This would help in improving performance, enable better services to be provided to the target groups, and make for greater accountability. Improving the environment is also of great importance in rural areas. Soil erosion, waterlogging and flooding, deforestation and water pollution, all adversely affect farmers and also reduce farm yields. Hence, effort has been made to provide environmental protection as an integral part of developmental activity. In the urban slums also, environmental conditions have been improved, resulting in a better life for more than nine million slum dwellers.

The allocations for education and health have not only been increased during the Seventh Plan period, but efforts are being made to improve the quality of services provided. The new educational policy seeks to provide opportunities to the brighter students in rural areas to obtain free education, boarding and lodging in public schools, where education of an improved level is imparted. In the early stages of implementation of the scheme there may be weaknesses and defects, but with experience they will be overcome, and the scheme assist in enabling the brighter students to develop themselves to their full potentiality. Government attaches great importance to human resource development, as literacy, education and health programmes release the creative energies of people, secure their participation in the development process, and increase productivity and efficiency. Sizeable allocations have also been made for outlays on adult education, destitute homes, community centres, and female education. It would be readily appreciated that since increase in female literacy—and Kerala provides empirical evidence—is the surest safeguard against population growth, improvement in health and education, particularly of females, not only promotes social justice and equity but also supplements the family planning programmes. The importance of education in the development process also stems from the fact that it facilitates application of science and technology to agriculture, and adoption of scientific methods for improving productivity through the utilization of improved seeds, fertilizers, and other inputs.

Considerable progress has been made during the Sixth and Seventh Plan periods in promoting social justice and equity, reducing poverty, increasing employment, and setting up the institutional framework, particularly in rural areas. The following steps are needed to provide a thrust and edge to make the programmes more effective:

1. The process of decentralization should be speeded up

and necessary structural reforms in the rural administration effected. This would help in deriving the maximum benefit from decentralization both in the development process, as also implementation of social welfare measures. Efforts should be made to link up agricultural production plans with poverty alleviation programmes to make them more effective. As Sukhamoy Chakravarty[4] said, 'The solution to the problem of rural poverty will require that small farmers must also be given access to land-augmenting innovation, along with a programme of well-conceived public works. Many of the specific tasks will need to be done on a decentralized basis.'

2. District level monitoring bodies should be set up to ensure that the outlays under the various poverty alleviation and employment-generation programmes, as also the minimum needs programme, reach the targets group in full and leakages and wastage of funds are reduced and gradually eliminated. Effective implementation and reduction in leakages could effect a substantial increase in benefits, and with the same outlay, far greater results could be achieved in ameliorating the condition of the poor and the unemployed. The Planning Commisson is considering shifting the focus of IRDP from individual beneficiaries to community groups to enable improved utilization of funds.

3. Improvement should be effected in the effectiveness of education, health care, and family welfare programmes. The quality of service provided in these sectors needs to be improved, and the performance assessed in terms of its ultimate effect on literacy, incidence of disease and mortality, nutritional levels and fertility rates.

4. The allocation for housing should be sizeably increased. Besides, increasing social welfare, employment, and incomes, it increases demand for house-building and construction materials, and also has a multiplier effect upon various sectors of the economy. Large-scale housing construction programmes should be implemented for the middle and poor classes. The houses need not be expensive, but they should be properly constructed, and the environment should be clean and wholesome. Further, maintenance should be such that they do not degenerate into slums, like those found in metropolitan cities, which are a blot on civilization.

5. The NREP should be linked with continuing rural development

works, so that permanent capital assets are created. It is also necessary that capital assets like buildings and roads already created in the countryside are properly maintained. Besides, it should be ensured that institutions like schools and hospitals continue in operation and are efficiently run.

6. The development strategy should aim at the creation of an abundance of wage-goods. The pattern of consumption is also important. A large number of basic consumer goods industries, catering to the production of goods consumed by the masses in the country have to be established. The textile mills in the public sector should concentrate on the production of cloth which is consumed by the poor and lower middle classes. The excise duty on such production should be brought down to a minimum, so that cloth—and other wage-goods—which are basic necessities of life, are made available to the masses at the minimum possible price.

7. Corporate enterprises should be encouraged to adopt villages and develop the areas in the vicinity of their factories, as also provide educational and health facilities. Such expenditure should be fully deductible for tax purposes.

8. The spread of the green revolution to the eastern, central, and other regions, and increase in agricultural productivity through better quality of inputs, rural credit, expanded irrigation facilities, and consolidation of holdings would assist in increasing incomes and raising the low level equilibrium in which these regions are enmeshed.

9. The scheme of crop insurance, skifully formulated and properly administered, could be a great boon to the farmers, and should constitute an integral part of the package of social welfare measures. If there are lacunae in the scheme and misuse, remedial measures must be undertaken.

10. Depending upon the funds position, the objective should be to provide increasing social security to the people. Unfortunately, with increasing population and the resources crunch, progress has been limited. The objective, however, should be kept in view in framing future plans.

11. Potential for employment-generation through small-scale industries is considerable. Institutional credit and bank finance should be made readily available to match the projects identified and formulated by government department or agencies set up for

the development of such industries. Here also, there should be close co-ordination between the authorities and finance bodies to provide single window facilities and clearances to small entrepreneurs.

12. Finally, it hardly needs to be emphasized that the impact of social welfare measures varies in inverse proportion to the growth in population. But increase in education, social welfare, and population are also interlinked in the reverse direction. As literacy, employment, and incomes increase, there is greater consciousness about limiting the family, and it has a salutary effect upon the rate of growth in population. The family planning programmes need to be stregthened and made more effective.

R. J. Chelliah,[5] has emphasized certain measures which deserve attention: (1) Agricultural development and stimulated export facilitates growth of industry and services, resulting in increased output and employment; (2) since plentiful supply of food and goods of mass consumption lead to poverty alleviation, development of wage-goods and consumer industries should be promoted and obstacles to their growth on account of licencing and other restrictions removed; and (3) a rural capital formulation scheme would create the necessary capital assets in rural areas and generate considerable volume of employment, which would generate purchasing power for consumption of the wage-goods produced.

It may be pointed out that the various social welfare schemes being implemented by government, together with the public distribution system and twenty-point programme have helped in making a dent in poverty and unemployment. The percentage of population below the poverty line is likely to be reduced to 26 per cent by the end of the Seventh Plan, and be brought down to about 5 per cent by the year 2000.[6] Thus the progress is considerable; what is needed is to enhance the effectiveness of such programmes through better implementation.

BALANCE OF PAYMENTS

While the Indian economy as a whole is progressing satisfactorily, a major problem is that of adverse balance of payments and decline in foreign exchange reserves. The policy framework for export promotion must identify thrust areas where India has comparative advantage and also marketing economies. Close cooperation between government and industry is necessary for the removal of hurdles in the path of accelerated export growth. Incentives conducive to diversion of products from the domestic to the export markets have to be formulated. Better cooperation between government and industry is vital in stimulating exports, and the Export Promotion Councils need to be dynamized.

A policy framework needs to be designed for the promotion of exports that would not only provide incentives for improving export performance in general, but also measures for removing constraints in respect of exports of leading exportable commodities, based on sector-specific analysis. The international environment, restrictive trade flows, and external factors have a definite constricting effect upon exports. That external factors did not affect Indian exports during the seventies is to a certain extent true, but there is no doubt that external constraints on Indian export performance have become highly significant during the eighties. Protectionism in industrialized countries, manifesting itself in rising trade barriers and elevated tariff structure, and stagnation in international trade flows, have resulted in increasing competition in export markets and erosion in the prices of exports of developing countries. Besides, certain countries like Bangladesh have been heavily subsidizing their export of jute goods, to the detriment of Indian exports of this commodity. Similarly also Sri Lanka has reduced prices of tea. The European Economic Community have imposed non-tariff barriers on the export of oil cakes; barriers have been raised against marine products in the United States, while the Multi-Fibre Agreement has placed restrictions on export of clothing. Export price realization has been adversely affected because of the fall in international prices of agricultural commodities and other primary products.

Various internal factors have also acted as constraints in export promotion. There are structural deficiencies and factors which adversely affect the competitiveness of Indian products in the international markets. Owing to increase in population and gradual rise in living standards, there is escalation in domestic demand, and with attractive price realization in domestic markets, goods tend to be diverted and consumed internally, and exports suffer in consequence.

Basically, the high cost of production of Indian industrial products is due to a variety of factors, including the high level and effect of interest charges, depreciation (based on escalating costs of capital equipment), and the network of indirect taxes, including sales tax, excise and custom duties, which enter into the cost of commodities. Besides, inadequate utilization of installed capacities, as a result of infrastructural and other bottlenecks, and low levels of productivity and operational efficiency, result in increasing the cost of production. Surpluses for export are not available because of the low volume of production.

Despite official inspection and other measures, complaints are often received of the poor quality of Indian goods exported. Lack of quality-consciousness is compounded by the indifferent quality of raw materials and other inputs. For instance, the poor quality of coal is cited by the steel, cement, and several other industries as being a constraint both on the quality and quantity of their production. Government should try to ensure that the quality of inputs for production of export goods is satisfactory, and impose discipline on exporters to ensure that the quality of exports is maintained, so that the acceptability of Indian goods in the export markets increases.

The strategy for export promotion and stimulation of inflow of invisible earnings should, *inter alia*, comprise the following measures:

1. Reducing the cost of production in export industries so that they are competitive in international markets. The high cost of production of Indian exportable goods is often attributable to higher prices of imported and other inputs, and failure to realize economies of scale. The high cost structure and poor productivity are a function of low efficiency of factors of production, management skills, level of technology, scale of production, high cost of raw materials and other inputs, and the constituent element of duties in such costs.

2. Removing infrastructural constraints in the economy and other bottlenecks and ensuring timely availability of raw materials and inputs at reasonable prices for export industries. Inadequacy of infrastructure and inability to obtain imported and domestic inputs when required, adversely affect production of goods and maintenance of delivery schedules.

3. Improving the quality of goods, marketing facilities, satisfactory packaging and execution of export orders in accordance with the scheduled delivery dates, as also providing efficient after sales service.

4. Compensatory policies and incentives as countervailing measures to the increase in tariffs in foreign countries against Indian exports.

5. Inducing large houses and other industrial complexes to increase their export commitments and in general to devise methods and instrumentalities for diversion of goods from the domestic to the export markets.

6. The increase in growth of certain selected export items should also be extended to other commodities.

7. Exports must be diversified to new areas. Indian consulates in various countries have their economic departments. They should explore markets in the respective countries and provide feedback to export councils at home for promotion of exports.

8. Modernization and technological upgradation of industry is necessary to reduce cost of production and increase the competitiveness of exports in international markets. Some liberalization of imports has taken place in order to increase the production of exportable goods.

9. Tourism is an important source of foreign exchange earning, and every effort should be made to stimulate its inflow. Tourist centres should be developed and constraints to the inflow of tourist traffic, as also inconveniences experienced by foreign tourists, as ascertained from travel agencies, should be removed.

10. Increase in the inflow of foreign investment capital, as suggested earlier, increases foreign exchange receipts on capital account and should be encouraged.

11. Various fiscal and other concessions given to Non-Resident Indians to stimulate the flow of deposits and investment are commendable. Constraints to such investment and difficulties experienced by NRIs should be ascertained and removed.

12. The Income-tax Act has liberalized the tax provisions. According to Section 80 HHC, export profits are entirely tax-free, which is a highly significant concession. Government has also provided, *inter alia*, for cash compensatory support to exporters, duty drawback and Replenishment import licences (withdrawn now), as also concessional interest and liberal export finance, and facilities for establishment of export houses and joint trading companies in India for export promotion. Difficulties experienced by exporters should be resolved and procedures simplified. A single form regarding exports, as in Korea and Hong Kong, should replace the present multiplicity of forms required to be filed.

13. Export of services is assuming importance as a foreign exchange earner and should be treated at par with merchandise exports for eligibility for exemption under Section 80 HHC of the Income-tax Act.

14. Profit from sale of REP licences should also be eligible for tax exemption under the aforesaid provision without elaborate formalities.

Taking an overall view, the increase in the volume of exports is satisfactory, even though the annual average ratio of current account deficit to GDP of about 2.2 per cent over the Seventh Plan period is a cause for concern. Measures for export promotion, import substitution, and curtailment of inessential imports are necessary to reduce the deficit on the balance of payments account. The foreign exchange position continues to be difficult, even though exports recorded a remarkable increase of 28.9 per cent in 1988–9 and 36.3 per cent in 1989–90. Imports also increased by 25.9 per cent and 25.6 per cent in the respective years.

TABLE 9.3 — *Balance of Payments* (in crores)

Item	1987–8	1988–9	Percentage Increase
Exports	15,741	20,295	28.9
Imports	22,399	28,194	25.9
Deficit	6,658	7,899	

SOURCE Compiled from *Economic Survey 1989–90*, pp. 115, 119.

During the first four years of the Seventh Plan, the average of current account deficit increased to 2.2 per cent of GDP from 1.3 per cent during the Sixth Plan period. Various factors contributed to this deterioration. Growth in production of oil decelerated, while debt-service payments on external debts increased. IMF and other loan instalments also came up for repayment.

External debt had reached a level exceeding Rs 81,000 crores[7] by the end of March 1990, and will rise to about Rs 1,00,000 crores by end of 1991. The debt service ratio had already touched the high level of 27 per cent and is likely to rise still further to about 30 per cent. That the country may be enmeshed in a debt-trap of the kind in which certain Latin American and other developing countries were enmeshed is not correct, but every effort is necessary to augment export earnings and conserve foreign exchange through rationalized imports. Concessional assistance has been inadequate and invisible earnings sluggish. As a consequence, there was erosion of foreign exchange reserves[8] which slumped to a low level of Rs 5,843 crores in June 1990.

CONTROL OF POPULATION

The growth in GNP and other economic gains in the country are being largely neutralized by the increase in population, with the consequence that per capita income in real terms rises at a snail's pace. Plan measures for improving health and social welfare have brought the death rate down appreciably from 14.9 per 1000 in 1970–1 to 11.1 per 1000 in 1985–6, but the birth rate has been reduced only from 36.9 per 1000 in 1970–1 to 32.6 in 1985–6. Life expectancy at birth has increased both for males and females. The overall picture in regard to control of population is not encouraging and the projections are that the population of India may reach 100 crores by the end of the century. It is relevant to point out that China, besides other measures, has adopted the norm of not more than one child per couple and it is believed that it has achieved far greater success than India in controlling population.

It is evident that the impact of the family planning programme has been insufficient in controlling population growth and drastic measures are necessary. The small family norm of two children per couple should be further reduced to one child. Secondly, a large number of abortion clinics should be established all over the country. They should be widely publicized and persons with one or more children should be encouraged to take advantage of the facility afforded. Sentiment should have the least consideration in economic matters; difficult problems call for drastic remedies, irrespective of personal predilections.

CONCLUSION

A basic question facing policy-makers and planners today is whether to allow the economy to move at the same pace or to aim, during the period of the Eighth and Ninth Plans spanning the last

TABLE 9.4—Targets and Achievements of Agricultural Production during the Seventh Plan

(million tonnes/bales)

Crop	1985–86 target	1985–86 achievement	1986–87 target	1986–87 achievement	1987–88 target	1987–88 achievement	1988–89 target	1988–89 achievement	1989–90 target
1. Rice	63.50	63.82	65.00	60.56	64.00	56.43	67.95	70.67	72.50
2. Wheat	49.20	47.05	49.00	44.32	50.00	45.10	52.32	53.99	54.00
3. Coarse cereals	33.00	26.20	32.00	26.83	32.00	25.85	33.00	31.89	33.75
4. Pulses	13.50	13.36	14.00	11.71	14.00	11.04	13.30	13.70	14.75
5. Total foodgrains	159.20	150.44	160.00	143.42	160.00	138.41	166.57	170.25	175.00
6. Oil-seeds	13.60	10.80	14.80	11.27	14.00	12.38	15.65	17.89	16.50
7. Cotton	8.60	8.73	8.80	6.91	8.80	6.43	9.80	8.69	10.00
8. Jute and mesta	8.60	12.65	8.50	8.63	8.60	6.78	9.20	7.70	9.50
9. Sugarcane	191.00	170.65	195.00	186.09	180.00	196.70	195.02	204.63	212.00

SOURCE Economic Survey 1988–9, p. 12; the last two columns are from Economic Survey 1989–90, p. 12.

decade of this century, at achieving a higher growth rate of 6 per cent during 1990–5 and 1995–2000. The level of poverty in the country, despite reduction in the Sixth Plan period to 37 per cent, is still very high, large-scale unemployment persists, and the population continues to increase at about 2.1 per cent per year (1981–6), thereby reducing the increase in per capita income to about 3.4 per cent. In our opinion, it is imperative that every effort should be made to ensure that the economy moves into a higher orbit of growth rate during the nineties. This is possible only if new strategies based on pragmatic considerations are adopted. We have indicated the broad parameters of the new strategy of growth which would stimulate development and enable the country to enter the twenty-first century with greater prosperity for the people, a reduced level of poverty and unemployment, and a resurgent, technologically advanced and dynamic economy.

REFERENCES

1. W. W. Rostow, *The Stages of Economic Growth*, CUP, Cambridge, 1960, p. 23.
2. Hans P. Binswanger and Joachim von Braun, 'Technological Change and Commercialization in Agriculture: The Effect on the Poor', in *The World Bank Research Observer*, World Bank, Washington, vol. 6, No. 1, Jan. 1991, p. 72.
3. Seventh Five Year Plan (1985–86 to 1989–90), Government of India, p. 5.
4. Sukhamoy Chakravarty, *Development Planning*, OUP, Delhi, 1989, p. 88.
5. R. J. Chelliah, *Seventh Plan Perspective*, ed. M. S. Adiseshiah, Lancer International/India International Centre, Delhi, 1985, p. 48.
6. *Seventh Five Year Plan*, Table on p. 22.
7. SOF: *Economic Survey 1989–90*, pp. 7, 8, 115, 119; *RBI Annual Report 1989–90*, p. 1.
8. Including Gold and SDRs.

10

Liberalization and Sectoral Growth

Emphasis had been laid upon the impact of liberalization on the growth of the industrial sector of the economy. We shall now proceed to explore the inter-sectoral composition of the national product, the linkages of industry with agriculture and the services sector, and the extent to which liberalization policies are capable of stimulating development of these sectors and the economy as a whole.

Agriculture, in industrially developed countries, generally accounts for between 2 to 10 per cent of GDP, while the industrial sector's contribution to GDP is usually between 30 and 50 per cent. The services sector accounts for between 45 and 65 per cent. The share of agriculture in India and China in GDP was 44 per cent in 1965 and 32 per cent in 1988, and that of industry 39 and 46 per cent respectively in the two years in China, and 22 and 30 per cent in India.[1] This is eloquent testimony that, as industrialization progresses, the share of agriculture declines. The figures for Korea are highly significant in this context. Between 1965 and 1988 its economy took great strides, and its GDP increased from 3000 million dollars in 1965 to 171,300 million dollars in 1988. The share of agriculture in GDP declined from 38 per cent to 11 per cent and that of industry increased from 25 to 43 per cent.

LINKAGES BETWEEN INDUSTRY, AGRICULTURE, AND SERVICES SECTORS

The inter-sectoral linkages between industry and agriculture are multi-dimensional, and increasing productivity in one sector supports the rise in production and growth in the other. It has been observed that in India a good monsoon year has a substantial impact upon the prospects of the economy; this is a reflection of the close linkages between the industrial and agricultural sectors. The increased generation of agricultural incomes provides the demand for consumer goods and semi-durables produced by industries. With rise in incomes, the proportion spent on food declines, and increasing amounts are spent upon other goods produced by industry. Besides, thanks to the multiplier effect, the demand for capital goods is also stimulated.

TABLE 10.1 — *Distribution of Gross Domestic Product* (per cent)

| | Agriculture | | Industry | | Services | |
	1965	1988	1965	1988	1965	1988
USA	3	2	38	33	59	65
UK	3	2	46	42	51	56
Italy	10	4	37	40	53	56
Japan	9	3	43	41	48	57
Korea	38	11	25	43	37	46
Thailand	32	17	23	35	45	48
China	44	32	39	46	17	21
India	44	32	22	30	34	38

SOURCE *World Development Report 1990*, World Bank/OUP, New York, pp. 182–3.

An analysis of agricultural and industrial production and wholesale prices over the past decades shows that the years of good monsoon and agricultural production are usually also years of good industrial production and increase in GNP, with low levels of inflation. For instance, 1979–80 and 1987–8 were drought years. Agricultural production fell sharply in both the years (*vide* Table in Chapter 2). Industrial production also declined during the two years, while inflation increased substantially. The Indian economy, at one time, was described as a 'gamble' on the monsoon. With far greater irrigation facilities than a few decades ago, the dependence of agriculture on the monsoon has diminished appreciably; but the linkage between the sectors is strong and a good monsoon and consequent spurt in agricultural production are almost prere-quisites for a normal rise both in industrial production and GNP, as also a subdued price level and low inflation. Agriculture also provides raw materials for various industries, including *inter alia*, textile, sugar, paper, and edible oil mills. Besides, agriculture supplies wage-goods (food) to the workers and others in the industrial sector.

Export of agricultural products increases the quantum of foreign exchange available for import of raw materials and inputs for industry. Besides, in the early stages of development, farm surpluses, the result of increased productivity, stimulate savings, and these can be diverted for investment in industry. In Japan, the Soviet Union, and several other countries, savings from the agricultural sector provided the principal source of funds and resources for capital accumulation and industrial development. Most landlords in Japan in early Meiji times had occupational interests outside agriculture and they provided a substantial proportion of capital to new industries. Actually, agriculture financed almost a quarter of the non-agricultural investment between 1888 and 1922. The land tax was the principal instrument in the hands of government for mobilization of farm surpluses, and the funds were channelized for industrial development. The Soviet Union, in the post-Revolution years, collectivized farms and extracted surpluses by keeping down the consumption of farmers (as also others), to be utilized for boosting investment in heavy machinery, machine tools and other industries in consonance with the Soviet model of planning. Increase in farm productivity enables additions to the labour force seeking employment in industry. As industry develops, it draws labour from agriculture, further relieving the pressure for employment in the farm sector.

The inter-sectoral linkage is functional in both directions. Various agricultural inputs like fertilizers, pesticides, irrigation pumps and pipes, as also tractors, threshers and other mechanical equipment and implements, and cement and steel for irrigation channels and dams, are manufactured by the industrial sector. Indeed, the Green Revolution would not have been possible without such inputs from industry. Both the sectors thus gain immensely from the linkages.

IMPACT OF LIBERALIZATION ON GROWTH OF AGRICULTURE

Government in September 1991 announced that the private sector would be freely permitted to establish power plants, which were earlier mostly reserved for the public sector, except as captive units. This is a measure of considerable significance for industrial and agricultural development. While the average plant-load factor in public sector electricity plants is about 56 per cent, it is considerably higher—above 80 per cent—in certain private sector plants. The portents are that within a period of about five to ten years, power shortage will be eliminated in the country, leading to increase in utilization of installed capacity. It would, besides, help in meeting the full requirements of agriculture.

The principal inputs for stimulating agricultural production, *inter alia*, are seeds, fertilizers, pesticides, tractors, and other agricultural machinery and implements, power, and credit. The growth of the fertilizer industry is vital, because if indigenous production is inadequate, imports are necessitated. The fixation of retention prices by government and inadequate returns on capital employed according to revised norms are having an adverse impact upon the growth of industry. Government should, as a part of its liberalization package, free the fertilizer industry from controls within a short period, as in the case of the cement industry. Installed capacity and production would then multiply and availability to agriculture would increase. For two or three years, till the new plants come into operation, fertilizer imports could bridge the gap between supply and demand.

Liberalization is a multifaceted concept; decentralization of authority, planning, allocation of resources and implementation, constitute a significant part of the process of deregulation. The tendency in an authoritarian or command economy is towards centralization of all economic powers; and as the transition towards a market economy progresses, central powers and authority are diluted and delegated to state and local governments. Actually, the degree of success in implementation of projects likely to be achieved greatly increases as decentralization occurs, and responsibility for executing schemes is squarely placed upon the state or local governments or the target groups themselves.

Experience has shown that centralized planning on a macro-level needs to be co-ordinated with decentralized planning at the regional, district, and even block levels. For a large economy like India's, the former leads to inefficiencies and wastages, and only part of the allocated funds reach the target groups. Balanced multi-level planning, involving devolution of funds and powers to the local authorities or elected bodies, is particularly necessary in the case of agriculture, land development, minor irrigation projects, local industries, dairy farming, fisheries, housing, water supply, sanitation and health, and schools. Since the local people have far better knowledge and familiarity with these subjects, giving them responsibility both in the planning and implementation of projects in the agricultural and allied sectors, infrastructural and social services sectors, yields far better results in terms of performance and benefits derived by the people, than from centralized planning.

Area planning agencies in the form of project formulation bodies should be established at the district or block levels. Raj Krishna[2] states that autonomous corporations and agencies such as dairy and fertilizer corporations, agricultural finance corporations, small farmers' agencies, and some banks have performed exceedingly well in area development work and have proved to be 'effective delivery systems.... They should be given a clear objective, substantial autonomy, sufficient finance and a fully professional management and technical expertise.' A high-powered, truly representative rural development planning and co-ordination body with the collector as the chairman, should be set up in all the districts, and it should have decentralized responsibility and power to formulate plans and ensure their successful implementation. Where there are elected panchayats, the funds and powers may be transferred to them.

Liberalization also needs to be extended to provide easy credit to the farming community. The rural banks, which presently are adjuncts of public sector banking institutions, should be converted into farmers' co-operative banks, owned and managed by representatives of farmers. The Central Government should, as a part of its decentralization programme, transmit funds directly to village panchayats for building up infrastructure and comprehensive rural development and social welfare. The greatest service it would render to this worthy cause would be to ensure that effective monitoring committees, composed of local citizens, are set up to ensure that leakages and wastages of funds are obviated, and the funds not only reach the target groups, but are properly spent for the intended purposes.

There is considerable disguised unemployment in the agricultural sector. If infrastructural development receives a stimulus, through liberalization measures, industrial growth and increased utilization of capacity would assist in transfer of part of the rural workforce to urban industry. Besides, the establishment of large-scale industry in a rural district leads to increasing employment of landless agricultural labour in industry. Gradually, skills develop and the burden of surplus labour on agriculture is reduced. For instance, the growth of the cement industry in Mandsaur district[3] in Madhya Pradesh has effected a positive change in this predominantly rural opium-growing area. During the last two decades, the occupational composition has registered a change.

This brings us to the linkage of large-scale and small-scale industries. The latter develop as suppliers of materials and goods to the principal industry. The provision of technology and finance, as in Japan, by large-scale industries, would enable them to develop along modern lines. The dynamism imparted by large-scale industries and their impact in stimulating the growth of various small and medium industries, workshops and transport, and other services, promotes, in ever-widening circles, industrial progress; this is all the more evident in backward areas. Small-scale industries have been pleading with the government for liberalization of regulations and controls. Particularly obnoxious are the number of inspectors from various departments of the government who periodically visit these small units. Government has responded, and such inspections have been reduced. The small units have also pleaded for reduced excise duties and taxes, and relaxation of norms, to which there are indications of positive government response.

The infrastructural sector, besides power, also needs liberalized policies. The coal industry, since nationalization, has effected a multifold increase in the price of coal, and most units are losing heavily. The average quality of coal is poor and this has deleterious effect upon the production of steel, cement and other user industries. Privatization, provided there are buyers, can greatly improve the functioning of this core sector industry. Railways have been effecting increases in fares and freight almost every year, but their functioning on the whole is not unsatisfactory, given the vast ramifications of their organization and services. An element of competition has been introduced in postal services. This is a commendable step.

The development of the industrial superstructure not only postulates the development of infrastructure such as power and other utilities, but also the extensive, although not so prominent, *services infrastructure sector*, comprising, among others, transport, communication, banking, insurance, shipping, storage and warehousing, and distribution, as also hotels, travel, advertisement, entertainment and other agencies and bodies. With increasing complexities of business, law and taxation, lawyers, accountants, tax experts, and a vast range of management and industrial advisers and computer operators and engineers, develop their expertise and services to assist entrepreneurs and industrial managers in the performance of their tasks. Variegated specialist services enable the industralist to focus his energies on basic developmental functions. The expansion and proliferation of the services sector is directly related to the growth in the complexities of business. As industrialization progresses, the higher income demand elasticity for services stimulates the development of this sector. For instance, in the early stages of industrialization, the in-house service officials catered to the need of industry for advertisement, sales promotion, distribution of goods and recruitment of staff. But, gradually, with the expansion of business, the need for specialized services in all the various fields was felt and the tasks were assigned to professional firms, and contractors in the case of distribution of products.

The construction business, normally regarded as a part of the services sector, accounts for an appreciable contribution to GDP, and is vital not only to industry, but also for providing housing, *inter alia*, to the officers and workers who run industries. Investment in construction and housing has a multiplier effect on industrial development; it not only provides employment to vast numbers, but also boosts demand for steel, cement, and other house-building materials, which stimulates development. With industrialization, urbanization inevitably increases and, as noted earlier, a backward district may blossom into a developed and urbanized area. This boosts the demand for other services such as sanitation, water supply, hospitals, schools, civic administration, police, and various services. As women begin to participate as industrial workers, domestic services are commercialized.

With global integration on the increase, not only have the less developed countries, such as Korea, Taiwan, Singapore, Brazil, and India, provided the West and the Middle East with a workforce, but also exported labour-intensive products, with comparative cost advantage to them. In turn, they have imported from the industrialized countries various services such as banking, insurance, airways, shipping, engineering, computer software, and above all, science and technology. Countries like India and Pakistan have provided developed economies such as the UK and USA with engineers, technologists, doctors, and academicians. Here, however, the developing countries are losers, in that they forego the benefit of the expenditure on training and education of these specialized professionals, which accrues to the countries utilizing their services. However, remittances from citizens working abroad help in increasing the invisible exchange earnings of the parent countries.

Liberalization and the Services Sector

Nationalization by government of various services sectors, such as banking, insurance, and airways, and establishment in the public sector of hotels and shipping companies have given the government sizeable presence in the services sector, but with mixed results. The banking sector has developed considerably, and also extended credit to priority sectors, but some weaknesses have developed: certain large banks are reported to be sick and the quantum of bad debts has considerably increased; loans are not always given on merit; customer services have deteriorated; and due to high administrative expenditure, interest rates remain at a high level and are largely inelastic. The Reserve Bank, however, has maintained a high level of efficiency, which is commendable. While life insurance is the monopoly of the LIC, general insurance comprises four companies competing with each other, with GIC as the apex supervisory body. Customer services have declined since nationalization, and claims settlement, particularly in the case of general insurance, causes difficulties. The shipping industry, particularly in the public sector, has incurred heavy losses. The operational efficiency of airways, a monopoly enterprise, is low, while costs and fares keep multiplying. The private sector should be allowed to re-enter this sector; competition may induce greater efficiency and improved customer service. Privatization of the services sector would lead to an improvement in customer service, and also obviate losses in the shipping and hotel sectors. But presently the possibility of privatization appears remote.

The transport industry in the public sector, particularly bus services, are incurring heavy losses, which constitute a burden on state budgets. Since it is most difficult to generate surpluses, the only solution is to privatize them. The transport industry is also one of the most heavily taxed sectors; besides, licensing and other formalities cast a heavy burden. The various road transport authorities also give the operators a difficult time. Liberalization in rules and regulations, and nationalization of taxes, would contribute to improving the health of this industry, and reduce transport costs, which enter into the cost of raw materials for industry and commodities intended for public consumption.

Corporation taxes on residential and office premises in urban areas are escalating, while sanitation and health services, roads, water and electric supplies, and other services are deteriorating in most areas and cities in the country. Deregulation and increased competition could contribute to an improvement in services; and privatization, wherever possible, should be effected. The Thatcher government in the UK has privatized a number of utilities and service industries with advantage. Operational efficiency and return on capital employed have improved, while both capital and revenue budgets have benefited.

LIMITATIONS OF ECONOMIC LIBERALIZATION

While structural adjustment relating to domestic liberalization and relaxation of norms for inflow of foreign investment capital are commendable, a note of caution is necessary in regard to modification of the policy framework to effect, (a) financial openness and liberalization of the financial sector; and, (b) trade openness and outward orientation. Financial openness and sectoral liberalization (T. Banuri, 1991) imply the exposure of the domestic financial system to world capital markets and free international capital flows, freeing the domestic interest-rate stucture and relaxing controls over banks and various other financial institutions in the country. Trade openness and outward orientation indicate a degree of global integration, deregulation, and liberalization in regard to imports and exports, reduction in protective tariffs, devaluation, and exposure of markets to the international economy.

Freeing interest rates and permitting banks to charge the customers such interest as they deem proper, keeping in view the creditworthiness of borrowers, may theoretically sound attractive, but in actual practice it may result in distortions—since bankers have far greater clout, in that each bank may exercise its discretion according to its own perceptions, even predilections—

and with an increased interest burden, industrial product costs may sizeably escalate to the detriment of international competitiveness. As regards free capital inflows and outflows, they are fraught with danger in that the economy may be exposed in a far greater degree to the influences of international disturbances, of which more later.

The advocates of import liberalization argue that lowering the level of protective tariffs would result in more efficient allocation of resources and investment, in consonance with the country's comparative advantage, and it would facilitate stimulated exports on the basis of reciprocity. However, the practical aspect is that with the foreign exchange crunch, there are limits to the liberalization of imports or reduction in protective tariffs possible. If exports are stimulated and remittances from abroad and invisibles increase, it is always possible to relax imports. But the basic problem is to increase exports, particularly in the face of widespread international protectionism. Integration with the global economy and free rupee convertibility are fascinating concepts, but in actuality they do not appear feasible even in the medium term.

While both financial and trade openness increase vulnerability to external shocks, a distinction between the two must be made. Alan Hughes and Ajit Singh assert[4] that 'while trade openness does increase flexibility to cope with financial market shocks, financial openness reduces the ability to adjust to any exogenous shocks'. When a trade shock occurs, financial openness would lead to heavy flight of capital, which would aggravate the difficulties of adjustment. This is what transpired in Mexico and various other Latin American countries. Mexico recorded macroeconomic expansion and high growth rates during the sixties and seventies. To cope with the oil shock in 1973, the Mexican government resorted to heavy commercial borrowing on the international market—with bankers obliging—at reasonable interest rates. These loans were largely used for investment purposes and structural change in the economy. Mexico initiated greater global integration; and it expanded its exports—particularly of oil—by about 200 per cent during the period 1967–81. It also deliberately increased its imports very considerably after 1977. As a consequence, large current account deficits occurred, which were financed by further commercial loans. The debt service burden continued to rise.

These factors rendered the Mexican economy highly vulnerable. When another oil shock occurred in 1979, followed by world recession (1980–2), the economy was engulfed in a serious crisis. International bankers imposed a freeze on lending. These difficulties were compounded when in February 1982 the Government floated the currency instead of imposing exchange control. There was heavy flight of capital, including outflows by its own citizens. Despite devaluation, the rate of inflation escalated from 28 per cent to 100 per cent by August 1982 (later reduced to 60 per cent in 1985). Exchange control was imposed, which stemmed the outflow, but the damage had been done. Alan Hughes and Ajit Singh say,[5] 'with respect to the question of economic vulnerability, we have argued that compared with India and China, the poor economic performance of Mexico and Brazil during the 1980s may be ascribed to their large foreign borrowings and their greater integration with the world economy, particularly with the international financial markets'.

A consequence of liberalization and global integration was that the resumption of a normal growth rate in Mexico and Brazil depended not on domestic factors or internal dynamism but on international factors such as the rate of growth of the world economy, levels of international trade and interest rates, terms of trade for primary commodities, and the stability of the US dollar. Economic interactions between the USA, major European countries and Japan, would largely determine these factors. (Singh, 1984; Taylor, 1982). Interestingly, in the case of China—and India to a large extent—the growth rate does not essentially depend upon that of the world (although foreign exchange earnings and aid are important), but largely on the parameters of their economies, domestic factors determining growth of industrial, agricultural, and other sectors, institutional framework and policies, and the dynamics of their developmental processes. Unanimity does not exist in regard to the benefits accruing from financial restructuring and openness, and trade—particularly import—liberalization. It is opined that these measures have their limitations and the policy package formulated by international bodies should be structured to the requirements of the specific economy, keeping in view fundamental economic factors and operational trends, its institutional arrangements, economic and social, and historical background.

TABLE 10.2—*Mexico: Principal Economic Indicators 1977, 1980 & 1983*

Item	1977	1980	1983
GDP, real growth rate (% p.a.)	3.5	8.3	−5.3
Inflation rate (% p.a.)	29.0	26.4	101.9
Current balance/GDP (%)	−2.4	−4.5	3.6
Total Debt, US $ billion	31.1	57.1	93.7
Total Debt/GDP (%)	38.0	30.7	65.6
Debt service/exports (%)	45.4	33.5	40.4
Exports/GDP (%)	9.5	12.6	19.1
Imports/GDP (%)	9.4	13.8	8.9

SOURCE *World Bank Data Bank*, IMF, 1987; *World Debt Tables 1986–7*, World Bank, Washington.

REFERENCES

1. *Vide* Table 10.1.
2. Raj Krishna, *Facets of India's Development*, G. L. Mehta Memorial Lectures 1976–86, ICICI, Bombay, 1986, p. 59.
3. Mandsaur District in Madhya Pradesh. The author was elected to Parliament from this district in M.P.
4. Alan Hughes and Ajit Singh, referred to by Tariq Banuri (ed.), in *Economic Liberalization: No Panacea*, Clarendon Press, Oxford, 1991, p. 11.
5. Alan Hughes and Ajit Singh in *Economic Liberalization: No Panacea*, ed. by Tariq Banuri, Clarendon Press, Oxford, 1991, p. 97.

11

Internal and External Indebtedness: Scenario in the Nineties

The economy has made commendable progress during the Sixth and Seventh Plan periods (1980–1 to 1989–90), in that the rate of growth of national income exceeded five per cent per annum in real terms, but certain structural imbalances have emerged. We propose to analyse in this chapter internal and external indebtedness, which has considerably escalated during the eighties, and assumed such huge dimensions that it threatens eventually to enmesh the country in a debt-trap. According to budgetary statements, the aggregate of internal debt, external debt, and other internal liabilities (such as small savings schemes, provident funds, and others) amounted to Rs 2,66,913 crores in 1989–90 (R.E.).[1]

The large magnitude of indebtedness is revealed by the fact that while in 1980–1, total liabilities were 44 per cent of GDP at current market prices, they increased to about 60.3 per cent of GDP at the end of 1989–90. Besides, the interest charges payable by the central government increased from 11.6 per cent of total expenditure in 1980–1 to 19.2 per cent in 1989–90 (B.E.).[2] Borrowings are actually not harmful to the economy; they constitute, together with taxation, surpluses of public enterprises, BCR, and limited deficit financing, one of the important instruments for the economic development of the country. But the success of the borrowing programme postulates, (a) that moneys are utilized for creation of productive assets of public utility and, (b) the overall quantum of borrowings is within prudent limits. If the borrowed moneys had been productively used, they would have yielded adequate return which would have serviced the loans and covered repayment. If public enterprises, in which considerable moneys had been invested, yielded adequate returns on capital employed, the return flow of funds to the budget would have contributed to reduction of the deficit.

TABLE 11.1 — *Internal and External Debt*

Year	Internal Debt	Internal Liabilities	External Liabilities	Total Liabilities
1980–81	30,864 (22.7)	17,587 (13.0)	11,298 (8.3)	59,749 (44.0)
1984–85	58,537 (25.4)	38,267 (16.6)	16,637 (7.2)	1,13,441 (49.2)
1985–86	71,039 (27.0)	48,292 (18.5)	18,153 (6.9)	1,37,484 (52.4)
1989–90 (R.E.)	1,33,361 (30.1)	1,05,035 (23.8)	28,517 (6.4)	2,66,913 (60.3)

SOURCE Compiled from *RBI Annual Report 1989–90*, p. 89 (based on the Budget documents of the Government of India).

NOTES Figures in brackets represent percentage to GDP at current market prices.

FISCAL BUDGETING AND PSBR

The quantum of investment by the public sector increased substantially from around 1880 in industrialized countries and after 1940 in developing countries. Central government spending increased sizeably and in certain economies it exceeded 50 per cent of GNP.[3] A consequence of the increase in public sector activity has been the sizeable increase in Public Sector Borrowing Requirements (PSBR). Ordinarily, current expenditure is balanced or exceeded by current revenues; and a part of the capital expenditure is financed out of revenue surpluses. The capital expenditure remaining would largely be covered by borrowings and to a small extent by deficit financing. Proper utilization of funds would ensure that the interest charges for servicing and repayment of debts are covered by the income emanating from such investment in capital assets over a period of years.

There is, however, a serious structural imbalance in the Indian fiscal system. The current expenditure is so considerable that it exceeds the revenue-raising capacity of government and there is deficit on the revenue account itself, as a result of which the shortfall is covered by the capital budget. The total fiscal deficit consists of, (a) deficit on revenue budget, (b) financing of capital or developmental expenditure and, (c) loans to state governments and public enterprises. The PSBR would inevitably be very high, and if adequate loans and borrowings from the market and foreign sources are not available, considerable deficit financing would be required. If this occurs in a particular year due to exceptional circumstances, say financing a war, or extraordinary expenditure occasioned by natural calamities like floods, drought, or earthquake, the fiscal balance may be restored in one or more years, with some special effort in the form of a cut in expenditure, revenue mobilization, reduction in developmental expenditure, and external aid. But if the structural budgetary imbalance of the revenue deficit being financed out of the capital budget, with consequent extensive recourse to borrowings and deficit financing, tends to become a regular feature of the fiscal system, severe macroeconomic destabilization is inevitable. A large spiralling price inflation, high interest rates, and accumulation of public debts, not only adversely affect savings and investment, but also cause hardship to the vulnerable sections of society, leading to socio-economic discontent. Thanks to the linkages of internal and external stability, there would be a spillover effect upon the country's balance of payments also, with pressure on exports and spurt in imports. The high costs of capital equipment and technological inputs would adversely affect industrial and agricultural progress. Devaluation of currency becomes inevitable; and even this may not stem the falling internal value of the currency if exports are inelastic and import-intensive, and the international trade environment is protectionist—particularly in the developed countries.

An important aspect is that in order to service the large accumulated debt, taxes have to be raised. These taxes are a dead weight burden upon the community, and currently no benefit is derived from them. Besides, as debt accumulates, the quantum of taxes needed to service the debt continues to grow. Increase in taxes beyond certain limits has disincentive effects, with consequent adverse effect upon savings, investment, and economic growth.

It should be said that if debt is increasing, so is GDP. If the ratio of debt to GDP remains constant—both growing at the same rate—there may not be too much cause for concern (although if GDP declines in any year, accumulated debt would not proportionately diminish), but actually the ratio of internal debt and liabilities to GDP has increased during the eighties from less than half to over three-fifths of national income, and the ratio continues to rise. It is also sometimes argued that the internal debt is owed to ourselves and need not cause concern. This may be true, but beyond certain limits it may lead to a breakdown of the fiscal system, as happened in the post-War period in certain European countries. Part of the debts was repudiated, with widespread hardship and discontent with the state apparatus. The effect of inflation upon internal indebtedness is significant. Actually, a decline in the value of the currency leads to a reduction in real terms in the value of the debt. But if the nominal rate of interest on the debt rises, yielding higher income, depreciation in the real value of the debt would be lower. However, in the case of debt with long-term maturity and static interest rate, hidden repudiation of debt in terms of rupees, consequent upon inflation, is undeniable.

The central government's fragile budgetary position is likely to further deteriorate on account of, (a) the increase in the rupee component of the additional oil import bill; (b) cost of repatriation and rehabilitation of Indians from the gulf region; (c) shortfall in revenues if corporate production and profits decline, particularly in the case of industries with oil products as inputs; (d) escalation in the salaries and wages bill on account of the inflationary factor; and (e) the high burden of fertilizer and other subsidies.

Although government is making a considerable effort to reduce expenditure, past history shows that the possibility of substantial reduction in expenses is remote, primarily because its outlay on defence, interest charges, and subsidies is inelastic. Besides, it has to make provision for liabilities on account of remission of farmers' loans, additional transfer payments and expenditure for rural development and employment, and administrative expenditure which is highly responsive to inflation. What government can do is to improve the monitoring of plan and non-plan outlays to ensure that the money reaches the target groups, funds are not wasted in the pipeline, and money is utilized for creation of assets scheduled. In effect, reduced outlays could yield improved results in real terms.

Revenues should continue to be buoyant, as industrial production has been increasing in 1990–1 (half year) at about double the rate in 1989–90, and the profits of the corporate sector are satisfactory. A good monsoon provides a promising outlook for a bumper crop in regard to foodgrains and other products. With strong linkages between the industrial and agricultural sectors, this factor should also buttress industrial production and incomes. Government needs to make extraordinary efforts to, (a) improve the administration for collection of taxes; (b) widen the base of taxation by bringing within the tax net self-employed persons who do not pay taxes; (c) bring agricultural incomes within the scope of taxes through direct and indirect taxes; (d) increase user charges, particularly of power and other inputs to agriculture; (e) make land revenue progressive; and (f) reduce generation and proliferation of black money. Improvement in operational efficiency of public enterprises and increased return on capital employed would alleviate the burden of budgetary support to the undertakings.

The above measures would be instrumental in reducing the structural budgetary imbalance, and obviate the need for deficit financing. Giving greater responsibility for industrial development to the private sector and reducing the activities of the public sector would assist in reducing PSBR. This is vitally necessary if government is to obtain a firm grip on the problem of accumulated internal indebtedness during the nineties.

Privatization of certain public enterprises would also contribute to an incremental flow of funds to more effectively balance the budget. The Thatcher government in the UK was able to garner considerable resources through privatization of various public sector industries and utilities. Accruing gains from privatization are manifold. Besides strengthening the budgetary position and reducing PSBR, divestment of loss making public undertakings diminishes the burden of losses, which in effect have to be financed out of public revenues. If the enterprises turn the corner and generate surpluses after privatization, they contribute to general revenues in the form of taxes. If their cost of expansion, modernization, and technological upgradation is either borne by the concerns themselves, or raised from the capital market and its members, budgetary allocation would no longer be necessary. The government in India is hesitant about taking steps to privatize public enterprises, but the portents are that the decade of the nineties will witness the transfer of a few undertakings from the state to the private or joint sector. It is hoped that the proceeds will contribute towards reducing deficits and indebtedness.

EXTERNAL DEBT

The Gulf crisis of 1990 added a new dimension to India's difficult balance of payments position. As a net oil importer, the escalation in the import bill for oil, together with other losses, was estimated to aggregate $2.8 billion (Rs 4200 crores), taking the price of oil to $25 per barrel. The immediate effects of the crisis on the BOP position were, (a) a sharp escalation in the cost of oil entailing loss of foreign exchange; (b) a sharp fall in remittance by workers in the affected areas; (c) losses on account of cancellation or postponement of construction contracts, and decline in export of goods and services to the Gulf region; and (d) foreign exchange cost of repatriation and rehabilitation of Indians living in the Gulf areas. Unless India is able to secure IMF credits from the compensatory contingency financing facility (CCFF), to temporarily overcome the crisis, its difficulties are likely to be compounded. Prospects of bilateral assistance from the USA, UK, Japan, and other countries, and commercial borrowings have improved, although the latter entails high interest liability. If the price of oil rises further and oil imports have to be restricted, it would result in deceleration in industrial and agricultural production and general business activity, resulting in lower exports to industrial countries. This would exacerbate the BOP deficits. Some loans in the IMF CCFF account have been made available, while other loans are on the anvil. However, the entire volume of additional foreign exchange required is unlikely to be forthcoming, and development of some degree of self-reliance through increased exports over a period of three years is imperative.

A developing country's industrial growth postulates capital formation on a massive scale. The mobilization of internal resources needs to be buttressed by foreign capital or foreign exchange earnings. Multilateral assistance on concessional terms by the developed countries or international institutions is vital for the consummation of the industrial development programme. If the terms of the loan assistance are stiff, repayment of loan and servicing may impose a heavy burden, beyond its fiscal capacity.

The recipient country has a reciprocal obligation to utilize the foreign aid for productive purposes that generate sufficient surpluses, which would facilitate not only servicing the loan, but also its repayment. Presently, concessional aid has been declining, even though India's economic progress has been lauded by international authorities; and it has conservatively utilized foreign exchange, largely for development and essential purposes.

INTERNATIONAL TRADING ENVIRONMENT

The post-Second World War years 1950 to 1973, till the first Oil shock, witnessed unparalleled economic growth in the industrialized world, which was facilitated by access to cheap supplies of raw materials from third world countries. Almost 70 per cent of the world's output of nine major minerals (excluding oil) required to sustain an industrial economy were consumed by the developed countries. Industrial growth was accompanied by an upsurge in international trade. Besides, the necessity of multilateral assistance to underdeveloped countries was recognized, and concerted action taken, resulting in a sizeable transfer of real resources from the industrialized countries and multilateral institutions in the form of aid on concessional terms to developing countries.

With the first Oil shock in 1973–4, the scenario changed for the worse. GDP growth in industrialized economies, which had been about 5 per cent a year in the sixties declined to 3.1 per cent per annum in the seventies. Fiscal deficits and inflation grew owing to high incomes, large social security programmes, and rigidity in the operation of domestic markets, resulting in deceleration in growth. The third world countries however maintained their average growth rate of about 5.4 per cent per year in the sixties, during the seventies. The growth was heartening, but it was accompanied by, (a) huge budgetary deficits, inflation, currencies with inflated values, and extraordinary incentives to accelerate industrial and agricultural growth. These domestic imbalances rendered many of the economies more vulnerable to external economic shocks and exogenous factors; (b) many of the countries accumulated large external debts and servicing burdens beyond their capacity.

The prospect of the world economy in 1978–9, on the whole, was one of cautious optimism, and it appeared that both the developed economies and third world countries had successfully overcome the adverse effects of the Oil shock and were well set towards resurgence of industrial activity in the case of the former, and steady progress by the latter. But destiny willed otherwise. The second Oil shock in 1979 resulted in mounting price inflation; this was however accompanied by unemployment and stagnation—stagflation in short—during the years 1980–2. Anti-inflationary monetary policies were adopted, resulting in a severe recession. Most industrial countries recorded a decline in overall growth rates (touching a low of—0.4 per cent per annum in 1982). One effect of these developments was disillusionment with Keynesian policies, and initiation of the trend towards liberalization, which manifested itself in, (a) reduction in state intervention and deregulation of private enterprise; (b) a diminished role for the public sector and privatization of industry and; (c) liberalization of financial markets and other sectors of the economy. Besides, in the USA, considerable tax-cuts were effected, while public spending increased, leading to high budgetary deficits. Meanwhile, developing countries, which had accumulated huge foreign debts in the seventies, faced grave economic crisis. A sea change occurred in the international trading and economic environment: diminishing commodity prices due to world-wide recession and reduced world trade, high interest rates and severe diminution in not only concessional assistance but also bank financing, as during the period 1980–1 to 1983–4, commercial banks withdrew their support. An outcome of financial disequilibrium and external payment imbalances in the eighties—with the USA following stimulation in fiscal policy and large current account deficits, and other developed countries pursuing policies of budgetary consolidation—has been a decline in foreign aid to developing countries and resurgence of protectionism. Developing countries have been forced to seek alternative avenues for financing their deficits, including commercial borrowing at high rates of interest. India's external debt increased from Rs 69,681 crores[4] in March 1989 to Rs 81,168 crores at the end of March 1990.

An analysis of the BOP position during the last two decades shows that three important factors, *inter alia*, contributed to the sharp escalation in foreign indebtedness and increase in the debt-service ratio: (1) the two Oil shocks of 1973–4 and 1978–9, which necessitated heavy borrowings to finance the increased cost of oil; (2) decline in multilateral concessional assistance leading to increased recourse to commercial borrowings on stiffer terms; and (c) the world depression during 1980–1 to 1982–3, deterioration in the trading environment, and subsidence in international trade, on account of which Indian exports were constricted, while due to upsurge in industrial development within the country, imports increased. The terms of trade also became unfavourable to developing countries' exports. Another factor has been the steady devaluation of the rupee *vis-à-vis* other currencies, particularly sterling and the dollar. This has undoubtedly assisted in stimulating the country's exports, but the outstanding loans and interest obligations have automatically multiplied in rupee terms, entailing greater liability.

The first Oil shock in 1973 increased India's oil import bill, but thanks to certain favourable factors and good economic management, the economy was able to overcome the adverse effects of the shock. Concessional aid and foreign resources' inflow continued during the seventies (as during the sixties) at satisfactory levels. Besides, there was an upsurge in remittances from abroad and other net invisible inflows. Macroeconomic policy measures, initiated by government in 1973–4 contributed to conversion of the trade deficit into a surplus in 1976–7. It was a remarkable performance, even though the deflationary measures had a dampening effect upon output and incomes. The second Oil shock in 1979 occurred in the context of an international diminution in concessional foreign aid, which continued in the 1980s. Besides, erosion had taken place in the favourable inflows of the seventies; remittances and transfers as also other invisibles had decelerated. Inadequacy of concessional loans necessitated resort to commercial borrowings, which were expensive in terms of high interest charges, and inflow of NRI deposits was induced by offering high rates of return.

The stagnancy in exports during the period 1980–1 to 1983–4 reflected the worldwide slump in international trade, owing to recession in most industrialized economies. Meanwhile, as a result of the spurt in oil prices, imports grew by 34.2 per cent in 1979–80 and 37.3 per cent in 1980–1; while exports in the corresponding period grew by 12.1 per cent and 4.6 per cent only. Trade deficits during the first half of the eighties amounted to between Rs 5390 crores and Rs 6060 crores in each of the five years. The overall effect was that debt obligations and the debt service ratio increased considerably, the latter touching 13.6 per cent in 1984–5. It is significant that at the end March 1980, India's outstanding external debt was Rs 13,430 crores, which included commercial borrowings of Rs 1252 crores only. At the conclusion of the Sixth Plan in 1984–5, the external debt had escalated to Rs 35,800 crores, including commercial borrowings of Rs 6908 crores and IMF dues of Rs 4888 crores.

Two developments during the Sixth Plan period are significant in regard to their impact upon the BOP. Domestic production of oil soared and this helped in keeping down the oil import bill. Imports however continued to increase to meet the requirements of a fast growing economy. Import of industrial raw materials and capital goods equipment sustained the progress of industrialization. But economic management was not flawless. Certain avoidable imports were permitted. Import of inessential luxuries and consumer durables need to be kept down. Bulk imports of fertilizers could have been much less if the industry had been allowed to attain its normal rate of growth. Table 11.2 vividly illustrates the BOP position and the state of foreign indebtedness during the last five years of the eighties, corresponding to the period of the Seventh Five Year Plan.

The average debt-service ratio envisaged in the Seventh Plan was 17.6 per cent while the actual average for the first four years of the Plan works out to 21 per cent, which is considerably higher. According to the *R.B.I. Annual Report 1990*, external debt as a proportion of GDP at market prices increased from 12.5 per cent at the end of March 1980 to 17.8 per cent at the end of March 1989. The various fiscal and other measures taken by government to increase exports yielded dividends and there was ground for optimism that the tempo of growth would be maintained. The continuing devaluation of the rupee *vis-à-vis* other currencies facilitated the promotion of exports. The most disturbing feature, however, was the growing external indebtedness and rise in the debt-service ratio, which was estimated to be in the vicinity of 30 per cent by the end of 1990. Part of this accumulation of external debt was attributable to the decline in aid on concessional terms, necessitating recourse to commercial borrowings at high rates of interest. The cumulative burden of interest payments partially neutralized the invisible inflow of remittances, which were, however, on the decline. While domestic consumption of petroleum

TABLE 11.2 — *Current Account Balance and Debt-Service Ratio*

Years	Exports in crores of rupees	Growth Rate of Exports (percentage)	Imports in crores of rupees	Growth Rate of Imports (percentage)	Trade Deficit in crores of rupees	Foreign Indebtedness	Debt-Service Ratio (percentage)
1984–85	11,744	20.2	17,134	8.2	–5390	35,725	13.6
1985–86	10,895	–7.2	19,658	14.7	–8763	39,691	16.0
1986–87	12,452	14.3	20,096	2.2	–7644	48,348	22.0
1987–88 (P)	15,741	26.4	22,399 (PR)	11.5	–6658	54,409	24.0
1988–89 (P)	20,295 (P)	28.9	28,194 (PR)	25.9	–7899	68,831	23.0
1989–90 (P)	27,681 (P)	36.5	35,714 (P)	26.7	–8033	81,168	—

SOURCE Compiled from *Economic Survey 1989–90*, Table S-90 & S.73; *RBI Annual Report 1989–90*, p. 135; *1988–9*, p. 99.

(P) = Provisional.

(PR) = Partially Revised.

products had been rising, oil production in the country could not be further stimulated.

The export performance during the last three years of the Seventh Plan had been heartening; however, the adverse trade balance had also been considerable and exceeded Rs 8000 crores in 1989–90. This had occurred due to the maintenance of the high momentum of industrial growth during almost the entire period of the Seventh Plan, as also in agriculture (except during the drought year 1987–8). A growing economy required extensive imports of capital goods and technology, besides industrial and other raw materials, intermediates, and oil and petroleum products. Bulk imports of fertilizers were necessary to sustain agricultural growth, while that of edible oil was unavoidable.

Perspective for the Nineties

What is necessary during the nineties is to reduce internal budgetary imbalances, control inflation, improve quality and reduce costs of products through technological upgradation, restrict imports to the bare minimum, and stimulate exports through determined efforts and better marketing. The import intensity of exports also needs to be curbed, as it tends to partially neutralize export gains. Import of raw materials and capital goods should be restricted, with some obligation on industry to increase exports. With efficient economic management, there is considerable scope for a stimulated export drive and import substitution. Despite comparative advantage in certain commodities, if the internal value of the rupee were to decline and price parity with other trading countries was disturbed due to inflation, exports and balance of payments would be adversely affected, necessitating further devaluation of the rupee.

The substantial deficit on the foreign trade account and sizeable foreign indebtedness are likely to have far-reaching consequences in the foreseable future. Repayment of commercial borrowings and interest payments on loans and deposits would increase the foreign exchange outgo. The IMF loan would provide temporary respite, but it would be repayable during the nineties, and the effect then would be similar to that indicated above. Maintenance of the tempo of growth would necessitate sizeable imports of capital goods, as also of industrial raw materials as necessary, to keep the wheels of production in motion.

Even though the Gulf crisis was a passing phase, oil prices will take some time to return to pre-crisis levels. The burden of oil imports will therefore continue to be high. Rationalization of imports is imperative and some degree of belt-tightening will be necessary.

Import substitution wherever possible has been necessary to conserve foreign exchange. It was not a question of choice, but of necessity. The industrial structure has become so diversified and absorption of technology has improved sufficiently to enable the country to manufacture, with some effort, innovation, and encouragement from the authorities, many goods which were being imported. Besides, repetitive imports of technology have to be avoided. Developing countries need to imbibe lessons from Japan in the matter of adaptation of advanced technology imported from developed countries. Of this, more later.[5]

Exports recorded commendable growth during the last three years. Not only has the tempo to be maintained but to be further accelerated. Various measures of export promotion are indicated in Chapter 9; we would only mention here that, (a) there are countries with whom the country's trade is either non-existent or infinitely small, including Jamaica, Fiji, Malta, the Bahamas, and certain African countries. They include a number of Commonwealth members. Their requirements should be explored and efforts stimulated to reach out to newer markets with more diversified commodities; (b) Japan, the EEC, and developing countries constitute a vast market for Indian exports, which need to be developed; (c) the stage has come when India should import raw materials and export finished products to developing countries; (d) consulates and commercial attachés in foreign countries should be assigned the task of assisting in export promotion and weightage should be given to their contribution in this effort when assessing their efficiency and performance. It hardly needs to be emphasized that the development of Bombay High for production of oil enabled the country to successfully withstand the Oil shock in 1978–9; that it is imperative to further step up domestic oil exploration at this critical juncture. Success in this direction would greatly alleviate difficulties.

The scope for enhanced foreign exchange earnings from tourism is almost unlimited, liable to rise directly in proportion to efforts. An imaginative approach, leading to development of new tourist centres, with improved infrastructure for tourism, including greater internal travel, hotel accommodation, and other facilities are necessary. Internal peace and stability, however, is a prerequisite to increase tourist traffic which has been very adversely affected by disturbances and exaggerated reports of these.

ALTERNATIVE SCENARIO: IMPACT ON GROWTH

An alternative scenario may also be considered. If oil prices rise further and inadequate increase in exports results in compulsory diminution in imports, the consequences for growth could be serious. Scaling down the import of oil would adversely affect industrial production. If inflow of raw materials, metals, scrap, and intermediates necessary for industry have to be severely curtailed, the utilization of installed capacity would be severely affected, leading to decline in output and profits. Factories may have to close down, with consequent effect upon employment. Pruning of imports of capital goods would have a direct impact upon industrial growth, establishment of new industries, and expansion and diversification of exising units. If technology imports are affected, it would lead to obsolescence in production processes and apparatus, and further impair the competitive capacity of Indian industry in international markets.

The agricultural sector would not be immune to the impact of serious foreign exchange shortage. A reduction in the import of oil and fertilizers would have a direct impact upon agricultural production and productivity. Besides, if other industries supplying inputs to agriculture are adversely affected, the repercussions on agriculture would be similar. Logically, if there is an adverse impact of foreign exchange shortage upon agricultural and industrial production, it would pose a threat to internal price stability. Latent inflationary forces are present in the economy and reduction in critical imports could trigger serious inflation in double digit figures.

This gloomy scenario is not likely to emerge, as the country should be able to overcome the present BOP crisis. The World Bank and IMF authorities are fully seized of the impact of the Gulf situation on the Indian economy and inflow of loans on CCFF account on concessional terms has commenced. Meanwhile, efforts at export promotion and conservation of foreign exchange, and

TABLE 11.3 — *Debt Indicators in Developing Countries, 1975 to 1987* (percentage)

Country group and debt indicator	1975	1980	1981	1982	1983	1984	1985	1986	1987[a]
All developing countries:									
Debt-service ratio	13.7	16.2	17.9	21.0	19.7	19.5	21.8	22.6	21.0
Debt–GNP ratio	15.7	20.7	22.4	26.3	31.4	33.0	35.9	38.5	37.6
Highly indebted countries:									
Debt-service ratio	24.0	27.1	30.7	38.8	34.7	33.4	33.9	37.7	32.7
Debt–GNP ratio	18.1	23.3	25.6	32.4	45.4	47.5	49.5	54.1	55.9
Low-income Africa:									
Debt-service ratio	10.2	13.6	14.6	14.2	14.2	15.1	17.9	19.9	34.7
Debt–GNP ratio	25.2	39.8	44.2	48.0	55.1	62.0	68.9	72.1	76.2

(a) Estimated.

NOTES Data are based on a sample of ninety developing countries. The debt-service ratio is defined as the dollar value of external debt payments (interest and amortization) on medium- and long-term loans expressed as a percentage of the dollar value of exports of goods and services. The debt–GNP ratio is defined as the dollar value of outstanding medium- and long-term debt expressed as a percentage of dollar GNP.

SOURCE *World Development Report 1988*, The World Bank/Oxford University Press, New York, p. 31.

reduced consumption of oil and other products are being intensified. These efforts should bear fruit and the crisis be resolved without adversely affecting growth or aggravating inflationary pressures.

REFERENCES

1. Receipts Budget, GOI, 1989–90, pp. 40. 41.
2. 'White Paper on Economy', Government of India (Dec. 1989), para 26; *RBI Annual Report 1988–89*, p. 86.
3. *World Development Report 1988*, World Bank/OUP, New York, p. 5.
4. *RBI Annual Report 1989–90*, p. 135.
   RBI Report on Currency & Finance 1980–81 and
   RBI Bulletin Nov. 1988; revised from provisional estimate of Rs 68,831 crores, *see* Table 11.2.
5. *Vide* ch. 13.

12

Foreign Capital and Investment Climate

The developmental role of foreign investment capital in accelerating investment can hardly be over-emphasized. As W. Arthur Lewis says, 'One can think of no country, including Britain, Russia and Japan, where foreign business did not play a major role in the initial stages of development, both by providing extra income, and also by imparting new techniques'.[1] We have attained a stage of growth where we require not an indiscriminate inflow of foreign capital, but investment in industries based on sophisticated technology. Government is right in regulating and channelizing the inflow of foreign capital into sectors where it is most needed, and in encouraging imports of newer generation machinery and technology. What is particularly reassuring is that it does not discriminate between foreign and Indian capital.

Two contradictory trends, however, are in evidence in the country today. While on the one hand, there is an increase in foreign collaborations and inflow of foreign investment capital together with modern technology, on the other there is liquidation of existing investments and transfer of some leading industrial concerns to Indian nationals. That such transfers have some virtues is not denied, but funds which would otherwise have been available for establishment of new industries are being absorbed in the acquisition of existing units. Besides, this involves repatriation of capital and consumption of foreign exchange.

Prerequisites for Foreign Equity Investment

The remedy is not to impose restrictions on repatriation of capital, but to create an investment climate in which the foreign investor feels safe and a suitable environment exists in which to secure a fair return on capital investment, commensurate with the risks involved. What the investor seeks is reasonable security of tenure and opportunities for building an industrial complex over a period of years. The foreign investor would hardly risk his capital in expansion or new projects if the future outlook for industry in general, be it due to economic or political causes or state intervention and controls, is gloomy.

The levels of corporate and personal taxation and the administration of taxes have an important bearing in this context. The basic corporation tax for public companies has been raised to 51.75 per cent, even though investment allowance has been withdrawn. This compares unfavourably with the UK, where corporate tax rate has been progressively reduced to 35 per cent, and in 1991 to 32.5 per cent. Besides, shareholders in the UK obtain credit for part of the tax paid by the company under the imputation system of taxation. There is a correlation between GDP growth and tax rates. According to a detailed World Bank study[2] over a period, the average annual rate of growth of GDP was 7.3 per cent in the low tax group of countries and 1.1 per cent in their highly taxed counterparts.

The other side of reducing tax levels is government's anxiety to cleanse the tax system which is understandable. But widespread raids, and the attendant publicity and prosecution in certain cases, have an unsettling effect upon industrial activity, and slow down the tempo of industrial growth and corporate expansion. Besides, they give rise to tension and apprehension among the business community, leading to an adverse effect upon the investment climate. Of even greater significance is that the image of the Indian business community is tarnished in other countries, as a result of which foreign collaborators tend to be somewhat wary of entering into agreements. The list of those involved in tax cases includes highly respected persons and reputable companies, including multinationals. Without entering into the controversy as to whether the I.T. department's actions were justified or not, it would suffice to say that if the impression is formed among collaborators and multinationals abroad that by and large Indian businessmen are dishonest, or that any company operating in India and its officials are liable to be subjected to raids and perhaps also prosecution, the inflow of foreign capital may slow down. Government proposes to lay down ground rules for raids and collateral action in consultation with industry. This aspect of the matter may also be kept in view in formulating guidelines.

A multinational corporation may choose to effect certain variations in its product mix and the range of products initially sanctioned. Government would like to retain the power to decide what departure it would permit from the originally created pattern of production. But one should not put an enterprise into a straitjacket; it should be encouraged to expand to its fullest potential. Any successful industrial undertaking must have the opportunity for growth and reasonable diversification. This is also something government should bear in mind when modulating its industrial regulation policies.

Fortunately at the present juncture the pendulum has swung to the other extreme and instead of nationalization, the world trend is towards privatization due to the failure of the public sector to deliver the goods. However, in India, a state government has evinced keen interest in nationalization of certain textile mills, some of which are sick. Instead of curbing this tendency, the Centre promised funds for the venture, as also for modernization in the future, despite the poor performance of textile mills nationalized in the past. What is of greater relevance is that adequate compensation must be paid in all cases of nationalization. Unfortunately, Article 31 of the Constitution was amended, substituting the word 'amount' for 'compensation', thereby dispensing with the concept of a 'just equivalent', and rendering compensation non-justiciable. Shareholders of most coal companies have suffered due to extremely poor compensation.

However, government policy is basically against nationalization, although it is hesitant about privatization—now proceeding apace in the UK, Japan, and several European countries.

REFERENCES

1. W. Arthur Lewis, *The Theory of Economic Growth*, George Allen & Unwin Ltd., London, 1957, p.258.
2. Keith Marsden, *World Bank Study, Finance and Development*, IMF & World Bank, Washington, Sept. 1983, p.40.

13

Role of Technology for Growth: Japan's Success Story

Government has rightly focused attention upon the imperative need for modernization and upgradation of technology. Several industrial units in cement, steel, sugar, paper, textiles, and other industries were established more than 25 years ago and modernization has become urgently necessary; besides, even with regard to newer industries like electronics, computers, and telecommunications, technology is fast changing and the ability to remain internationally competitive postulates technological upgradation on a continual basis. The fiscal policy, in consonance with this objective, has emphasized the need to import appropriate technology and accelerate the development of indigenous knowhow. Various measures, including rationalization of excise and customs duties for electronics, computers, and similar industries, and spreadover knowhow fees over six years for tax purposes, have been taken by government to implement this policy.

JAPAN'S EXPERIENCE

It is relevant to observe that in the post-War period, half of the fast paced real growth of 10 per cent per year achieved by Japan is attributable to technological innovation. Since Japan entered late into the ranks of industrialized nations, it was more economical to import foreign technology from overseas sources and make further improvement to the basic imported knowhow. Toshio Shishido writing on *The Japanese Economy* regards 'imitation as a very important positive factor for economic development, essential for countries trying to catch up with advanced countries'.[1] Japan has been able not only to adapt foreign technology, but to improve upon it to derive tremendous advantage. It has consequently attained a technological level almost equivalent to that of the USA, and in certain industries like steel, automobiles, and electrical home appliances it has achieved a march over the United States.

Certain important factors have contributed to the phenomenon of an adaptor surpassing the inventor. Japan developed a new technological trend, and this is where India has most to learn from her. Not only did it adapt the technology of large-scale industry and mass production, but also ushered in the 'era of miniaturization'. Progress in miniaturized technology has its impact not only on electronics but various industrial fields, and this new technology was successfully implanted in mass production industries. Small-scale industries were nurtured by large industries and it was ensured that modern technology and quality control permeated the ancillary units which supplied components to parent factories, producing, for example, automobiles and television sets. 'Small is beautiful' is not merely a concept of Professor E. F. Schumacher but a significant aspect of Japanese industrial culture.

Having achieved outstanding success in its technological development programme, Japan's rate of dependence on imported technology was brought down to 10.9 per cent in 1983 from 16.7 per cent in 1970. Japan now invests 2.5 per cent of its GNP on research and development (R & D) — an impressive percentage exceeded only by the USA and the Soviet Union. There are two interesting aspects: firstly, Japan has become a net exporter of technology during the 80s and secondly, Japan's R & D policy is characterized by a fusion of efforts by government and private industry, similar to its industrial policy, which is marked by close co-operation between the two.

Science Cities

Japan is also establishing science cities, similar to California's high-tech Silicon Valley, 'where cross-pollination between university and industry researchers produces thousands of new ideas and products and often spawns new companies'.[2] At Kumamoto, which is being developed by Japan as a leading high technology research centre, the authorities have established a state-of-the-art laboratory, affiliated to the university, which is also utilized by research scientists from commercial establishments. When some new innovative ideas are conceived, the research complex provides incubators in the form of small laboratories to assist corporate entities to utilize the ideas for the development of commercial products. Like Rome, science cities cannot be built in a day, but it is expected that by the year 2001, probably eight or ten science cities will be functioning.

Tshkuba near Tokyo has about 7000 scientists in more than 100 national laboratories and another 1000 scientists in private laboratories. It is virtually known as the City of Brains and has provision for a wide spectrum of scientific facilities and apparatus ranging from a $600 million Particle accelerator to a Space Centre and Mechanical Engineering Laboratory for developing mobile robots which could be utilized for repair of nuclear power plants. Industrial complexes are also making determined efforts at R & D. They are bringing American research scientists to their laboratories to give innovative activities an edge and a push.

The great advantage accruing to Japan over the USA is that less than 10 per cent of the government's research budget is spent on military technology, while in the USA the corresponding figure is 70 per cent. Corporate R & D budgets in the USA are being starved of funds, as the objective of corporate planning is to obtain high short-term financial gains. According to *Newsweek*,[3] in mid-1988 the United States was lagging behind Japan in commercializing high-temperature superconductivity, which was potentially one of the most vital technologies of the eighties. The Japanese are stealing a march over the United States in area after area, and this is a challenge that the latter must face. The Japanese as a nation are a determind people, and having once decided to attain a high level of proficiency in the art of innovation, it would not be surprising if by the end of the century they significantly transform themselves from imitators and adaptors into innovators.

LEVELS OF EMPLOYMENT NOT ERODED

Fears have been expressed that technological progress may result in erosion in levels of employment. That pure process innovation may lead to a reduction in labour input is true, but that does not imply an overall decline in employment.[4] There are several reasons: (a) the consequential reduction in price should contribute to an escalation in demand for the final product and a larger share of the domestic market, which in turn should partially offset the reduction in labour input per unit of output; (b) lower costs may increase competitive capacity, leading to higher exports; (c) the impact of major innovations transcends the industry in which they occur. The use of radios, telephones, and television not only stimulated employment in the manufacture of these items, but also that in communications and broadcasting. With the development of computers, electronics and telecommunications, vast employment opportunities have been created; this is also the case with growth of petrochemicals; (d) negatively, in the absence of technological upgradation, inability to face foreign competition would lead to closure of industry and reduced employment; and (e) product innovations lead to the production of new and improved quality goods, thereby stimulating demand and manufacture of higher value output and greater inputs. During the eighties, computers and electronics are expected to increase employment in the United States. Half the jobs created during this period would be in the services sector, including computer and data-processing services.

It is expected that computer-chip based technologies would, in the long run, result in higher employment levels through a new explosion of economic growth; and there is no historical evidence with regard to significant loss in employment. Improved technology stimulates the aggregate demand for labour by increasing consumption and providing gainful investment avenues. Besides, rapid high-tech growth is usually synonymous with economic prosperity. Even in India it is not true that the application of modern technology is likely to lead to reduction in employment. Initially, a modern sophisticated automatic plant may utilize fewer workers for production than ordinary plants, but the establishment of such an industry, together with various ancillary and tertiary industries that generally come up in contiguity to such a plant, and the stimulus it gives to the services sector, including transport, housing, education, medical and recreational facilities, and markets, leads to increases in employment.

As provided in the fiscal policy, the Indian government has set up a venture capital fund to provide equity capital for pilot plants seeking to adapt imported technology to wider domestic application, and commercial exploitation of indigenously developed technology. To partly fund this a five per cent R & D levy is being imposed on all royalty and lump-sum payments for imported equipment, drawings and designs. Government is setting up an autonomous technology assessment and forecasting council to monitor technological developments in India and abroad. Its role is to ensure the import of the latest technology, conducive to increased consumption, efficiency, and productivity and obviate the induction of equipment and know-how which is obsolete or tending towards obsolescence in the next decade. We would suggest that it should be made obligatory for each large industry to develop at least five ancillary industries, reinforced with modern technology. Maruti has taken the initiative in this direction, which is commendable. This should also provide stimulated employment.

Government is also establishing a high-powered National Science and Technology Commission (NSTC), with the objective of synchronizing science and technology with planning in order to bring about a sea change in the country's socio-economic scenario by the year 2001. It is proposed that linkages be developed between the NSTC, Planning Commission, and State-level science and technology commissions. Later the linkage would be extended to district and blocks within the state. The Science Advisory Council suggested that higher technology should *inter alia* be utilized in the areas of industry, agriculture, infrastructure, food, human resource development, and pollution control. In the field of industry, the quality and efficiency of production must improve, and productivity should be enhanced. Higher technology is imperative, particularly in areas where we enjoy comparative cost advantage, in order to stimulate exports. To improve food production, higher technology should be utilized for intensive agriculture, better water management, upgradation of the genetic production potential of major crops, exploration of the ocean for seafoods, and reforestation to prevent soil erosion and flooding.

A multi-pronged technological strategy needs to be forged. The technology developed in other countries should be imported and adapted, and further research undertaken. If imported technology is not available on reasonable terms, we should make intensive efforts to develop our own. Since there is the constraint of resources for research, there should be a perspective selection of areas and objectives; funds should be concentrated on research projects which are result oriented, and the research should include a delivery system which would make the technology available both to the producer and the consumer. The considerable progress and advancement of Western countries, as also the newly expanding economies of the East, like South Korea and Taiwan, have been achieved with the help of modern technology. If Indian industries are to remain competitive, both internally and internationally, and the country is to progress, there is no alternative to deployment of advanced technology and its periodic upgradation.

REFERENCES

1. Toshio Shishido 'Japanese Technological Development' in *The Japanese Economy* by Toshio Shishido and Rynzo Sato, Auburn House Publishing Co., London, ch. 15, p. 200.
2. 'Breeding New Ideas', *Newsweek*, vol. 112, 8 Aug. 1988, p. 54.
3. Ibid., p. 55.
4. Lynn E. Browne, 'New Technologies and Employment' in *Economic Impact*, No 49, 1985/1, International Communication Agency, USA, Washington.

14

Institutional Finance

The development banks in the country have played a catalytic role in promoting industrial development. They have provided industrial finance for new projects, expansion and modernization of industry, and have assisted not only the established industrial houses, but also nurtured the growth of new entrepreneurs. Highly discriminating as these institutions have been in financing projects on the basis of the threefold criteria of matching production capacity creation with potential demand, financial viability, and the economic priorities of the country, they have also played a pivotal role in allocation of scarce means and resources, in consonance with the broad framework of policies designed to accelerate the momentum of growth. The IDBI, IFCI, and ICICI and several other Central and State finance corporations have made a sterling contribution and deserve every praise. Certain aspects of institutional policies, however, need to be modified to stimulate development and facilitate financing of projects.

Debt–Equity Ratio

Reduction in corporate taxation should increase residual post-tax reserves and contribute to self-financing of industries to a greater degree. But in order to accelerate capital formation by the corporate sector, the debt–equity ratio needs to be substantially relaxed, particularly in the case of capital-intensive industries like cement, fertilizer, paper, and others. The norms (1991) for availability of finance adopted by financial institutions provide for a debt–equity ratio of 2:1. Where, on the basis of overall appraisal, the institutions feel that the project would be only marginally profitable, the ratio may be 1.5:1, requiring a greater proportion of equity. The debt–equity ratio may be relaxed in the case of both new and existing priority sector projects and highly capital-intensive industries, depending upon the quality of management. Institutions, however, seek to induce entrepreneurs to increase the promoters' contribution to as high a level as possible in order to maximize their stake in the project.

An important institutional norm is that the promoter should generally contribute 20 per cent (relaxable to 17.5 per cent for backward areas and 15 per cent and below for core sector industries) of the total project cost. But difficulties arise because the listing of shares for quotation with the Stock Exchange postulates that the public should be offered at least 60 per cent of the issue. With a debt–equity ratio of 2:1 for new projects, 40 per cent of equity works out to 13.33 per cent of the project cost. In order to obviate this difficulty, promoters are generally required to provide loans to make up the shortfall. Recently, the Stock Exchange Rules have been modified so that promoters can initially subscribe to and hold 70 per cent of the shares issued, but within three years they have to divest themselves of holdings in excess of 40 per cent equity share capital. As a result of the inflationary rise in prices of plant and machinery the world over, project costs have escalated to astronomic levels. A million tonne cement plant may cost between Rs 250 to Rs 300 crores and a fertilizer plant producing 4.5 lakhs tonnes of ammonia and 7.5 lakhs tonnes of urea per year, based on offshore gas, may cost between Rs 800 and Rs 900 crores. The debt–equity ratio in the case of gas-based fertilizer plants may be relaxed to 4:1. While government does permit some relaxation for capital-intensive industries, the quantum of promoters' contribution is very considerable in such cases and beyond the capacity of even some of the middle-ranking big houses. It is significant that during the post-war reconstruction period in the fifties, Japan permitted a debt–equity ratio of 10:1. As Herman Kahn writes, 'From the viewpoint of companies competing and expanding, the high debt–equity ratio means that the Japanese firm gets its capital for expansion more cheaply than the American firm does. The money paid in interest on Japanese debentures is not only a tax deductible expense but it is usually much less than the corresponding profits a US or Japanese firm would have to earn if it expanded by increasing its equity.'[1] Even now in Japan, a debt–equity ratio of between 4:1 and 5:1 is common and is often relaxed to further stimulate corporate growth.

We are of the view that the standard debt–equity ratio in India should be 3:1 and in tlie case of capital-intensive industries, it should be relaxed to 6:1 to facilitate financing of projects. The institutions may, however, enforce intensive monitoring and exercise greater vigilance during the gestation period of aided industry. As regards the promoter's contribution, it should be 10 per cent of the project cost with oscillation of 2.5 per cent on either side, depending upon the quality of management.

CONVERTIBILITY CLAUSES

Quite often financial institutions insist on a clause providing them the option to convert upto 20 per cent of their medium-term and long-term loan into equity at par or at a pre-determined premium, which is often much less than the market value of shares at the time of conversion. The clause operates to the disadvantage of shareholders. The lending institutions have the best of both worlds. The institutional viewpoint is, of course, that since they share the risks involved in setting up new enterprises, they should also share the prosperity of a successful venture. Since institutions quite often take up equity shares in concerns they finance, either by underwriting them or by way of firm allotment, they share the fruits of success. The convertibility clause often acts as a deterrent to borrowing, particularly in the case of existing concerns or those seeking loans for modernization. It may also contribute to watering down capital. This aspect of the policy needs reformulation. (Recently, this stipulation has been dispensed with, *vide* ch. 22.)[2]

The personal guarantee of promoters is often insisted upon by lending bodies. But where a concern incurs heavy losses, quite often recovery is not possible despite such guarantee. It is a deterrent to free borrowing and industrial expansion or modernization, and also needs reconsideration.

NEW INITIATIVES

It was provided (now withdrawn) that companies would be allowed to issue convertible debentures bearing a maximum interest of 14 per cent, and 12.5 per cent in case of FERA and MRTP companies, which would increase their marketability. A new instrument in the form of convertible cumulative preference shares carrying a right to 10 per cent dividend has been introduced in order to diversify the market, and enable new companies to raise capital. However, the latter has not met with good public response. It is, however, relevant to observe that convertible debentures, in lieu of the public issue component of equity capital, as instruments for raising capital, have an inherent superiority over convertible preference shares. Debenture interest, as already indicated, is a charge against profits, while preference dividend is an appropriation out of post-tax profits. The implication is that companies would have to allocate profits before tax equivalent to 20 per cent of the preference capital. Besides, debenture interest paid during the construction period could be capitalized. This would obviate to a certain extent delay in payment of equity dividend.

Government has adopted a pragmatic policy designed to liberate the economy from excessive controls and impart dynamism to the processes of growth. In a move to dismantle controls, a number of industries have been delicensed, so that in areas where additional capacity is necessary, procedural delays are reduced to a minimum. The assets limit for MRTP companies has now been abolished (*vide* ch. 22) in consonance with the considerable increase in the cost and economic size of projects. Cognizance appears to have been taken of the fact that Indian companies are small compared to their western counterparts and growth in size to augment competitive capacity is desirable. Government has taken measures to prescribe a minimum economic size for new units in specified industries to ensure that they achieve economies of scale.

Securities of listed public companies are to be made freely transferable. A 'Code of Take-overs' has been formulated to regulate take-overs and discourage corporate transfers through cornering and surreptitious deals. Conversion of closely-held companies into listed public companies is being encouraged by permitting them to enlist by offering only 40 per cent of their equity capital in two stages over a period of three years, and capitalize the greater portion of their free reserve prior to making the public issue. Bonus shares guidelines are being relaxed and non-FERA companies in existence beyond ten years, or which have been making profits for more than five years, would be allowed to capitalize prior to the public issue, reserves upto a maximum ratio of 5:1 as compared to 1:1 allowed at present. Such companies, numbering over a hundred, have a high rate of profitability and considerable resources. If they take advantage of this liberalization, and enlist themselves, they would add equity shares with a face value of about Rs 400 crores to the stock exchanges. The conversion of such companies into public bodies would facilitate their expansion and modernization by enabling them to garner resources through public issues and easier accessibility to institutional finance. Measures are also being formulated to reduce the prevailing cost of public issues. Companies are allowed to retain 15 per cent excess subscription beyond the amount sanctioned by the Controller of Capital Issues.

Term lending rates were in August 1991 increased by the financial institutions from 14 per cent to 18.5 per cent and above as a part of the current liberalization package (including freeing bank interest rates) in regard to the financial sector recommended by the World Bank, and to regulate the projected increase in demand for funds in the context of a liquidity crunch they had been facing for some time. But this hike in interest may have serious repercussions in regard to increasing the cost of projects, having a cascading effect on the cost of the final product and militating against export competitiveness. The debt–equity ratio has also been reduced from 2:1 to 1.5:1, while enhancing the effective promoters' contribution to 25 per cent. This may have an adverse impact upon development.

South Korea, as a measure of state policy, has consistently maintained low interest rates on long-term loans for project financing so as to ensure low cost industrial growth, conducive to enhanced international competitiveness. Recent liberalization of industrial and foreign investment policies were intended to increase the momentum of industrial growth and stimulate exports. A sharp increase in institutional lending rates at this juncture may prove counter-productive.

High interest rates enter into the cost of commodities and outprice them in the international market. Prime lending rates in most OECD countries are much lower than in India. It is evident that commercial banks' lending rates need to be reduced in India, so as to reduce the cost of production and improve the competitive capacity of goods in the export markets.

Government also seeks to promote technological innovation and upgradation of technology in industry through selective incentives. The electronics, plastics, telecommunication, and sunrise industries should provide the thrust, and their lateral and forward linkages should give a boost to development. Customs duties over a wide range of raw materials and components have been reduced or abolished to make industry more competitive. There is a strong case for reduction in customs duty on imported capital goods, and abolition of excise duty on machinery produced indigenously. Reduction of project costs is vital to the strategy of export promotion.

Certain new initiatives have been taken by financial institutions in regard to promotion of technology, energy conservation, and pollution control. Venture capital funds have been set up by the IFCI and ICICI. Loans, which are interest free but commanding royalty in case of successful implementation of new technology, have been introduced. If the technology fails, the loans are written off. This is a signal development, which should stimulate induction of new technology and growth of entrepreneurship.

Evidence of the positive impact of the government policy of liberalization, and improvement in the investment climate and the capital market is available. Opening up the economy, giving freer rein to the private sector and streamlining procedures will not only enhance efficiency but also facilitate collaborations. India provides a vast and expanding market, and possesses a large pool of trained technicians. That is a perfect recipe for the transfer of technology. It could be an export base for American companies in joint ventures.

Greater responsibility devolves upon financial institutions in the context of dismantling industrial licensing and controls; their role in the efficient allocation of resources becomes crucial. The principal institutions possess the requisite infrastructure and have attained a high level of proficiency in project appraisal and financing. A greater degree of transparency coupled with competition appeared to be necessary. Towards this end, it has now been decided to allow the IDBI, ICICI, and IFCI to independently appraise and finance projects upto Rs 50 crores instead of in a consortium; thus the borrower now has a choice. If the World Bank does not allow us to follow the policy of subsidized interest rates, the borrowers should have the option of freely negotiating the rates of interest in their project loans with the institutions, subject to an upper limit.

CAUSES OF SICKNESS OVERSIMPLIFIED

The Finance Ministry's proposals that management deemed to be responsible for mismanaging an industrial unit will be debarred from having access to funds from financial institutions even for new projects and that bad managers, like bad currency, have to be kept out of circulation, are highly controversial. The onus for reporting sickness has been placed on the managements themselves. If 50 per cent of the net worth of a company is eroded, it would be obligatory for it to seek a fresh mandate from its shareholders; and when the company loses its entire net worth, the existing directors or owners may under certain circumstances have to relinquish its management. Government has over-simplified the issue. Transfer of management may have justification in cases where malafide intentions are proved and sickness is attributable to fraudulently siphoning off funds. But in most cases, industrial sickness may be a consequence not necessarily of bad management, but of financial constraints, recalcitrant labour, changes in technology or external factors beyond management control. This is particularly so in areas where power and other infrastructural deficiencies have made it difficult for industries like jute, textiles, and shipping to maintain their viability, and they suffer from endemic sickness. The cement industry was in bad shape for a considerable period because of inadequate retention prices determined by government; with partial decontrol (subsequently full decontrol) there has been a sea change in its prospects. In such cases, the solution to industrial sickness lies elsewhere than in changing managements. The basic problems afflicting the industry need to be effectively resolved.

To whom the management should be transferred is another important question? Past experience bears out that take-over of sick industries by state or central corporations has not restored viability to the units; most of them have sunk deeper into the red. The only solution that appears to be practicable is to effect their merger with healthy units. In this context, the setting up of a Board of Industrial and Financial Reconstruction (BIFR) of sick units, and the reconstitution of the IRCI to IRBI[3] (new Bank) with a reinforced armoury of powers, are steps in the right direction. The BIFR would be the apex body for coordination of efforts for rehabilitation of sick units. Powers have been conferred on it to prepare schemes for merger, lease, and even sale or closure of sick units. It is opined that speedy clearance of amalgamation and similar schemes in respect of industries found viable after thorough scrutiny by the BIFR would be possible, as reference to High Courts and the MRTP Commission may be obviated by having them sanctioned by the Board. With simplification of procedures and involvement of large industrial houses in rehabilitation of sick units, as stated by the Chairman of IRBI, a breakthrough is visualized. The Bank has formulated a package of guidelines, comprising reliefs and concessions, for financial institutions and banks to revive sick units. Three years' working experience has shown that speed is of the essence in revival of sick units; this aspect requires urgent attention by BIFR if it is to live up to the needs of the economy. In Japan, as noted earlier, a large firm in real financial trouble would be assisted wholeheartedly by the government (*vide* ch. 7). Since we are preparing the economy for the twenty-first century, and seek to encourage induction of new and advanced technologies in industry, with its attendant risks, we should develop a similar industrial culture of assistance to industry, whatever be the circumstances.

REFERENCES

1. Herman Kahn, *The Emerging Japanese Super State*, Penguin Books, Harmondsworth, 1973, p. 121.
2. The Finance Minister in his Budget Speech (1991–92) announced the abolition of the mandatory convertibility clause for new projects (*vide* ch. 22).
3. IRCI = Industrial Reconstruction Corporation of India.
   IRBI = Industrial Reconstruction Bank of India.

PART II

FISCAL POLICY FOR GROWTH
IN DEVELOPING ECONOMIES

15

Fiscal Policy and Plan Finance

Government enunciated in December 1985 a pragmatic and comprehensive Long-Term Fiscal Policy, calculated to accelerate the momentum of economic growth and employment, secure adequate resource mobilization for the Seventh Plan, and rationalize the tax structure, so as to strengthen the inbuilt revenue-raising capacity of the tax system. Several measures have been taken to achieve these objectives; it is desirable to assess the implementation of the policy, and indicate corrective steps for stimulating growth without inflation.

CRITERIA FOR EVALUATING IMPLEMENTATION OF FISCAL POLICY

The implementation of the fiscal policy may be evaluated on the basis of the following criteria as to whether, (1) it has assisted in increasing revenue productivity, contributed to formulation of a rational expenditure policy, and provided for adequate financing of the Seventh Plan; (2) it has stimulated savings and investment, and promoted economic growth and welfare; (3) it has increased efficiency in resource allocation; (4) it has contributed to price stability; and (5) it has promoted stability, simplicity, and equity of the tax structure, as also increased voluntary tax compliance.

The fiscal policy was intended to strengthen the 'operational linkages between the fiscal and financial objectives of the Seventh Plan and the annual budgeting exercises'[1] and to serve as a bridge between plan targets and annual budgets. Fiscal policy, in this context, has to subserve plan objectives and to provide the framework for mobilization of adequate resources. While formulating estimates for the Seventh Plan, emphasis had been laid on keeping budgetary deficits and monetary expansion low. Public savings in the form of surpluses generated by the budgets and public undertakings had been assigned a more important role than borrowings, which, however, have been buoyant. While the shares of domestic borrowings and net external finance in the Seventh Plan were likely to approximate those in the Sixth Plan at the rate of 5.1 per cent and 1.4 per cent of GDP, public sector savings were scheduled to rise to 3.6 per cent (aggregating 10.1 per cent) as against 2.8 per cent of GDP for the earlier plan.[2] In monetary terms, public sector enterprises were expected to generate surpluses totalling Rs 35,485 crores; besides yielding further revenues at the central level in the form of additional resource mobilization through increase in administered and other prices. At the state level, state electricity boards and transport corporations were to convert their expected losses into surpluses over the plan period.

According to the *Economic Survey* for 1988–9, internal resources generated by public undertakings amounted to Rs 7,022 crores on a capital employed of Rs 58,125 crores in 1987–8, yielding 12.08 per cent as compared to 11.60 per cent in 1986–7.[3] On a five year basis, the resources should have amounted to about Rs 35,100 crores. It was expected that there would be a distinct improvement in the working of public undertakings and the portents were that the rise in operational efficiency would be progressive. The actual generation of resources by public undertakings amounted to Rs 23,115 crores over the Seventh Plan period, falling short of the target by Rs 12,370 crores. However, government was able to raise Rs 7,484 crores through the issue of bonds by certain leading public undertakings, although the effective interest rates were high.

Government is considering adoption of a policy decision to reduce the strength of labour with a golden handshake, in the case of over-staffed units, and to close down concerns which were perennially in the red and incapable of achieving viability. Government also proposed to adopt a multi-pronged strategy, including organizational changes, improved management methods, workers' participation, and appropriate financial and pricing policies. We would suggest that the autonomy of public enterprises, once budgets are finalized, should be almost inviolable, and stability in the tenure of top officers, who should be mostly technocrats, ensured. The twin system of 'hire and fire' and reward for good work should be introduced on a pilot basis and later extended if successful. Basically, improvement in capacity utilization and productivity, inventory rationalization, and upgradation in technology are necessary. Induction of experts in financial management at the overall monitoring level appears to be imperative.

The buoyancy in market borrowings and small savings, confirmed by increase in the growth rate of commercial bank deposits at 19.4 per cent in 1989–90 and the Sixth Plan experience has been a positive factor, contributing to the success of plan financing. This has been reinforced by incentives and instruments for savings devised by government. It has been making every effort to mobilize savings in the rural areas and the buoyancy in savings is likely to be maintained. The target of Rs 73,062 crores at 1984–5 prices on this account in the Seventh Plan, as expected, was exceeded and the aggregate market borrowings and small savings amounted to Rs 99,460 crores (including the aforesaid public sector bonds). The fiscal policy stated that the balance from current revenues would be reduced from minus 0.4 per cent of GDP in 1985–6 to a positive balance of 0.2 per cent of GDP in 1989–90. The Seventh Plan provided for a negative balance of Rs 5,249 crores on this account. The Central budgets during recent years show increasing deficits on revenue account. The actual balance on current account in the Seventh Plan amounts to minus Rs 12,213 crores.

TABLE 15.1 — *Non-Plan Expenditure, 1987–9*

	Actuals 1987–88	Revised Estimates 1988–89	Increase	Percentage Increase	*In crores of Rupees* Percentage of Non-Plan Expenditure (1988–89)
Interest	11,236	14,150	2,914	25.93	28.95
Defence	11,968	13,200	1,232	10.29	27.01
Major Subsidies	6,279	7,790	1,511	24.06	15.94
	29,483	35,140	5,657	19.19	71.90
Other Non-Plan Expenditure	11,308	13,737	2,429	21.48	28.10
Total Non-Plan Expenditure	40.791 (62.69%)	48,877 (64.5%)	8,086	19.82	100.00
Plan Outlay	24,277 (37.31%)	26,906 (35.5%)			
Total Expenditure	65.068 (100%)	75,783 (100%)			

SOURCE Receipts Budget, 1989–90, Government of India, pp. 67, 68. Figures in brackets in columns 2 and 3 represent percentage to total expenditure.

TABLE 15.2—*Financing the Seventh Plan (Public Sector)*
(At 1984–5 Prices)

| Original Estimate | Percentage | | In Crores of Rupees | |
			Estimated Actuals	Percentage
(−) 5,249	−2.9	Balance on Current Revenue	(−) 12,213	−6.5
35,485	19.7	Contribution from Public Undertakings	23,115	12.3
73,062	40.6	Market Borrowing, Small Savings etc. & Loans from Institutions	99,460	52.9
44,702	24.8	Additional Resource Mobilization	33,388	17.7
18,000	10.0	Foreign Aid	16,348	8.7
14,000	7.8	Deficit Financing	28,381	15.1
—	—	Centre's Assistance to States (Difference)	(−) 290	−0.2
1,80,000	100.0		1,88,189	100.0

SOURCE Adapted from *RBI Bulletin*, June 1990 (Supplement), p. 103.

An analysis of the Union Budget on the expenditure side shows that Defence accounts for 27.01 per cent, major Subsidies 15.94 per cent, and Interest 28.95 per cent, aggregating 71.90 per cent of non-plan expenditure as compared to 67.2 per cent in 1984–5. While non-developmental expenditure as a component of total expenditure has risen from 57.96 per cent in 1981–2 to 64.5 per cent in 1988–9, the developmental expenditure works out correspondingly to 42.04 per cent in 1981–2 and 35.5 per cent for 1988–9. The fact, as R. N. Malhotra, former Governor, RBI, emphasizes is that 'interest payment on debt incurred for productive investment should not normally be problematic. However, a rising part of borrowed funds are in recent years being utilized for meeting current expenditure which does not generate any income'.[4] There is almost a vicious circle operating which needs to be broken, namely revenue deficits, larger borrowings, and higher interest payments, leading to further budgetary deficits and borrowings.

The major subsidies on food, fertilizers, and exports are increasing every year. Diminution in subsidies should constitute a significant component of the strategy of expenditure control, but here the fiscal policy maintains a low key, on the ground that food and fertilizer subsidies benefit the poor. Actually, subsidies should not be necessary for the affluent farmer or consumer. The fiscal policy seeks to reduce the residual non-plan revenue expenditure from 3.6 per cent of GDP in 1985–6 to 3 per cent in 1989–90 and proposes substantial economy all round through the modern method of explicit multi-year budgeting of expenditure.

The White Paper on the Economy[5] refers to the mismatch between revenue receipts and revenue expenditure. The important point is that while the Centre's tax revenue is increasing by about 17 per cent annually, its revenue expenditure has increased by 18.4 per cent during the eighties.

STRUCTURAL BUDGETARY DEFICIENCY

A striking feature of the Union Budget 1988–9 (R.E.) is that despite buoyancy in tax revenues, there is a budgetary deficit of Rs 11,030 crores on revenue account and a surplus of Rs 3,090 crores on capital account (net deficit Rs 7,940 crores). There is a structural deficiency in that the capital budget finances a part of the revenue budget. In the seventies, the surplus on revenue account financed the deficit on capital account; this trend has been reversed during recent years. The continuation of this disturbing trend implies increasing absorption of resources for current expenditure, including interest payments, instead of spending on development. The evolution of a medium-term strategy to correct the structural deficiency of the capital budget supporting the revenue budget, and a review of expenditure policies to reasonably contain the deficit, is necessary.

TABLE 15.3—*Growth in Revenue from Principal Taxes*

	1984–85	1987–88	1988–89 R.E.	In Crores of Rupees Increase in 1988–89 over 1984–85
				(Percentage)
Corporation Tax	2.556	3.433	4.270	67.06
Income Tax	1.928	3.187	3.660	89.83
Customs	7.041	13.702	15.812	124.57
Union Excise Duties	11.151	16.426	18.547	66.33
	22.676	36.748	42.289	86.49

SOURCE *Receipts Budget 1989–90*, Government of India, p. 68.

During the Seventh Plan period, taxes have been further reduced. However, revenues have increased substantially. The aggregate increase amounts to 67.06 per cent in the case of Corporation Tax, 89.83 per cent for Income-tax, 124.57 per cent for Customs Duty and 66.33 per cent for Excise Duty over the four years. The overall revenues in respect of these items increased from Rs 22,676 crores in 1984–5 to Rs 42,289 crores in 1988–9 (R.E.), which works out to an impressive increase of 86.49 per cent over this period. Reduction and rationalization of taxes and Modvat have contributed to, rather than detracted from, increased revenues.

BRACKET INDEXATION

With the inflationary rise in prices, the intrinsic value of the rupee had appreciably declined, and in order to counter the phenomenon of 'bracket creep', the income brackets in tax schedules needed to be revised upwards from time to time, and exemption limits raised. Besides, the world trend was towards lowering tax rates and simplification of procedures. The highest marginal tax rate on personal incomes in the UK and USA has been pared to 40 per cent and 28 per cent respectively. The highest marginal rate in India should in stages be brought down to 30 per cent applicable to over Rs 2 lakhs income, and the tax schedule adjusted downwards. We are confident that revenues would increase as a consequence of such reduction in tax rate, both on account of increased productivity, incomes, savings and investment, and less avoidance. Past experience in India and abroad bears this out.

It is significant that the revenue deficit has been arrived at after providing for Rs 10,662 crores (B.E. for 1988–9) as States' share of income-tax and excise duties, as compared to the actual figure of Rs 7,490 crores for 1985–6. Thus over a period of three years, there has been an increase of 42.35 per cent in the devolution of resources to the states in consonance with the recommendations of the Eighth Finance Commission. The states should not have cause for complaint on this account.

The economy during the Sixth Plan period has achieved an average growth rate of 5.5 per cent per annum as compared to about 3.5 per cent per annum during the seventies, which is a positive achievement. The savings and investment rates during the Seventh Plan period are in excess of 21 and 23 per cent respectively. Infrastructural facilities (power) have recorded an improvement of above 10 per cent and the plant–load factor has improved to about 56 per cent from 46 per cent in mid-1984. The industrial growth rate has also increased appreciably. There is room for optimism with regard to improved industrial performance in the nineties, given government's liberal economic and tax policies and better capacity utilization, expansion, and modernization. Real national income during the Seventh Plan period increased by 5.6 per cent, which is more than the growth rate projected in the Seventh Plan and fiscal policy. The maintenance of this growth rate during the nineties is within the realm of possibility, but it postulates *inter alia* political stability, sustained implementation of the liberalized framework of economic and industrial policies, reasonable foreign exchange availability, and viable balance of payments position.

TABLE 15.4 — *Budgetary Deficits*

At Current Prices	In Crores of Rupees	
1985–86	4,937	
	+1,628	(Given to States to clear overdraft with RBI.)
1986–87	8,261	
1987–88	5,816	
1988–89	5,642	
1989–90	11,750	
At 1984–85 Prices	38,034	
	28,381	

SOURCE *RBI Annual Report 1989–90*, Table on p. 86, col. 5.

DEFICIT FINANCING AND INFLATIONARY POTENTIAL

The Seventh Plan provided for deficit financing of Rs 14,000 crores but the deficits during the five years from 1985–6 to 1989–90 (R.E.) aggregate Rs 38,034 crores (Rs 28,381 crores at 1984–5 prices). Although the economy on the whole is in good shape, there are inflationary forces ready to assert themselves to the detriment of price stability. Besides, periodic upward revision in administered prices—coal and steel prices have been increased—add to cost–push inflation. The Wholesale Prices Index increased by 10.6 per cent in 1987–8; 5.7 per cent in 1988–9, and 9.1 per cent in 1989–90 on point to point basis. That this large increase in prices occurred despite a good *kharif* crop, following a bumper harvest in 1988–9, does not augur well for the nineties; inflationary rise in prices may distort plan financing. It is significant that the rate of inflation in September 1991 was about 15.2 per cent and it appears to be gathering momentum.

The essence of the matter is that non-plan expenditure, particularly interest charges, subsidies, and defence expenditure have to be controlled, so that deficit financing and growth in money supply are restrained, and investment is matched by resources. On the supply side, adequate availability of goods has to be ensured. As the World Bank stated,[6] 'the quality and composition of public spending strongly influence development' and should improve. Improvement in the efficiency and effectiveness of public spending requires reform of fiscal planning, budgeting, implementation, and monitoring. The factors of production must be fully and efficiently utilized so as to achieve optimum productivity. This would reduce the capital–output ratio. The entire macroeconomic policy framework should be such that adequate equilibrium is maintained over a period between money supply and aggregate output. Fiscal and other economic policies should also be so attuned that they have an anti-inflationary bias. Considerable incomes have gravitated to the rural sector; it is necessary that it also yields adequate revenue. Certain classes of persons, like those having large agricultural incomes, do not pay income-tax. They should be brought within the tax net. The reservoir of savings in rural areas is large, and intensive efforts should be made to mobilize such savings. The potentiality is great; it needs to be exploited.

The Seventh Plan provided for additional resource mobilization

(ARM) of Rs 21,262 crores and Rs 23,440 crores through increase in administered and other prices and surpluses of state electricity boards and transport corporations. The actual pattern of financing the Plan (*vide* Table 15.2) shows that actual ARM at Rs 33,388 crores fell short of the target by more than 25 per cent. Despite substantial increases in administered prices of oil and petroleum products, coal, and other commodities and services in various years—which have added to cost inflation. ARM targets could not be achieved, largely due to the following: (a) non-tax revenue sources have not been fully exploited by government and user charges for various economic and infrastructural services have been provided below cost of production—particularly in rural areas. Power, irrigation, betterment facilities, and agricultural inputs are instances in point; (b) agricultural incomes have not been adequately taxed and the rich farmers have been acquiring tax-free incomes, accentuating the inequity of the tax system; (c) given the narrow tax base and widespread evasion—partly due to high tax rates and the complex network of controls—the yield from direct taxes has not increased to the extent envisaged. As the *Economic Survey* for 1990–1 states, 'the resolution of this problem would need a more effective tax administration and enforcement system, in conjunction with reasonable tax rates that would need to be combined with simplicity in tax laws, regulations and procedures, situated in the wider context of a comprehensive tax reform';[7] and (d) many state electricity boards, transport corporations, and public enterprises in the state sector continued to incur heavy losses, and the resolution of the microeconomic problems of these complexes proved to be a task often beyond the capacity of state governments.

Besides, although the Sixth Plan targets on account of ARM were exceeded, automatic growth in revenues in response to rise in national incomes was less than unity, and as a result additional resource mobilization was restrained. The fiscal policy had taken cognizance of this aspect and inbuilt measures to increase revenue elasticity of taxes were improvised but proved ineffective. In consonance with the decision to promote self-reliance, only 1.4 per cent of GDP was to be financed by funds from external sources, amounting to Rs 18,000 crores. In any case, the inflow of foreign aid and commercial borrowings showed a more or less stable trend. During the Seventh Plan period it amounted to Rs 16,348 crores, being marginally lower than the target.

The Seventh Plan document states that the ratio of tax to GDP which was 15.6 per cent in 1980–1 increased to about 18 per cent during the second half of the eighties. This compares unfavourably with other countries, where the percentage of tax to GDP is much higher: UK 37.8, USA 29, Japan 27.7, and Turkey 18.8 (OECD figures for 1983). While the fiscal policy ascribes the low level of aggregate revenues, *inter alia*, to the restricted tax base, given the low incomes of large sections of the population, deductions in tax laws and evasion, a prime factor is that while incomes during the last three decades of planning have gravitated to the agricultural sector owing to massive plan investment, the contribution of this sector to general revenues has not been proportionate to the investment made. Land revenue and agricultural income-tax are state subjects; they are neither elastic nor progressive, and have not yielded adequate returns. The fiscal policy does not strive to resolve this problem, although efforts are to be made to tap rural savings. Government's categorical assertion that it would not tax agricultural incomes because of the conceptual and administrative problems involved leaves a major lacuna in the Indian tax system, which will continue to distort the ratio of direct to indirect taxes and to GDP.

Table 15.2 shows estimated actuals in the financing of the Seventh Plan and the original estimates. A comparative study reveals, (a) the heavy reliance placed upon market borrowings at 52.9 per cent and deficit financing at 15.1 per cent, as compared to 40.6 per cent and 7.8 per cent respectively of the total outlay; (b) the negative balance on current revenues increased from (−) 2.9 to (−) 6.5 per cent; (c) contribution from public undertakings was 12.3 per cent as compared to 19.7 per cent and, (d) additional resource mobilization was 17.7 per cent as against 24.8 per cent envisaged. The conclusion is inevitable that expenditures have been rising faster than revenues, public enterprises have yielded inadequate returns, borrowings have been substituted as means of financing outlays for additional resource mobilization, and the pattern of financing the Seventh Plan has been inflationary. However, on the credit side, the Seventh Plan has exceeded growth targets, and the momentum of industrial and agricultural production and power generation built up should stand the economy in good stead, particularly during the critical period ahead in the wake of the Gulf crisis.

The thrust of the Long-Term Fiscal Policy is towards providing an environment of fiscal stability and open budgeting, conducive to long-term corporate planning, stimulated capital formation, and modernization. Since the proportion of indirect taxes to total taxes has increased from 73.4 per cent on an average during the five years ending 1979–80 to 77.4 per cent during the Sixth Plan, and that of direct taxes has declined, the government seeks to increase the share of direct taxes in revenue. This is proposed to be effected through built-in measures to increase revenue elasticity of income-tax in response to growth in incomes. Increased revenues are scheduled to emanate from more effective tax implementation and a broader tax base rather than escalation in tax rates. The success of the government's taxation policy is evidenced by the good results achieved in buoyancy in tax revenues. Government expected the gross tax collections during the period of the Seventh Plan to exceed the targeted figures by Rs 10,000 crores.

TRANSCENDING NURKSE'S THESIS: DISTRIBUTIVE JUSTICE

Government, in formulating the fiscal policy, has not ignored the distribution aspect. It stated that fiscal policy must ensure adequate availability of resources to fund social expenditure which benefits the poor. Current economic thought has transcended Ragnar Nurkse's thesis that increasing capital formation and not change in 'interpersonal income distribution'[8] is the primary aim of public finance in developing countries. The goals of growth and human welfare need to be simultaneously pursued. E. J. Mishan may not be right when he questions 'whether continued economic growth can be expected to enhance social well-being',[9] but it is now obvious that growth in GDP by itself is not enough; conscious effort is necessary to ensure that the benefits of development percolate to the poorest sections of society. Government's poverty alleviation programmes and public distribution system, despite shortcomings in implementation, are steps in the right direction.

On an overall assessment, it may safely be asserted that the implementation of long-term fiscal policy has successfully contributed to resource-generation, economic growth, and an equitable tax structure; but there is evidence of shortfall in plan resources and escalating non-plan expenditure, and hence greater reliance on borrowing, deficit financing, and higher administered prices which add to cost–push inflation. Inflation ranges in double digit figures.

What is necessary is to reduce the capital–output ratio, check budgetary and current account deficits and monetary expansion, improve operational efficiency of public enterprises to yield surpluses, and increase efficiency in resource mobilization. However, in view of the various constraints under which government had to operate, this was perhaps the most appropriate fiscal policy that could have been formulated; it emphasized both mobilization as well as efficient resource allocation.

REFERENCES

1. *Long-Term Fiscal Policy*, Dec. 1985, Ministry of Finance, p. 4.
2. Ibid., Table 3, p. 11.
3. *Economic Survey 1988–89*, Government of India, Table on p. 86.
4. R. N. Malhotra, *L. K. Jha Memorial Lecture 1988*, Fiscal Research Foundation, Delhi, p. 19.
5. *White Paper on the Economy*, Economic Advisory Council, Government of India, Dec. 1989, para. 28.
6. *World Development Report 1988*, The World Bank/OUP, Ner York, p. 6.
7. *Economic Survey 1990–91*, Government of India, p. 183.
8. Ragnar Nurkse, *Problems of Capital Formation in Underdeveloped Countries*, Basil Blackwell Oxford, 1955, p. 147.
9. E. J. Mishan, *The Economic Growth Debate*, George Allen & Unwin, London, 1977, p. 11.

16

Tax System for Developing Economies

ROLE OF FISCAL POLICY

Economic growth postulates capital formation and fiscal policy has a vital role both in regard to generation and mobilization of resources, and their investment in real capital assets. Fiscal policy can also influence the inflow and development of technology, the building up of adequate infrastructure—on which depends the superstructure of industrial growth—and the development of human resources. Government's expenditure policy and allocation of resources for building up social overheads such as education, vocational training and health facilities, employment, social security and poverty alleviation programmes, all contribute towards creating an environment in which industrialization and agricultural advance can take place. A structural transformation of the socio-economic institutional and legal framework, conducive to rapid industrial growth, needs to be effected if a developing economy is to achieve take-off and reach the stage of self-sustaining growth in the shortest possible time. Since the economy has to raise its rate of savings from a low level of about 3 to 5 per cent in traditional societies to a minimum of 12 to 15 per cent, fiscal incentives for saving and investment and measures to curb consumption—both through direct and indirect taxation—assume vital importance.

FUNCTIONAL FINANCE

The role of the budget is no longer regarded as neutral with regard to growth. The 'functional' approach has invested it with far greater importance; it is now a vital instrument for stimulating economic development. The principal role of budgetary policy in the pre-Keynesian era was to raise sufficient revenues for the activities of the state, and expenditure was intended to maximize satisfactions. The Keynesian theory revolutionized the entire concept of public finance, and it was widely recognized that the budget was an important instrument for influencing the level of economic activity, incomes, and employment through variations in effective demand.

The maintenance of internal stability, which implies price-stability and a high level of employment, postulates an adequate level of aggregate demand, which depends upon the level of expenditure and receipts. Aggregate demand should be adequate to provide the purchasing power for the goods produced by a fully employed economy and should expand with economic growth. If there is excess of aggregate demand, there would be inflation; and if there is deficiency in demand, output would be less than the potential, with inadequate utilization of capacity. If there is depression or slackness in the economy, the expenditure should be in excess of revenue, so that unutilized resources are used and the economy expands. Deficit budgeting is desirable to increase aggregate demand. The modern principle of 'compensatory finance'—essentially applicable to developed economies—is now being accepted as being also applicable to developing economies. Actually, a certain amount of deficit financing and moderate inflation are regarded as means of accelerating growth in developing economies.

The basic difference between the objectives of fiscal policy in developed and underdeveloped economies is that in the former fiscal policy is primarily intended to check cyclical fluctuations in the economy, maintain full employment and check inflation. Fiscal policy in an underdeveloped economy needs to be devised to maximize the ratio of savings to national income and to channelize these into productive channels of investment for maximizing economic growth. Maintaining stability in prices, securing proper allocation of resources, and ensuring distributive justice (corresponding to Musgrave's stabilization, allocation, and distribution functions) are no doubt also objectives of fiscal policy, but the predominant goal is maximization of growth and other objectives are secondary to this.

The basic concept of modern fiscal policy, as applicable to developing economies, is the mobilization of revenues and expenditure for maintenance of a high level of economic activity and growth, and the budget need not be balanced. Government's expenditure should be allocated to fulfilling the purposes of state policy, to increase employment and welfare, to develop infrastructure, and to promote or take up such investment as the private sector may not be willing or able to do. The function of taxation is not merely raising revenue for the state, but principally curbing private consumption, stimulating savings and investment, checking inflationary potential, modifying the pattern of investment, and assisting in securing a favourable balance of trade. Since revenues are generally insufficient to meet the needs of the State, governments usually resort to borrowings and deficit financing, as necessary, to achieve rising levels of economic growth. A balanced budget is almost an anachronism, and deficit budgets the norm.

Coordinated fiscal and monetary policies within the macroeconomic framework are necessary to achieve the objectives of economic growth and stabilization. Tax reform should aim at formulating a tax structure which provides for elasticity of tax revenues. As GNP increases with economic growth, revenues should automatically increase more than in proportion to such escalation in income. Revenues should also rise with increases in the price level. Income tax, excise duties—*ad valorem* particularly—and sales tax should, *inter alia*, provide the requisite elasticities to the tax structure.

As regards external stability, imports should be regulated by a structure of import duties, and excise and sales tax should be applicable largely to domestic goods. Incentives should be provided for exports. Thus, the grant of subsidies and tax concessions to exports in relation to domestic products would boost exports; similarly, higher taxation of imports as compared to indigenous products would discourage imports.

The multifaceted role of fiscal policy may now be delineated:

1. The structure and level of taxation, and the incentives for saving and investment inbuilt in the tax structure, constitute, *inter alia*, crucial determinants of the level of private and corporate savings, the inducement to invest, and the volume of investment in real capital assets. The structure of taxation influences the curtailment or restriction of consumption and transfer of resources for capital formation, and assists in maximizing the incremental-savings ratio.

2. The revenue productivity of the tax system is an important determinant of the quantum of resources available with the state for its various traditional activities, building up economic and

social infrastructure, and its welfare and developmental activities. The transfer of savings from private to public coffers through taxation, however, has a wide-ranging effect upon private disposition of income and the people's capacity to save and invest. If taxation leads to transfer of resources from private consumption to public saving, it is a gain to society; but if it results in transfer from private saving to public consumption, it is a loss to the economy, of which more later.

3. The tax system may be so formulated as to increase the efficiency of resource utilization and influence the pattern of investment in the economy.

4. The allocation of resources through plan and non-plan expenditure, the distribution of welfare benefits and transfer payments, and the tax structure and policy could assist in reducing economic inequalities, and ensuring social justice and percolation of the benefits of growth to the lowest strata of society.

5. The structural framework of taxes on imports and exports, such as customs *vis-à-vis* taxes on domestic production like excises, would influence the volume and pattern of foreign trade and contribute towards stability in the balance of payments.

6. The investment climate, which is influenced by economic and fiscal policies, incentives, and tax treatment of foreign investment capital would largely determine the inflow of foreign equity investment into the country.

LIMITS TO COLLECTIVE SAVINGS AND HIGH TAXES

The Indian tax structure during the last few years has been reoriented to the increasing demands of a planned developing economy in which the state has a decisive role to play. Increase in taxes in such a context perhaps becomes an inevitable concomitant of economic development; yet a good tax structure for an underdeveloped economy must conform to certain basic principles: it must not offend equity, it should promote efficiency, it should not siphon off funds which would have gone into productive investment, and it should promote development. Economic growth postulates capital formation and, in this context, the maintenance of incentives to work, save, and invest at a high level constitutes a prime objective of taxation policy.

An increase in national income and higher standards of living constitute the test of successful planning. But the chief requirement for developing countries is that of accelerating the pace of capital formation, so that the vicious circle of low savings and low investment is broken and the country reaches the stage of self-sustaining growth. It may be possible for a totalitarian country to pin down standards of living, while saving the total increment in real incomes for investment purposes. But for a democratic country like India, where poverty is extreme, planning must also allow for rise in the standards of living. Besides, the effect of the increase in population has also to be offset. The implication is that the increase in incomes must be substantial enough. This implies a very high level of capital formation and what is necessary is that the capacity to save must increase. The country's fiscal policies must be attuned to maximizing savings with corporations and the public. The reorientation of the tax structure during the last few years has resulted in a squeeze in corporate savings. No doubt finance corporations and credit institutions have assisted in development by providing long-term loans and capital, but ploughing back profits is the best form of industrial finance, and this has been adversely affected by increased taxation of the corporate sector.

Some policies are dictated by ideological considerations. The words of Dr Ludwig Erhardt,[1] the architect of German reconstruction, in his book *Prosperity through Competition*, are remarkable in this context: 'The successful rehabilitation of my country must serve as clear documentary evidence to put before the still vacillating and doubting peoples, of the fact that only by firmly rejecting socialist dogmas, of whatever complexion, and by affirming a free economic order can mounting prosperity and genuine security be achieved.' Tax concessions given by the Government in West Germany stimulated industrial activities. Within a short period of less than a decade, the country, aided by the Marshall plan, reconstructed its economy and is today industrially ahead of all the European countries. The German government wisely acted on the principle that tax concessions provide the scope and incentives for saving and investment, leading to capital formation at an accelerated growth-rate. Besides, on balance, a government does not lose on account of tax concessions. Economic expansion and increased real incomes provide increasing revenues to it, and the total volume of taxes is higher at the lower rates. The increased revenues sustain a higher rate of public expenditure and investment.

This doctrine applied to India would imply that centralized planning should be replaced by indicative planning, and allocation and utilization of scarce means and resources should be left to market forces. The regulations and controls binding private enterprises should be relaxed so as not to stifle initiative and enterprise, and thereby hamper economic growth. The present liberalization policy is highly commendable and should be pursued to its logical conclusion.

Higher taxation is often sought to be justified on the ground that, in a community in which the propensity to consume is high, taxation reduces consumption and not investment, and productive resources are released for development in the public sector. This proposition is largely true in the case of the poor and middle classes, whose consumption in relation to incomes is very high because of low earnings; but as income increases, the propensity to consume diminishes, a larger proportion is saved and, provided the investment climate is favourable, invested. Increased taxes in the case of persons in the higher income brackets, largely drawn from the industrial community, may curb their consumption to a degree but the greater portion of taxes would be paid by reducing savings and investment. It is said that taxation is a form of compulsory savings and is desirable. But it must be realized that taxation by itself only leads to a transfer of funds from private to public coffers, and not necessarily of funds which would have gone into consumption. Its effectiveness in promoting capital formation is limited by the extent to which the increased revenues are used for productive investment. If they are absorbed by an increase in administrative or non-development expenditure, the capital is virtually lost to the economy. Experience has shown that a sizeable part of the enormous increase in revenues due to increased taxation did not ultimately result in capital formation.

High levels of taxation, besides reducing the capacity to save at corporate and individual levels, have a disincentive effect upon investment. The decrease in the net marginal productivity of capital, besides inhibiting domestic investment, also adversely affects the flow of private foreign investment capital into the country. What is necessary, and this is important, is to carry taxation only up to the stage where its adverse effect upon private savings and the inducement to invest is balanced by the benefit that can be derived by the economy through public investment for capital formation.

So far as this country is concerned, that stage has been reached and the level of direct taxation appears to have reached its limits.

The emphasis on collective savings in the past has resulted in high rates of taxation. It has also been supported by the principle of ability to pay. It is urged that because of the principle of diminishing marginal utility as applied to incomes, there should be a progressive scale of taxation. Besides, progressive taxation is regarded as an instrument for reducing inequality in society. During the last few decades before the eighties, the tendency had been to increase taxation to the maximum possible levels. The Taxation Enquiry Commission[2] recommended the principle of collective savings and reduction of inequalities through heavy income taxation; it stressed the desirability of striving in stages to implement a ceiling on personal incomes.

The entire concept of collective savings and reduction in inequalities through high rates of taxation suffers from deficiencies. The modern trend in taxation is to reduce the level of taxes and simplify the structure. Firstly, high taxation reduces incentives, while for a developing economy it is imperative that savings, investment, and incomes increase to the maximum to stimulate growth. Secondly, progressive taxation has failed to reduce inequalities. If taxes are taken to levels which are almost confiscatory, people feel that the tax system is inequitable and unjust, that they have no moral obligation to comply with its laws, and voluntary compliance suffers.

If the concept of a mixed economy is accepted and it has to function effectively, and economic growth has to take place, there is no alternative but to provide incentives for private savings and investment, though it may lead to some inequalities in income and wealth. The main objective is to raise the standards of living of millions of people and some degree of inequality has to be tolerated. After all, provisions for social welfare schemes and social security to the people at large—indeed all transfer payments—can only take place if the state has sufficient revenues, and incomes and savings can be buoyant only if there is economic growth. The concept of economic power has lost much of its significance since there are many checks and balances, particularly with the enormous powers of regulation of the state. Banking and insurance have been nationalized. Besides, a number of financial institutions and mutual funds with command over large resources have emerged; they are mostly under the control and direction of the state. Actually, a large-sized industry can hardly be set up in the private sector without some degree of institutional finance. The so-called 'concentration of economic power' is largely illusory.

ATTRIBUTES OF A GOOD TAX STRUCTURE:
MEADE COMMITTEE (UK) PROPOSALS

Keeping in view the above objectives, we may consider what the principal characteristics of a good tax structure are. The tax system should have stability which is conducive to realistic corporate planning. Frequent changes in tax structure and rates of taxation lead to dislocation in the budgets and projections of corporations. Stability in tax laws is necessary for industrial growth and corporate planning. The Meade Committee, constituted to examine the Structure and Reform of Direct Taxation in the UK, stated[3] that

in addition to being efficient and just and compatible with the country's international position, a good tax system should also be coherent, simple and straightforward.... Tax burdens which are disguised by inflationary movements of prices, or by complexities in the devising or the administration of the tax, or by uncertainties in its application cannot properly meet this criterion of simplicity.

It should be clear to the taxpayer what is and what is not taxable; there should be certainty about the amount of tax payable; and it should be acceptable to the public. Other aspects of simplicity are ease of administration, ease of understanding by the taxpayer, and ease of compliance by him. Judged by the above criteria, our tax system can hardly be described as simple; quite the contrary.

The essential point is that the tax structure should be acceptable to the public. If the tax system is too complex and the tax rates very high—almost confiscatory—the public may feel that they have no moral obligation to pay taxes which are inequitable and unjust. It would lead to large-scale evasion and avoidance. But if the tax structure is reasonable and simple, it would definitely encourage voluntary tax compliance. The experience in many countries which have reduced taxes is that it leads to better revenues, both on account of increased work, incomes and savings, and also because of improved compliance. Besides, if the taxes are reasonable and low, the gains from tax evasion and avoidance are so marginal that people prefer to pay taxes rather than face penalties and prosecution. For an underdeveloped economy, the principal objective of taxation policy is to achieve economic growth through capital formation. The quantum of total tax revenue raised and the methods of raising revenue should be such that they do not adversely affect economic opportunities and incentives.

There are two aspects of the effects of a tax: the income effect and the substitution effect. If the taxes are very high, a person may work harder to increase his post-tax income so as to compensate for the loss due to taxes. This is described as the income effect. However, a high marginal tax rate reduces the net spendable income which obtains from an extra day's work and this reduction in his command over extra goods owing to extra work will have a tendency to make him prefer to work less. This is known as substitution effect, and it leads to inefficiency and waste. An industrialist may not expand his activities, leading to more efficient use of resources, because the increase in his profit after tax is unattractive. He may substitute an easy life for hard work and consumption of energy. If income derived from savings is heavily taxed, a person may opt for present consumption rather than to save. High wealth tax and estate duties may have a similar effect. Since economic growth postulates accumulation of capital and its investment in productive assets, this principle is of importance, particularly for underdeveloped countries.

CANONS OF TAXATION FOR DEVELOPING COUNTRIES

Adam Smith[4] laid down certain canons of taxation which are largely valid even today, both in developing and developed countries, and may be considered. According to the Principle of equality, the subjects of every State ought to contribute towards the support of the government, as nearly as possible, in proportion to their respective abilities; that is, in proportion to the revenue which they respectively enjoy under the protection of the State. This is based on the principle of ability to pay. The quantum of tax payable should be definite, so that there is no scope for exercise of discretion or arbitrariness, as this may lead to corruption in administration and harassment of the taxpayers. This is the principle of certainty. The tax which each individual is bound to pay ought to be certain. The time of payment, the manner of payment, the quantity to be paid, ought all to be clear and plain to the contributor and to every other person.

The payment of taxes should be so staggered that the mode and timing of payment cause the least inconvenience to the taxpayer. The modern system of 'pay as you earn' (PAYE) or advance payment of tax, are in accordance with this Principle of convenience. But for tax deduction at source from salary and advance payment of tax, taxpayers would be faced at the end of the year with a huge liability and would experience considerable difficulty in paying the taxes. The cost of tax collection should be the absolute minimum. Adam Smith, emphasizing the Principle of economy, says that if taxes are wasted in the form of excessive expenditure on collection, taxpayers would try to evade them.

R. J. Chelliah[5] has expounded certain principles which are highly relevant to underdeveloped economies. He has emphasized the mobilization of economic surplus. The development process results in increase in incomes. The surplus in a person's income comprises the excess above the level needed to maintain the minimum consumption necessary for maintaining efficiency and incentives. An effective tax structure should identify the surplus and either through taxation or incentives for investment channelize the surplus into productive investment. According to Chelliah, the principle is that 'each person should be made to contribute to taxation in accordance with his unused capacity or ability to contribute to economic development'. This ability is reflected in that portion of the economic surplus which he is not utilizing for productive investment. Consumption should not be allowed to increase proportionately to rise in incomes. The incremental savings ratio should be maximized.

The tax structure should have built-in income-elasticity, so that taxes automatically rise in response to increase in national income. It is necessary, in order to impart the requisite flexibility to the tax structure, to impose indirect taxes on commodities which have a high income-elasticity of demand. Besides, the scale of income-taxes should be progressive, so that the marginal rate of tax is higher than the average rate, and government's intake of revenues increases more than in proportion to a rise in incomes. The burden of development must be equally distributed among various sections of society. Taxation involves sacrifice and people, in similar circumstances and utilizing the surplus similarly, should be treated equally for tax purposes. This is in accordance with the Principle of horizontal equity. According to Chelliah, the Indian tax system does not satisfy this criterion. The tax system should provide a broad and diversified base for raising revenue for the activities of the state. Low rates of tax over a large tax base cause less distortion than raising the same revenue by imposing high rates of tax on a few activities. Government has therefore to rely on a tax system which is constituted of a number of different taxes, rather than to rely only upon one or two taxes; this helps in keeping down the marginal rates of tax. When the tax system is diversified, it is necessary to ensure that the various direct taxes constitute a coherent whole; that they do not impinge on each other and there is no inconsistency between the rules framed for their implementation. This may be illustrated. The rules for valuation of properties for wealth tax, estate duty (now abolished), and gift tax should have uniformity. This would also contribute to simplicity of the tax structure.

The tax system should be so devised that it is productive of revenue, sufficient for the needs of the various activities of the State. This is the principle of revenue productivity. The modern state has ceased to be just a law-enforcing agency with defence and external affairs as adjuncts; today its operations embrace a large range of functions. Above all, the concept of the welfare state has been universally accepted, and government's activities cover a broad spectrum, ranging from poverty alleviation programmes, provision for infrastructure, economic and social, and accelerating economic growth, to running selected industries with sophisticated technology, atomic power plants, implementing space and scientific research, and producing defence equipment, besides the traditional functions. The tax system has to provide for the collection of adequate revenues for these multifarious activities and provide for transfer payments.

NEW CANONS FOR STIMULATING GROWTH

We have discussed the beneficial effects of tax cuts upon economic activity. It is somewhat anomalous that in certain developing countries, the tax levels both on personal and corporate incomes are higher than in developed countries. Actually, taxes in the former should be low so as to provide incentives for capital formation, as also inflow of foreign investment capital. We are of the distinct opinion that the tax levels in economies which are in the transitional or pre-take off stage and the take off stage, should utilize a part of incremental revenues for purposes of reduction in the burden of taxation. This would stimulate savings and invest- ment in the household sector, accelerate development, and consti-' tute an important factor in enabling the economy to reach and transcend the stage of self-sustaining growth and speed up its drive towards maturity.

In this context, we would advocate two canons of taxation for developing economies: one relates to reduction in taxes for stimulating growth out of incremental revenues. As increment in tax revenues takes place from year to year in response to stimulated growth, a certain percentage should be set apart for reduction in personal and corporate levels of taxation. Thus the excess of revenues in any year over the revenues of the previous year should be appropriately divided—say in the ratio of 20: 80—between tax reduction and increased public expenditure. This would reinforce the contributory factors to growth and stimulate economic activity. This canon is based upon practical experience. Japan achieved excellent economic progress during the period 1960–9, when its GDP grew on an average by above 10 per cent per annum. The Tax Commission[6] in its Interim Report in 1960 stated, (a) that the tax burden should be limited to about 20 per cent of national income; and (b) that a part of the increase of revenue resulting from high economic growth should be used as resources for reduction of taxes every year. The Japanese Tax Bureau, Ministry of Finance,[6] states 'Thus, throughout this period [sixties], one of the characteristics of the major tax policies was a series of tax reduction programmes, in accordance with the recommendations of the succeeding Tax Commissions, which all insisted on allevia- tion of income-tax burden'. The spectacular growth of the Japanese economy during this period bears testimony to the beneficent effects of this programme, although no doubt this was only one of the principal contributory factors.

The other canon of taxation is that for developing economies, in order to maximize the incremental corporate savings ratio, that is, the ratio of savings or profits transferred to reserves for being ploughed back into business to the total profits after tax, *the tax on undistributed profits should be less than the tax on profits distributed as dividends.* Thus, if corporate tax is 50 per cent, the tax on the amount transferred to reserves should be about 30 per cent. This measure, in-built in the tax system, would automatically provide the incentive to plough back profits for expansion, modernization, and growth. The Government in Greece has recently (1989) proposed that 25 per cent undistributed profits of companies for the years 1988–91 would be exempt from taxation, provided they are wholly invested by the companies by the end of 1992. If the investment is in high technology sectors the exempt portion would increase to 35 per cent. This reinforces our plea.

The tax authorities should engender in the assessees the feeling that they will receive fair treatment and will not be harassed. The prime requisites for this are that the tax structure is equitable and fair; taxes are administered in a reasonable manner; the assessees' rights and interests are protected; and, above all, the administration itself develops a degree of trust in the taxpayer. The system that has been adopted recently in India, namely of accepting the returns of the assessees without scrutiny is a move in the right direction. If the assessee feels that unnecessary disallowances will not be made by the department, he would be more likely to make an honest declaration. Of course, the department continues to conduct detailed scrutiny of a certain percentage of returns and where evasion is noticed, deterrent penalties are levied. The system allows time to the assessing officers to concentrate their energies upon difficult cases. The scheme as a whole is commendable and should encourage voluntary compliance.

LEVEL OF TAXES AND GDP GROWTH: WORLD BANK STUDY

Conducting a survey of the experience of the impact of taxation on growth in twenty countries, covering almost the entire spectrum of world incomes, Keith Marsden,[7] in a World Bank Study, notes

In all cases, the countries that imposed a lower effective average tax burden on their populations achieved substantially higher real rates of GDP growth than did their more highly taxed counterparts. The average (unweighted) annual rate of growth of GDP was 7.3 per cent in the low-tax group and 1.1 per cent in the high-tax group'.

The low-tax countries included Japan, Spain, Singapore, Korea, Brazil, and Thailand, while the high-tax countries, *inter alia*, included the UK, Sweden, New Zealand, Chile, Jamaica, and Peru.

While tax–GDP ratios rose in most of the countries during the period under study, the relative tax position between low-tax and high-tax countries remained almost the same. The average tax–GDP ratio in the low-tax countries increased from 13.3 per cent at the beginning of the decade to 15.2 per cent at the end, while it rose from 21 per cent to 23.9 per cent in the high-tax group. This rise in the low-tax countries mainly reflected a widening of the tax base, rather than an increase in tax rates, although it coincided with a general reduction in the rate of economic growth (GDP) during the second half of the seventies.

Consequent upon high rates of economic growth in low-tax economies, higher levels of consumption and substantial rise in real living standards were achieved. High growth rates and increased revenues, associated with expansion of the tax base, provided funds for considerable increase in social welfare expenditure by governments in these countries. Besides, the argument that distribution is more equitable in high-tax countries than those with low taxes, is not borne out by the study. The share of the poorest 40 per cent of households in total income remained relatively high between 16.9 per cent and 21.9 per cent in five fast growing, low-tax countries such as Japan, Korea, Malawi, Spain, and Thailand. The growth in investment averaged 8.9 per cent annually for the seventies in low-tax countries, as compared to a decline of 0.8 per cent annually in high-tax countries. There is correlation between tax–GDP ratios and investment growth. A rise in the tax ratio of 1 per cent was associated with a reduction of rate of growth in investment of 0.66 per cent, and amongst various taxes, high corporate income-tax was the strongest deterrent to investment. The US experience confirms the results of this study: progressive reduction in corporate profit taxes would increase both business investment and capital stock substantially.

High taxes affect growth in two ways, according to the study: by adversely affecting the aggregate supply of the main factors of production by lowering their net return after tax, and by reducing the efficiency of resource utilization (total factor productivity). The more significant effects of taxes on growth in the lower income countries may be attributable to greater scope for productivity gains from the induction of modern technology and skills, transfer of capital and labour to more productive sectors, and 'externality effects'. In the higher income countries, productivity differences between sectors are much less and the existing levels of efficiency higher. Structural rigidities have a restrictive effect upon the mobility of resources and inhibit the introduction of new techniques. These factors restrict their 'potential for tax-induced gains'. The Marsden study further shows that inflation rates were higher in high-tax countries in seven out of the ten pairs during the decade and seem to have exacerbated the negative effects of taxation on growth.

Harvard Professor Lawrence Lindsey concluded from an econometric research study that among people with taxable incomes above $200,000, by lowering tax rates the US Government in 1984 collected $8 billion more in revenue than it would have if taxes had remained at 1979 levels. Lindsey concluded that tax cuts pay their way and revenues increase. There is some kind of Laffer curve in operation. This curve established the relationship between taxes and revenues (and production) and is in the form of a parabola. There exists an optimum point on the curve where the taxes will maximize revenues and GNP. In countries with high rates of taxation, if the taxes are reduced, buoyancy in revenues increases because tax cuts induce people to work harder and there is stimulated economic activity, increased productivity and incomes. However, according to Prof. Lindsey,[8] this accounts for only one-third of the increase in tax revenue. He believes that the balance two-thirds of increased revenues came from business and self-employed people who responded to lower taxes by cutting costs to maximize earnings. He believes that the highest rate at which governments are likely to maximize the tax take is at around 40 per cent.

It is now clear that the era of high taxes—the socialist shibboleth—is over. They have been thoroughly discredited on various counts. They adversely impinge upon business enterprises and growth, and militate against buoyancy in revenues; they give a fillip to evasion and avoidance, and check voluntary compliance with taxes; and they encourage laxity in expenditure and reduction in cost consciousness, as more than two-thirds of the expenditure is in effect borne by the revenue department. With winds of change sweeping over developed countries, who are virtually engaged in a race to cut taxes, developing countries have little alternative but to follow suit. Besides, so long as tax cuts pay their own way and result in increasing revenues through enhanced GNP and better compliance, it is in the interest of the exchequer to reduce them. The taxpayers are responsively happy, government revenues acquire buoyancy and, above all, the momentum of growth is accelerated. No Finance Minister can afford to ignore this triple-benefit formula, at least not in the present fiscal world environment.

TABLE 16.1 — *World Changes in Personal Income-Tax Schedules*

| | Tax rates in: | | Number of bands | |
	1985	1986 or later	Before	After
Australia	30–60	24–49 (1987)	5	4
Belgium	24–72	24–60 (Proposed)	14	4
Britain	30–60	25–40 (1988)	6	2
Canada**	6–34	17–29 (1988)	10	3
France	5–65	5–50 (1988)	10	10
Ireland	35–65	35–58 (1986)	3	3
Japan	11–70	10–50 (1988)	15	6
New Zealand	20–66	24–33 (1988)	5	2
Sweden*	35–80	35–60 (1988)	16	3
United States**	11–50	15–28 (1988)	15	2
West Germany†	22–56	19–53 (1990)	—	—

* Federal only.

** Includes employees' social-security contributions levied on an income-tax base.

† West Germany's tax schedule uses formulae, not bands.

SOURCE OECD. Cited by *The Economist*, London, 20 Feb. 1988, p. 62 (adapted).

INFLATION AND BRACKET CREEP: INDEXATION OF TAXES

The Meade Committee[9] suggested indexation of taxes to preserve the real, as distinguished from monetary, structure of taxation and to prevent the rate of inflation from becoming an arbitrary form of taxation, giving rise to inequities and distortions. Income and wealth by and large constitute the bases for assessment of taxes; two distinct types of indexation are required in regard to them. Since modern taxes are progressive, both the threshold and the tax brackets in the rate schedule of income-tax and wealth-tax need to be indexed. Besides, indexation for capital–income adjustment is necessary in order to reflect the real values of assets and liabilities and to determine real income. This includes adjustment in respect of depreciation, capital gains, stocks, and other items.

Indexation for capital–income adjustment implies the ascertainment of the proper size of the income which should form the basis for taxation. If a person earns Rs 1,500 interest on a deposit of Rs 10,000 and owing to inflation prices rise by 10 per cent, he must save Rs 1,000 for addition to his deposit account in order to maintain intact in real terms the value of his capital. Thus his net income after indexation for capital–income adjustment would be Rs 500 only which should be subject to tax. Income tax and wealth tax are progressive in nature in this country. Certain initial levels of income and wealth are exempt from taxation. If due to inflation, the price level rises, it would be equitable to raise the respective thresholds proportionately to the rise in prices, i.e. the thresholds should be adjusted in terms of the real values of income and wealth.

The tax brackets in the rate structure also need to be adjusted. Take the case of income tax. Each income bracket point from which the tax starts or from which a higher rate of tax is applicable, needs to be multiplied by a general price index in order to maintain the *status quo* in regard to the rate of progression of the tax in real terms. The amount of goods and services that a particular amount of wealth in money terms commands would be reduced if the price level increases. If the same rate of progression in wealth tax is to be maintained, then wealth brackets in the schedule for different wealth tax rates have also to be multiplied each year by the general prices index. This would ensure that wealth tax liability in real terms remains the same and the effect of inflation through an artificial increase in the money value of assets does not lead to an increase in the wealth tax burden.

Although indexation of the tax structure has not been formally adopted by many countries with a developed tax system, they have taken cognizance of the factor of inflation, and certain adjustments have been made in order to mitigate the inequities and hardship imposed by an inflationary rise in the price level. Thresholds for tax exempt incomes have been raised, personal allowances and social security payments—a form of negative taxation—have been increased. In Britain, 100 per cent capital allowances have been provided for new plant and machinery, while stock relief has been granted to reduce the rigours of tax liability arising from an inflationary rise in the value of stocks.

International tax harmonization is of great importance to European countries who are members of the European Economic Community, and the tax structure should be conducive to this. Efforts are being made in various continental countries in this direction, but progress is limited because each country seems to fashion its structure according to the needs of the state, the level of its social security system, and the economic environment within the country.

REFERENCES

1. Ludwig Erhardt, *Prosperity. through Competition*, Thames & Hudson, London, 1958, p. xii.
2. *Taxation Enquiry Commission Report*, GOI, Delhi, 1955, vol. 1, p. 154.
3. *The Structure and Reform of Direct Taxation*, Report of Committee, Chairman J. E. Meade (Meade Committee Report) (U.K.), 1978, George Allen & Unwin, London, p. 18.
4. Adam Smith, *The Wealth of Nations*, 1776, ed. Edwin Canon, The Modern Library, New York, pp. 777–9.
5. R. J. Chelliah, *Fiscal Policy in Underdeveloped Countries*, George Allen & Unwin, London, 1960, p. 66.
6. *An Outline of Japanese Taxes 1980*, Tax Bureau, Ministry of Finance, Tokyo, Japan, p. 10; Japanese Tax Commission cited by Tax Bureau.
7. Keith Marsden, *World Bank Study, Finance and Development*, IMF and World Bank, New York, Sept. 1983, p. 40.
8. Cited by Richard I. Kirkland jun., 'U.S. Tax Cuts Go Global', *Fortune*, 24 Nov. 1986, p. 132.
9. Meade Committee Report (*vide* Note 3 above), p. 100.

17

Evaluation and Reform of the Indian Tax Structure

Tax laws in most countries—developing and developed—have evolved over a period of time and are subject to modifications in response to the exigencies of economic, fiscal, and budgetary situations. Besides, there is a continuous struggle over the quantum of tax payable between the taxpayer and the revenue authorities; as a consequence, the tax structure acquires complexity.

We are reminded of a verse (108) by Omar Khayyam's in his *Rubaiyat:*[1]

Ah Love, could you and I with Fate conspire To grasp this sorry Scheme of Things entire, Would not we shatter it to bits—and then Re-mould it nearer to the Heart's Desire.

An Omar Khayyam or Nero may think in terms of complete demolition of the old structure to build a new one, conforming to their utopian dreams. That privilege is denied to lesser mortals; besides, it is also not necessary in the case of tax laws. The existing laws have withstood the test of time, and if there are complexities, avoidance, and evasion, the deficiencies are as much in implementation and levels of taxation as in the structure. A good tax system should have 'horizontal equity', which implies that persons with the same taxable capacity should be treated alike and bear equal tax burdens. Our tax structure suffers from certain infirmities: (a) the tax base is not sufficiently wide and does not cover large sections of persons who have assessable incomes; (b) certain classes of taxpayers, like those with high agricultural incomes, do not pay income-tax, while others with similar business or other incomes, have to bear the brunt of taxes; and (c) due to widespread tax evasion and avoidance, certain people pay less taxes than they should, casting a greater burden on those who do so conscientiously.

Revenues have to be raised without adversely affecting economic opportunities and incentives. Yet some distributional measures are also necessary in a society where a large percentage of the people are living below the poverty line. Since the criteria of efficiency requires low marginal rates of tax and vertical redistribution calls for high marginal rates on the richer classes, some conflict between these criteria is inevitable. A good tax system should minimize this conflict, and promote the desired level of redistribution with the least loss of efficiency.

Consumption versus Income as Base of Taxation (Kaldor's Scheme): Expenditure, Wealth and Gift Taxes, and Estate Duty

Nicholas Kaldor's scheme of tax reform (1956)[2] and government's paper on simplification and rationalization of tax laws (1986)[3] constitute milestones in fiscal history. Although expenditure tax—the *pièce de résistance* of Kaldor's proposals—was twice introduced and withdrawn, and his other proposals partially implemented and modified periodically, it cannot be denied that the scheme has left its imprint upon the tax structure. The Government's Scheme of Simplification and Rationalization of Direct Tax Laws is in the course of implementation, although some of the proposals have run into difficulties and have been withdrawn. It is proposed to broadly discuss and evaluate these schemes. Thereafter, we propose a comprehensive framework of tax reforms, directed towards rationalization of the tax structure, with a view to moulding it into an instrument for promotion of savings, investment, and growth, while rendering it equitable, efficient, and capable of inspiring trust in the assessees.

If innovative taxation is regarded as an index of progressive fiscal policy, the Indian tax structure would probably get the palm. Over the past few decades we have experimented with various kinds of taxes, and on the basis of experience some of the innovative measures have been subsequently withdrawn. A consequence of the fiscal experimentation was that at one stage the tax structure comprised not only of income tax and wealth tax, but also a formidable array of taxes including estate duty, expenditure tax, gift tax, and capital gains tax, as also wealth tax on companies. The bonus shares tax and dividend tax had also been improvised; they did immense harm to the capital market and were also subsequently removed from the statute book.

The 1958 Budget, based on Nicholas Kaldor's recommendations, imposed an annual tax on wealth, gift tax, and an expenditure tax. Kaldor's recommendation[4] that the introduction of these taxes should be accompanied by a reduction in the highest marginal rate of tax to 45 per cent (plus surcharge) was more or less ignored, although the maximum rate of income tax was brought down from 91.9 per cent to 84 per cent (including surcharge). Kaldor's recommendations were based on three principal grounds: (1) administrative efficiency would increase, as the assessee would have to file comprehensive tax returns in respect of wealth, income, and expenditure, and the need to maintain consistency in returns would ensure honest compliance. The efficiency of the system would also be enhanced as taxes would be levied both on income and property, which are interrelated. (2) Kaldor claimed that his system of taxation had the merit of equity; the ownership of property in the form of disposable assets endowed the property owner with a taxable capacity as such, in addition to the money income which that property yielded. Income alone was not an adequate yardstick of taxable capacity, and also between income from work and income from property, and between different property owners. Hence, wealth tax and estate duty were necessary so that taxes could be levied on the basis of this additional taxable capacity. (3) As regards economic effects, income tax discriminated against risk-taking, while taxes on capital did not discriminate against employment of capital in risky ventures. Kaldor wanted capital gains also to be included in taxable income. Since there was increasing urbanization, it was necessary to tax capital gains. Government, in implementing Kaldor's scheme of taxation, felt that it would also lead to distributive justice and reduce inequalities.

Theoretically, expenditure tax is ideal in that by taxing expenditure, the state should be curbing extra consumption. The basis of computing it is that taxable expenditure is generally regarded as income less approved investment, which is equal to expenditure plus investment in unapproved assets. Difficulties in computing expenditure arise because wealth at the beginning of the year and at the end of the year have to be worked out, which together with the mode of disposition of income during the year, gives the expenditure. Thus the taxable expenditure is a derived figure. This computation gives rise to various practical difficulties. Besides, if expenditure tax is not to replace income-tax, but is an additional tax, it adds to the burden of the taxpayer, causing considerable inconvenience; and the revenue yield is insubstantial. In an economy where there is a substantial amount of black money, a good part of the unproductive expenditure of assessees would be met out of it and expenditure taxation evaded. The same effect, more or less, as of the expenditure tax, can however be achieved by providing incentives for saving and investment in approved channels, while discouraging investment in unapproved channels like gold, silver, and land, which do not yield income but are subject to wealth tax. The Indian tax structure already provides such incentives, as also wealth tax.

The net effect of all the taxes imposed in 1958 was that the burden of taxation on assessees increased considerably, and due to the complexity of the tax structure and the number of returns that had to be filed, there was general dissatisfaction. Instead of the tax system being acceptable and inducing voluntary compliance, the entire scheme became counter-productive. What Kaldor had not envisaged was that if the tax structure was cumbersome and the tax burden heavy, it would tend to increase, rather than check, evasion. It was gradually realized by the authorities that the expenditure tax had failed to generate revenues commensurate with the effort on the part of the administration and assessees, nor had it fulfilled its objectives or rendered the system more equitable. The tax was withdrawn. Theoretically also, Kaldor's proposals were contradictory; his proposal to levy wealth tax and capital gains tax was in sharp contrast to his criticism of 'the double taxation' of savings.

Government's Discussion Paper on Tax Reform[5] seeks to achieve uniformity in the provisions of the three Direct Taxes Acts, which would be a precursor to the formulation of a single Direct Taxes Code, comprising Income-tax, Wealth-tax, and Gift-tax laws. Harmonization of procedural and other provisions in regard to definitions, methods of valuation, appeals, rules, and recovery proceedings should be brought about.

NEW TAX POLICIES FOR GROWTH

Certain distinctive features characterize the growth-oriented taxation policy formulated by government: promise of stability in the tax structure; openness as distinguished from secrecy to a certain extent and invitation to debate vital corporate tax issues; a degree of trust in the assessees as evidenced by the latest directive for acceptance of tax returns without scrutiny upto certain limits; and reduction in tax rates to encourage voluntary tax compliance, accompanied by penal measures for evasion. Government deserves kudos not only for its growth-oriented policies, but also for setting a new trend by inviting an open debate with regard to the scheme of corporate tax reform. Consequent upon rationalized rates of corporation tax in the Union Budget 1986–7, public companies were being taxed at 50 per cent (plus surcharge, since imposed on all classes of companies with income exceeding Rs 50,000), controlled companies, other than investment and trading companies, at 55 per cent, and the latter two categories at 60 per cent. Indicating his scheme of corporate tax reform, which included abolition of surtax in the third year (since withdrawn), the then Finance Minister proposed a further reduction of 5 per cent in corporate tax and withdrawal of surcharge (avoidable by deposit with the IDBI) during the next two years, but the trade-off was the phased withdrawal of investment allowance. (Corporate tax amendments in the 1990–1 Budget are discussed later.)

Investment allowance has a catalytic effect upon capital investment decisions and is a powerful incentive for industrial expansion. As assessment of the utility of investment allowance to the industrial sector of the economy must needs also take into account the problem of modernization and rehabilitation of machinery in the context of continual inflationary rise the world over in the cost of plant and machinery. As noted earlier, UK has extraordinarily liberal provisions of capital allowances on new plant and machinery. It was realized in the UK and other Western countries that the hiatus between the cost of machinery and the quantum of accumulated depreciation at the end of its useful life was large and made it most difficult for companies to replace machinery. This adversely affected modernization and technological upgradation, thereby impinging upon the competitive capacity of industry in the international market. Certain European countries like Holland, Belgium, and the UK moved towards adoption of inflation accounting and allowing depreciation on replacement cost basis.

The thrust of government's taxation policy is towards providing an environment of fiscal stability and open budgeting, conducive to long-term corporate planning, stimulated capital formation, and modernization. Since the proportion of indirect taxes to total taxes has increased from 73.4 per cent on an average during the five years ending 1979–80 to 77.4 per cent during the Sixth Plan, and that of direct taxes has declined, government seeks to increase the share of direct taxes in revenue. This is proposed to be effected through built-in measures to increase revenue elasticity of income-tax in response to growth in incomes. Increased revenues are scheduled to emanate from more effective tax implementation and a broader tax base, rather than escalation in tax rates. The success of the policy is evidenced by the good results achieved in buoyancy in tax revenues.

But in implementing the policy framework laid down in the Discussion Paper, government improvised certain measures, which proved to be neither simple and workable, nor acceptable. The provisions regarding, (a) a new scheme of taxation of partnerships, (b) assessment of charitable trusts, scientific research organizations, and others, (c) additional penal tax of 30 per cent of the difference between assessed and returned incomes, irrespective of whether the assessee had acted bona fide or otherwise and, (d) re-opening of assessments evoked considerable protests from the public, and government agreed to withdraw these proposals or suitably amend them.

The success of the experiment in reducing taxes is hardly in doubt; what is surprising is that governments have taken so long to appreciate their exhilarating effect upon economic growth. The Government in the 1990–1 Budget brought down the tax rate for public companies to 40 per cent plus surcharge of 8 per cent, equal to 43.2 per cent,* while abolishing investment allowance and backward areas tax rebate. In our opinion, investment allowance is indispensable to corporate growth, particularly that of capital-intensive industries. Government has abolished it, but phoenix-like, it would rise again in some form or the other. Even development rebate had to be resuscitated in the form of the investment allowance. History will repeat itself.

---

* With the Gulf Surcharge of 7 per cent imposed in 1990–1, basic tax rate increases to 46 per cent. This has been further increased in the 1991–2 Budget to 51.75 per cent (including surcharge).

It has been provided that payments made for acquisition of technical know-how would be allowed to be written off over a period of six years. If indigenously developed, in a recognized laboratory, university or institution, they may be written off in three years. This provision is a retrograde step in that, according to judicial decisions, the entire amount of consideration paid for acquiring know-how for modernization and technological upgradation was fully allowable in the year of payment. Government seeks to stimulate induction of modern technology; to this end, we suggest that the *status quo ante* be restored, and the new provision made applicable to payment for know-how of capital nature only.

The personal tax structure now conforms to some degree to certain norms which were unattainable previously: equity, simplicity, and easy compliance. Relief has been given in the taxation of personal incomes by simplifying and rationalizing both the income tax and wealth tax structures, and abolishing estate duty which barely yielded Rs 20 crores, part of which was absorbed by high cost of collection. With these modifications in the tax structure, gift tax to a great extent loses its *raison d'être*, and its abolition should be considered. The withdrawal of compulsory deposits, which had become an irritant and had outlived its utility, has also given relief to the taxpayer, although repayment due in 1985–6 had been postponed by a year. The objective of restructuring personal tax rates on a stable basis, while maintaining progressivity, is to ensure that the burden of the combined income tax and wealth tax rates does not lead to widespread evasion and avoidance, and prove to be counter-productive; that relief is provided to the middle classes and salaried earners, whose real incomes have been eroded by inflation; and that detailed scrutiny of selected small cases is generally substituted for routine examination of a large number of cases.

PERSONAL TAXES AND ALLOWANCES

Income tax is an important source of revenue for government and the yield from income tax amounted to Rs 1,440 crores in 1980–1, and is budgeted to yield Rs 3,660 crores in 1988–9. While the income tax was 11 per cent of gross tax revenue in 1980–1, it worked out to 8.7 per cent in 1988–9. The Indian Income-tax Act provides for an initial threshold of exempted income of Rs 22,000.

There are four slabs of income: the first slab ranges between Rs 22,000 to Rs 30,000 and the tax rate is 20 per cent, while the highest slab is on income above one lakh rupees and the tax rate on it is 50 per cent. There is a surcharge of 12 per cent in the case of persons having an income of above Rs 75,000 on all the slabs; thus the highest marginal rate is 56 per cent. Taking average income tax payable as a percentage of income, it is seen that on an income of Rs 50,000, the average tax is 15.2 per cent; on Rs 100,000 the tax is 30.91 per cent; on Rs 2 lakhs, it is 43.46 per cent; and on Rs 5 lakhs 50.98 per cent.

The structure of income tax is based on the principle that taxes should be pitched at high rates, but the scheme of allowances should be so formulated that efforts for reduction of tax liability induce savings in desired channels. Succinctly, the allowances include standard deduction for salaried classes—a kind of earned income allowance—and rebate on income tax in respect of provident fund, life insurance premia, housing instalments upto Rs 10,000, and six year National Savings Certificates and similar payments. Investment in equity shares of new companies, in whose case dividends are not received for the first few years owing to the gestation period, qualifies for rebate in income tax. Unfortunately this has been allowed to lapse. The amount contributed to the National Deposit Scheme also qualifies for deduction from income but on withdrawal of the deposit, the entire amount plus interest are fully taxed. However, premia paid for a Jeewan Akshay Yojana Policy to the LIC under the Section 80 CCA is not taxable, although the money is received back only after the death of the depositor. An important allowance is in respect of dividends, bank interest, and Unit Trust Income which are exempted upto Rs 13,000 in the aggregate. Complete exemption from tax is provided for export earnings. Besides, donations to eligible institutions qualify for 50 per cent allowance from income. These allowances no doubt contribute to a reduction in tax liability, but the general feeling is that a lowering of tax rates would lead to better tax compliance and increased business activity, and revenues would increase rather than decline on account of tax cuts. Government, with the objective of curbing evasion and avoidance, has stipulated that all companies and assessees must close their accounting year for tax purposes on 31 March, so as to facilitate inter-corporate verification with the aid of computers. Such uniform accounting year is not, however, compulsory under the Companies Act, 1956.

The Wealth tax Act provides for initial exemption of Rs 2.50 lakhs and another Rs 5 lakhs deduction from total taxable wealth. Agricultural property is exempt. Exempted assets within the aforesaid limit range from bank deposits, equity shares, Units of the Unit Trust and National Saving Certificates to one residential house, and moneys and assets brought into India by Non Residents for long-term retention in the country. Wealth tax is levied on net wealth, that is, assets less debts owed by the assessee. Wealth tax is payable at half per cent on net wealth (excluding the threshold of Rs 2,50,000) between Rs 2.50 lakhs and 10 lakhs; at 1 per cent of net wealth between the next 10 lakhs and 20 lakhs; and at 2 per cent on the balance of wealth above 20 lakhs.

The combined incidence of income tax and wealth tax is considerable in the case of higher bracket income tax and wealth tax assessees. A person with wealth of Rs 25 lakhs (net of initial exemption Rs 5 lakhs) and annual income of Rs 5 lakhs pays as income tax Rs 2,54,912 and wealth tax Rs 23,284, aggregating Rs 2,78,196, which works out to about 55.64 per cent of the annual income.

The Union Budget of 1990–1 provided for substitution of donee-based gift tax for the existing donor-based gift tax with effect from 20 March 1990, as an anti-avoidance measure, also designed to check conspicuous consumption. A basic exemption limit of gifts worth Rs 20,000 per year would be allowed: gifts between Rs 20,000 and Rs 50,000 in value would be taxed at 20 per cent in the hands of donees; gifts worth between Rs 50,000 and Rs 2,00,000 at 30 per cent and aggregate gifts above Rs 2,00,000 at 40 per cent. Gifts worth upto one lakh of rupees at the time of marriage, and those in foreign exchange, would be exempt from gift tax. The proposed Gift tax Bill is yet to be enacted. The revenue yield from wealth tax and gift tax amounted to Rs 67 crores and Rs 7 crores respectively in 1980–1, and Rs 130 crores and Rs 10 crores in 1988–9. Wealth tax worked out to 0.3 per cent of total revenue, while the yield of gift tax was negligible.

The yield from Estate Duty was Rs 24 crores in 1984–5 and Rs 14 crores in 1986–7. The duty was abolished with effect from 1985. However, an inheritance tax, which is much less complicated than Estate Duty and is essentially based on net wealth, was proposed but not passed, and the Bill has since lapsed.

Capital gains tax is levied on gains arising from short-term capital assets held for less than a year at normal income-tax rates; while capital gains arising from long term assets is entitled to concessional treatment. It is further provided that if the entire sale proceeds of long-term capital assets are deposited for three years with the Unit Trust or IDBI, they are wholly exempt from capital gains tax. We believe that if the period of three years is reduced to say one year, tax evasion on property transactions would be considerably reduced. Capital gains on sale of shares held for more than a year are in effect taxed at a concessional rate of about 20 per cent on highest slab. While the first Rs 10,000 (increased to Rs 15,000 in the 1991–2 Budget) gains are exempt, 60 per cent of the balance of gains also do not bear tax. Thus such gains of Rs 1,15,000 would bear tax of Rs 22,400 at the highest marginal rate of 56 per cent.

REVENUES NOT AFFECTED BY TAX CUTS

Direct taxes need to be pruned to stimulate growth, and to curb evasion and the generation of black money which contributes to inflation and other distortions in the economy. If cognizance is taken of this, the budgetary deficit should not act as a deterrent to the lowering of the personal and corporate taxes. The maximum personal income-tax rates were reduced in India from 97.75 per cent to 77 per cent in 1974–5, and to 66 per cent in 1976–7, for incomes above a lakh (instead of Rs 70,000 earlier). The revenues of the Central Government from income tax were estimated to decline by Rs 36 crores in 1974–5 and by Rs 60 crores in a full year. Actually, such revenues rose by Rs 130 crores from Rs 744 crores in 1973–4 to Rs 874 crores in 1974–5. The tax reduction in 1976–7 was also followed by an increase in revenue from Rs 965 crores in 1976–7 to Rs 1,025 crores in 1977–8. The Choksi Committee in its Final Report[6] found that 'Apart from the pecuniary gain to the Exchequer in terms of additional taxes mobilized and the gain to the economy from a reduction in the volume of unaccounted incomes, there is the more important gain in the improvement in the standards of public morality'. It concludes that, as in other parts of the world, the conditions in India also justify the 'progressive reduction in the rates of tax'.

The maximum marginal tax rate was reduced for individuals to 50 per cent from 61.875 per cent in the Union Budget for 1986–7.

The revenues of the government from income tax increased from Rs 2,509 crores in 1985–6 to Rs 3,660 crores (B.E.) in 1988–9, an increase of 46 per cent over three years.

In our view, the maximum rate of personal income tax should be reduced from 50 per cent (excluding surcharge of 12 per cent) at present to 30 per cent and the progression should be smooth and even at all levels. The maximum rate should be applicable at the level above Rs 2 lakhs instead of Rs 1 lakh at present. Allowances could be reduced. Higher rates of taxation, as we have noted earlier, do not necessarily result in higher revenues. A larger contribution to revenues can emanate from increased production. If a diminution in the excise duty on a particular commodity results in more than a proportionate increase in production, excise revenues would be larger. Besides, it may result in higher profits; consequently corporate tax revenue would also increase.

A deduction from taxable income of 50 per cent of the amount deposited with the Reserve Bank in fixed deposit, bearing the usual interest for ten years out of current income of upto Rs 20,000 per year may be considered for promotion of personal savings. The amount when received back should not be subject to taxation. Two principal shortcomings vitiate the National Deposit Scheme under Section 80 CCA and may hinder its success. While deposits qualify for 100 per cent reduction, their retrieval would entail 100 per cent taxation, and interest is taxable. If the scheme is to be a success, a time span of say ten years or age limit of about 65 years for maturity should be stipulated for tax-free withdrawal of deposits, so that some command over savings during an individual's lifetime is retained.

The LIC has clarified that according to legal opinion received by the corporation, the repayment of the principal after death under Jeewan Akshay Yojana—which has been framed under and has been integrated with Section 80 CCA Deposit—would not be subject to tax, although bonus and interest or pension would be taxable. The scheme may provide a credible alternative to the flow of surplus incomes into illegitimate channels to persons (such as film artistes) with concentration of incomes during a few years of active working life, as also to assessees with intermittent windfall profits or fluctuating incomes. Tax planning through regulation of deposits and withdrawals, as incomes rise and fall, may assist in evening out the incidence of taxation over a time span; the scheme would function as a kind of safety valve. But it must be clarified that the scheme in effect provides for deferral of tax, and as such is of limited relevance. It is suggested that the deduction from taxable income should not exceed 50 per cent of the quantum of deposit, while withdrawals should not be taxed. In its present form, with 100 per cent deduction from profits, government is losing considerable revenue without commensurate benefit. We feel it should be withdrawn and tax rates reduced.

The concept of reducing discretion in the hands of taxing officers should lead to a healthy tax system. The new scheme of mandatory interest and additional tax should be subject to certain safeguards: (a) The Commissioner should have power in all cases to waive interest or additional tax in case of genuine hardship. The provisions of Section 273A should be suitably amended and the powers of the Commissioner strengthened. They should have full discretionary power of waiver of interest, additional tax or penalty, if any, and in prosecution of cases, the power to compound or compromise, and withdraw cases. (b) There should be no automatic levy of additional tax, where the assessee has acted bona fide or where there is difference of opinion regarding assessability of income. (c) The assessee should have the right of appeal against additional tax or interest.

The new provisions regarding advance payment of tax are well-conceived and should contribute to better voluntary tax compliance even in cases where the assessee discovers after the close of the year that his income is substantially in excess of his earlier estimate. The rate of penal interest, however, should not exceed 18 per cent. Provision for advance payment of taxation of capital gains which cannot be anticipated is anomalous and should be amended.

The tax base in respect of income tax and wealth tax should be widened. A large number of self-employed persons, including traders and shopkeepers both in the urban and rural areas, have assessable incomes but do not pay taxes. It is necessary that through intensive surveys, such persons are brought within tax purview. Many persons derive incomes from supplying goods and services to government, public undertakings, and limited companies. Such persons should be asked to submit Income-tax Permanent Account Nos. before payment is made to them. This would ensure automatic filing of tax returns. Besides, a large number of traders and shopkeepers do not pay income tax, although many of them pay sales tax. A list of sales tax assessees should be obtained from Sales tax departments of state governments, and it should be ensured that they file income tax returns.

Various monetary limits to tax exemptions need to be revised upwards as, owing to inflationary rise in prices during the last few decades, the real value of such limits has declined. For instance, the basic exemption limit for income tax may be increased to Rs 24,000 and the initial exemption from long-term capital gains should be increased to Rs 20,000. The qualifying amount of investment in prescribed channels for tax rebate under section 80C (now §88) should be increased to Rs 60,000 from Rs 40,000 and the quantum of rebate on different slabs of qualifying amount revised upwards.

Many industrial units in the small and medium scale sectors are organized in the form of partnership concerns and closely held companies. The tax system has been so formulated that closely held companies, partnerships, and proprietory concerns are taxed at rates that discriminate against them. Actually, a small company with income of less than Rs 5 lakhs should be taxed at lower rates. Partnership firms are subjected to double taxation of income, both in the hands of the firm and in the hands of partners. It would be equitable if the firm tax is abolished and the income is allocated directly to the partner in whose hands it would be taxed at the appropriate rates. Alternatively, the entire tax should be levied on the firm after deducting salaries to partners, and the amount of residual profit allocated to the partner could then be free of tax. If this system is adopted, a minimum salary of Rs 5,000 per partner should be permitted, so that working partners could be adequately remunerated. The balance of incomes may be taxed in the hands of the firm at reasonable rates. The basic idea, in either case, is that the same income does not suffer tax twice. Till such time as the expected tax reform for partnership firms is given shape by government, the high tax rates schedule in respect of registered firms should be revised downwards.

The penal tax of 20 per cent on the difference between assessed income and returned income should not be applicable where the assessee has acted bona fide. If due to difference in opinion between the assessees and the taxing officer, certain expenditure is disallowed, it does not prove that the assessee has avoided tax. It is only where *mens rea* or guilty mind is proved, that penal tax should be levied.

The new system, whereby the assessee filing his Return of Income, will be issued a tear-off acknowledgement slip containing necessary details of the return filed by him which would be equivalent to an order, is in pursuance of the principle of placing greater faith in the assessee and is commendable. It would also minimize the contact between the assessee and the Income-tax Officer in a large number of cases, which would be a healthy development. The cases, to be chosen by random sampling, for detailed scrutiny should be selected at the Commissioner's level.

System of Appeals: Is Modification Necessary?

The existing system of appeals is working satisfactorily and should not be changed. Since Commissioners (Appeals) have been provided for, the institution of AACs may be abolished. Otherwise no change is necessary. The existing I.T. Appellate Tribunals, working under the jurisdiction of the Law Ministry, have been doing excellent work and dispensing justice to the taxpayer. The Tribunals should not be disturbed in any manner. What government can do is to ensure that the quality of departmental representation before the Tribunals is upgraded and becomes more effective. The power of Appellate Authorities to stay recovery proceedings during pendency of appeal should continue. Alternatively, where the Income Tax Officer does not grant stay of recovery, the Commissioner should be given the necessary authority to stay recovery proceedings till appeals are disposed of. The National Court of Direct Taxes should be a division of the High Court and under the jurisdiction of the Law Ministry. Where different benches of the NCDT give differing judgements, a Central Bench of three members should be created to consider the different bench judgements and give its final verdict, applicable all over India.

The proposed scheme of establishing a high-powered appellate body under Article 323B or Entry No. 95 of List I of the 7th Schedule to the Constitution to be known as the National Court of Direct Taxes (NCDT), would have the effect of reducing the highest court of appeal in respect of direct taxes to the status of an Administrative Tribunal. Its stature, compared to the High Courts, whose functions it would take over, would be greatly diminished and the right of appeal of the assessees would be diluted. Since the Department would appoint the members of the NCDT, the judges may not enjoy the same autonomy and freedom as High Court Judges, which may influence their judgements. In any case, if government implements the scheme, the following safeguards are absolutely essential: (a) There should be provision for appeal to the Supreme Court against the orders of the NCDT, besides the power of the Supreme Court with regard to Writs under Article 32 and special leave petitions under Article 136 of the Constitution; (b) the writ jurisdiction of the High Courts should continue; (c) the NCDT should not be under the purview of the administrative Ministry (Finance Ministry in this case), but under the aegis of the Law Ministry, which should have the power of appointment of judges of the NCDT; (d) even with regard to incentive provisions under Chapter VI A or any other section, there should be provision for appeal to the NCDT; (e) the fees for filing Appeals before ITAT are adequate and should not be increased. The same fee should cover identical appeals for different assessment years.

Taxation of Agricultural Incomes

(a) Agricultural incomes should be brought within the orbit of taxation. Agricultural incomes need to be transferred from the 'State List' to the 'Concurrent List' by amendment of the Constitution. Since many states are not utilizing their powers, they should not have any objection to such transfer. The Centre can thereafter, either through the Income tax Act or a new Act, impose Agricultural income-tax, and the proceeds could be shared with the states.

(b) Land revenue should be restructured and rendered progressive. The present structure of land revenue is outdated and the revenue yield is inelastic.

(c) Commodities which enter into the expenditure budgets of upper and middle income farmers and other persons in rural areas should be subjected to higher rates of excise duties.

(d) Agricultural inputs should be subjected to higher indirect taxation. It may be argued that this may adversely affect the small farmer, and impinge upon agricultural production. The marginal farmers may be given some form of compensatory assistance, but the basic idea is that prosperous farmers and landlords should be made to contribute to revenues. The fear that agricultural production may be adversely affected is unfounded, as there is adequate margin of profitability, owing to economies of scale. Larger holdings should bear additional taxation.

(e) A joint committee consisting of experts from the Finance and Agriculture Ministries should be appointed to study the problem of mobilization of taxes and savings from the rural areas. If necessary, the committee could visit district and tahsil headquarters and hold discussion with district and panchayat officials about the best means of mobilizing resources. The reservoir of incomes and savings in rural areas is large, and considerable mobilization can take place. Efforts should be both extensive and intensive. Every single household should be approached and brought within the network of the small savings movement. This would also assist in improving the overall ratio of savings to GDP.

COMPOSITION OF TAX STRUCTURE OF VARIOUS COUNTRIES WITH DIFFERENT PER CAPITA INCOMES

An analysis of the composition of the tax structure of various countries with differing levels of per capita incomes shows that in countries with per capita income of between $200 and $300, income taxes and taxes on property comprise 17.5 per cent and 3.9 per cent of total tax revenue, while customs and excise duties account for about 62.5 per cent. The picture is sharply different in the case of countries with per capita income of between $500 and $900. Income taxes account for 24.7 per cent of tax and property taxes 7.5 per cent, while customs and excise duties provide only 22 per cent of tax revenue. In the case of a highly industrialized country like the USA, revenue from income taxes amounts to about 48.2 per cent, payroll taxes 24.1 per cent, and property taxes 9.4 per cent, while revenue from customs and excise duties accounts for only 14.4 per cent of total tax revenue. Thus while indirect taxes yield the major portion of taxes in developing countries, as per capita income rises, income tax and other direct taxes assume increasing importance; and in developed countries, they yield the major portion of taxes, while the contribution of customs and excise duties is proportionately less.

INDIRECT TAXES: EXCISE, CUSTOMS, AND SALES TAX

Indirect taxes have to be so structured that they subserve the basic objectives of tax policy in underdeveloped economies:

1. taxes on commodities should be productive of adequate revenue for the consumption and investment functions of the state,

TABLE 17.1— *Average Composition of Tax Structures for Sample of Countries at Various Level of Per Capita Income*

Per Capita Income in Dollars	Income Taxes	Taxes on Property	Taxes on International Trade	Taxes on Production and Sales	Total Excluding Payroll Taxes	Payroll Taxes	Total
			AS PERCENTAGE OF TOTAL REVENUE				
Under 100	16.3	4.1	38.5	28.0	96.7	3.3	100
100–200	19.6	2.0	33.4	33.8	96.3	3.7	100
200–300	17.5	3.9	35.2	27.3	91.3	8.7	100
300–400	22.3	5.9	27.9	30.6	81.8	18.2	100
400–500	23.4	8.4	34.7	29.2	84.9	15.1	100
500–900	24.7	7.5	13.5	8.5	85.3	14.7	100
United States	48.2	9.4	0.1	14.3	75.9	24.1	100

SOURCE: R. A. Musgrave and P. B. Musgrave, *Public Finance in Theory and Practice*, 4th Edn., McGraw Hill Book Company, Singapore, p. 795.

and they should be revenue elastic in relation to increase in GDP. Taxes on goods with high income elasticity of demand would serve this purpose, as revenues would increase more than proportionately as incomes increase.

2. They should curb consumption from rising proportionately to increase in productivity and incomes, and contribute towards increasing the incremental-savings ratio; they should stimulate growth by increasing the ratio of capital formation to GDP; and they should assist in mobilization of a portion of the growing surplus in rural areas for developmental purposes; and

3. they should be progressive and equitable, and promote distributive justice.

The structural framework of commodity taxation has to be so designed as to effect additional taxation of luxuries and semi-luxuries at high rates, and broad-based taxation of commodities of mass consumption at comparatively low rates. This would, (a) secure progressivity in taxation; (b) curb consumption from absorbing the entire increase in incomes and productivity, particularly in the case of persons with low incomes whose propensity to consume is almost near unity, and divert resources for public investment; and (c) secure adequate revenues from commodity taxation for the purposes of the state. As the Taxation Enquiry Commission, stated[7] 'An extension of the taxation of necessaries appears unavoidable, if significant results by way of diversion of resources for financing public investment, are to be secured'.

There will undoubtedly be some conflict between the principle of progressive taxation and taxation of necessities; between distributive justice and curbing consumption of the lower and middle classes, whose standards of living are already low. But these dilemmas have to be faced and conflicting objectives reconciled as best they can, in structuring the framework of commodity taxation. R. J. Chelliah[8] believes that to secure the policy objectives, diversion of resources and purchasing power is necessary in certain directions from the private to the public sector; from consumption goods industries to production goods industries in the private sector, and diversion of demand from imports to domestically produced goods. Taxation of luxuries and exemption of capital goods would encourage such diversion. Besides, high import duties on luxuries would curb demand for imported goods, and also support domestic industries against foreign competition.

Taxes on commodities tend to be inflationary. It has been observed that increase in excise duties in the annual Budget often leads to some price rise. If excise duties are increased on a large scale they will have an inflationary impact, particularly on account of the cost–push factor. Rise in prices may lead to higher levels of wages and a consequent further increase in prices. Commodity taxes do reduce purchasing power in the hands of the people, but this is partly neutralized by the factors noted above. Excise duties are convenient to administer and collect as they are imposed upon organized manufacturing industries, whose products constitute the taxation base. But value added tax (VAT) is far superior, as it avoids the cascading effect of excise duties on intermediate products which constitute the raw materials of other industries.

Sales tax, imposed by State governments in India, constitutes multiple taxation of the same product both at the point of manufacture and the point of sale. Since there is widespread evasion of sales tax, and much less of excise duty, additional excise duty in lieu of sales tax is imposed by the Union Government in the case of cloth, sugar and tobacco, and the proceeds are distributed among the states. Extension of this to other commodities would increase the overall revenues of the State governments, but on grounds other than fiscal, the latter are reluctant to replace sales tax with additional excise administered by the Centre. The Tripathi Committee in October 1983 recommended the replacement of sales tax by additional excise duties on five more commodities: vanaspati, drugs and medicines, cement, paper, and petroleum products. The Finance Minister assured the states that this would not be imposed against their will; and revenue from these items would be maintained even after replacement, but the proposal is facing difficulties in implementation.

Sales tax is not only productive of revenue for the states but also has flexibility. It is however highly regressive, in that both the rich and the poor have to pay the same tax on a commodity. Some progressivity, however, can be secured by imposing a higher rate of tax on luxuries and lower rates on items of mass consumption. Sales taxes are imposed at differential rates by different state governments, and this causes distortion in prices. The Union Government should persuade the states to agree to uniformity in sales tax rates throughout the country.

Modvat

The simplification of the indirect tax structure and merging of various excise duties into a single basic rate (while retaining cesses as separate levies) is intended to promote economic growth, equity, simplicity, and built-in revenue-raising capacity. Rationalization of customs duties would lead to greater efficiency in the allocation of resources.

The Union Budget 1987–8 extended Modvat to all industries, except tobacco, textiles, and petroleum. Excise duty was not increased to neutralize the relief in duty owing to reduction of the cascading effect. With the changes effected in the Modvat scheme, government claims that it has successfully eliminated the cascading effect of excise duty and given a measure of excise relief. Thanks to accelerated growth, excise duties are bound to grow sizeably.

Scheme for Disclosure and Utilization of Unaccounted Money

While estimates of unaccounted money circulating in the economy vary widely, it is indisputable that large hoards of black money exist and are being continually generated. Various efforts have been made periodically, in the form of disclosure schemes, capital bonds, demonetization and, of course, raids, to discover and bring it into the purview of taxation, but the success achieved so far has only been marginal. It is now increasingly recognized that low rates of taxation, simplification of the tax structure, and placing trust in the taxpayer are the best methods of dealing with this problem, combined with deterrent punishment for evasion. The carrot and stick policy has definitely resulted in making the cost of evasion high, while the net benefit from evasion has been reduced, and as a result the level of generation and circulation of black money has declined. But the problem of bringing out black money into legitimate circulation and its utilization for industrial development and other nation-building activities is far from resolved. The problem is a complex one but it may be worthwhile if a simple scheme for disclosure and constructive utilization of such money, could be devised.

The basic difficulty is that if the maximum marginal rate of tax is 50 per cent, it would be inequitable and unethical to charge a lower rate on black money disclosed. In a complete restructuring of tax rates, the maximum marginal rate of tax should be brought down to 30 per cent, in line with the general trend internationally. Such a move would encourage voluntary compliance with tax laws and reduce creation of black money. If this proposal were implemented, a simple scheme could be formulated. It may be provided that an assessee could at any time during the year credit unaccounted money in his books, subject to the following conditions:

1. He simultaneously informs the ITO by a notice in the prescribed form that he has credited such money in his books of accounts and has deposited 70 per cent thereof in his bank account.

2. He pays 30 per cent of the amount credited in the books in the form of tax into the Reserve Bank or authorized banks to the credit of the government account, through a *challan* obtained from the Income-tax Department, within a period of seven days and forthwith deposits the receipted tax *challan* with the ITO.

3. He intimates to the ITO that such money less tax would be utilized by him within a period of six months in the purchase of one or more of the following assets:

   (a) Low-cost housing,
   (b) plant and machinery,
   (c) shares of new companies,
   (d) National Savings Certificates,
   (e) Unit Trust Scheme Certificates.

4. Such assets shall be held by the assessee for a minimum period of three years.

5. If he fails to invest the money in any of the approved channels, he will be liable to pay additional penal tax at 25 per cent of the gross amount disclosed.

The advantage of the scheme to the assessee lies in its simplicity, in that he is not liable to payment of penalty or interest. He does not also have to explain the source of the money or be questioned by the authorities. Besides, he is able to utilize the unaccounted money either in his business, in housing, or for purchase of shares, units or saving certificates, which are productive. The inestimable advantage of the scheme, from the point of view of revenue, would be that the parallel economy would be reduced and black money channelized into nation-building activities, rather than be spent on consumption or investment in undesirable channels, leading to inflation. The assets created and incomes generated would be subject to wealth tax and income tax, and would be productive of revenue.

TABLE 17.2a — *Growth of Central Taxes (By Major Heads)*

Sl. No.	Head of Tax	1981–82	1984–85	1986–87	1987–88	1988–89	1989–90
1.	Corporation Tax	1970	2556	3160	3433	4270	4500
2.	Taxes on Income other than Corporation Tax	1476	1928	2878	3187	3660	4000
3.	Customs	4300	7041	11475	13702	15812	18000
4.	Union Excise Duties	7421	11151	14470	16426	18547	21910
5.	Other Central Taxes of which:	372	342	247	200	264	266
	a) Wealth Tax	78	107	174	101	120	120
	b) Interest Tax	—	—	—	9	—	—
	c) Expenditure Tax Act, 1987	—	—	9	6	36	36
	d) Gift Tax	8	11	14	8	10	10
	e) Estate Duty	20	24	50	8	5	3
	f) Other Taxes & Duties	266	200	564	68	93	97
6.	Taxes of Union Territories	277	410	564	665	768	862
7.	Gross Tax Revenue (Total: 1 to 6)	15816	23428	32794	37613	43321	49538
8.	Less States' Share	4274	5777	8475	9578	10669	12054
9.	Net Centre's Tax Revenue	11542	17651	24319	28015	32652	37484
10.	Non-tax Revenue	3081	5319	8143	8719	9772	13508
11.	Total Revenue	14623	22970	32462	36734	42424	50992

TABLE 17.2^b — *Percentage Share in Tax Revenue*

Sl. No.	Head of Tax	1981–82	1984–85	1986–87	1987–88	1988–89	1989–90
1.	Corporation Tax	12.45	10.91	9.64	9.13	9.86	9.08
2.	Taxes on Income other than Corporation Tax	9.33	8.23	8.78	8.47	8.45	8.07
3.	Customs	27.18	30.05	34.99	36.43	36.50	36.34
4.	Union Excise Duties	46.92	47.60	44.12	43.67	42.81	44.23
5.	Other Central Taxes of which:	2.36	1.46	0.75	0.53	0.61	0.54
	Wealth Tax	0.49	0.46	0.53	0.27	0.28	0.24
	Interest Tax	—	—	—	0.02	—	—
	Expenditure Tax Act, 1987	—	—	—	0.02	0.01	0.01
	Gift Tax	0.05	0.15	0.03	0.02	0.08	0.07
	Estate Duty	0.13	0.10	0.04	0.02	0.03	0.02
	Other Taxes & Duties	1.69	0.85	0.15	0.18	0.21	0.20
6.	Taxes of Union Territories	1.76	1.75	1.72	1.77	1.77	1.74

SOURCE: Computations based on data available in Budget Papers 1989–90 (Feb., 1989), Ministry of Finance, Government of India.

TABLE 17.3 — *Centre's Revenue Receipts and Revenue Expenditure*
(As percentage of GDP)

	1980–81	1981–82	1982–83	1983–84	1984–85	1985–86	1986–87	1987–88	1988–89 (RE)	1989–90 (BE)
1. Tax Revenue (Net of States' share)	6.9	7.3	7.4	7.5	7.7	8.1	8.3	8.4	8.4	8.9
2. Non-Tax Revenue	2.5	2.5	2.8	2.4	2.9	3.0	3.4	3.1	3.0	3.7
3. Total Current Revenue (1+2)	9.4	9.8	10.2	9.9	10.6	11.1	11.7	11.5	11.4	12.6
4. Total Current Expenditure	10.0	9.9	10.9	11.1	12.1	13.2	14.4	14.3	14.2	14.2
(a) Interest payments	2.0	2.0	2.2	2.3	2.6	2.9	3.1	3.4	3.6	4.0
(b) Subsidies	1.2	1.2	1.3	1.3	1.6	1.8	1.9	1.8	2.0	1.9
(c) Defence expenditure	2.6	2.6	2.7	2.7	2.8	2.9	3.4	3.0	2.8	2.4
(d) Grants to States & UTs	2.1	1.7	2.0	2.1	2.3	2.7	2.6	2.8	2.6	2.6
(e) Others	2.2	2.4	2.6	2.6	2.8	3.0	3.3	3.3	3.2	3.4
5. Revenue Account Surplus (+)/Deficit (−)/(3−4)	−0.6	−0.1	−0.7	−1.2	−1.5	−2.1	−2.7	−2.8	−2.8	−1.6

SOURCE: *Economic Survey 1989–90*, GOI, Delhi, p. 77.

TABLE 17.4—*Budgetary Transactions of the Central and State Governments and Union Territories*
(Including extra-budgetary resources of public sector undertakings for financing their plans
in crore rupees)

	1980–81	1981–82	1982–83	1983–84	1984–85	1985–86	1986–87	1987–88	1988–89 (BE)	1988–89 (RE)	1989–90 (BE)
I. Total Outlay	36845 (27.1)	43738 (27.4)	52747 (29.7)	60829 (29.4)	72825 (31.6)	83961 (32.0)	100790 (34.4)	112169 (33.7)	127780 (32.7)	132081 (33.8)	149223 (34.7)
(a) Developmental	24426	28653	33591	39274	48085	53397	63778	68801	78107	81153	92165
(b) Non-Developmental	12419	15085	19156	21555	24740	30564	37012	43368	49673	50928	57058
II. Current Revenue	24563 (18.1)	30425 (19.1)	35795 (20.2)	40989 (19.8)	47098 (20.4)	56773 (21.6)	64823 (22.1)	73485 (22.1)	86036 (22.0)	84301 (21.7)	103623 (24.1)
(a) Tax Revenue	19844 (14.6)	24142 (15.1)	27242 (15.3)	31525 (15.2)	35813 (15.5)	43267 (16.5)	49540 (16.9)	56976 (17.1)	64147 (16.4)	65443 (16.7)	76041 (17.7)
(i) Direct Taxes	3268	4133	4492	4907	5329	6252	6890	7483	8804	8966	10337
(ii) Indirect Taxes	16576	20000	22750	26618	30484	37015	42650	49493	55343	56477	65704
(b) Non-tax Revenue	4719	6283	8553	9464	11285	13506	15283	16509	21889	19358	27582
III. Gap (I-II)	12282 (9.0)	13313 (9.5)	16952 (9.6)	19840 (9.6)	25727 (11.2)	27188 (10.4)	35967 (12.3)	38684 (11.6)	41744 (10.7)	47280 (12.1)	45600 (10.6)

TABLE 17.4—*Continued*

	1980-81	1981-82	1982-83	1983-84	1984-85	1985-86	1986-87	1987-88	1988-89 (BE)	1988-89 (RE)	1989-90 (BE)
Financed by:											
(i) Domestic Capital Receipts	7161	9493	13012	16094	18765	21899	24439	29415	29653	35210	33671
(ii) Net External Assistance	1670	1301	1591	1611	1857	1850	2378	3765	3735	3217	3723
(iii) Budgetary Deficit	3451	2519	2349	2135	5105	3439	9150	5504	8356	8853	8206
	(2.5)	(1.6)	(1.3)	(1.0)	(2.2)	(1.3)	(3.1)	(1.7)	(2.1)	(2.3)	(1.9)

SOURCE: *Economic Survey 1989–90*, p. 76. Figures in Brackets are percentages of GDP.

REFERENCES

1. E. Fitzerald, *The Rubaiyat of Omar Khayyam*, Collins, London, p.160.
2. Nicholas Kaldor, *Indian Tax Reform—Report of a Survey*, Ministry of Finance, Delhi, 1956, various chapters.
3. Discussion Paper on *Simplification and Rationalisation of Direct Tax Laws*, Ministry of Finance, Government of India, Delhi, 1986.
4. N. Kaldor's *Report*, p. 15.
5. Discussion Paper on Direct Tax Laws (*vide* Item 4 above), p. 1.
6. *Direct Tax Laws Committee* (Choksi Committee) *Final Report*, Sept. 1978, Ministry of Finance, Government of India, Delhi, p. 16.
7. *Taxation Enquiry Commission Report*, Vol. 1. p. 149.
8. R. J. Chelliah, *Fiscal Policy in Underdeveloped Countries*, George Allen & Unwin, London, pp. 90, 91.

18
Corporate Tax Reform

Corporate income tax in India is almost as ancient as Income tax and vestiges of the former are traceable even in the 1860 Income-tax Act. The 1922 Act, as amended in 1939, partly accepted the imputation principle in regard to corporation tax, which implies that a company pays income tax on behalf of its shareholders. Till the 1959–60 Budget, dividends received by shareholders were grossed up by 46 per cent in their hands, and the amount of grossing up was considered to be tax paid by the company for its shareholders, to be deducted from the latter's personal tax liability on total income (including the grossed up dividends).

The 1959–60 Budget adopted the classical scheme of taxation, according to which the company pays tax on its own account and the shareholder does not receive any credit for the tax paid by the company. When the new scheme was introduced in 1959, grossing up of dividends was abolished and the corporation tax rate was reduced from 51.5 per cent to 45 per cent in the case of Indian companies. It was proposed that the overall tax rate applicable to Indian companies would be so fixed that the yield would be equal to the annual gross yield less the annual credit given to the shareholders. The tax liability of the shareholders would no longer be related to the tax borne by the companies.

The corporation tax structure and the rates during the last three decades have undergone several changes, but basically the classical system has continued to be operative. Before we analyse the corporate tax system in India, it is desirable to have an overview of modern analytical thinking in respect of the classical view and integrationist view of corporation tax, and the Meade Committee (UK)'s recommendation for replacement of corporation tax by a tax on corporate tax flows.

J. A. Kay (March 1990)[1] argued that the income of companies is ultimately that of shareholders and ideally that income should be attributed to them and taxed accordingly. That is the integrationist view, but it has not been wholly accepted anywhere in the world. However, recent reforms in Australia and New Zealand have achieved to an extent integration between personal and corporate income taxes by providing for equivalent individual and corporate tax rates and a high degree of imputation. Complete integration of corporate and personal income taxes is more an academic concept than a practical proposition as, (a) the company is a separate legal entity distinct from its shareholders and the latter have no claim or right upon the company's reserve until distributed or capitalized; (b) it is inequitable to include in the shareholder's income a portion of the company's retained profits which have not been received by him; (c) shareholders buy and sell shares in companies and the company's members' list is in a continuous state of flux (except during the period of book closing). A person who is a shareholder on the record date for distribution of dividend and ceases to be a member after a month may be taxed on an amount which he has neither received nor will ever receive.

CLASSICAL SYSTEM

The United States and India have adopted the classical scheme of company taxation; and there is complete dichotomy between the corporation tax on companies and income tax on individuals. In this system, dividends are taxed twice: once in the hands of the company as its income, and secondly as dividends to the extent of distribution in the hands of the shareholders (subject to partial tax exemption in respect of dividends). However, in the UK, France, and Germany, corporate taxation is based on the system of partial imputation, according to which the shareholder receives credit for some part of the tax liability of corporations through grossing up of dividends.

TAXES ON CASH FLOWS MOOTED

Suggestions have been made for tax reform in the UK to include the replacement of corporation tax by a tax on corporate cash flows, which would imply that all capital investment would be allowed as a deduction from profits in the year in which the acquisition of plant, machinery, and other assets takes place. The corporation's inflow of cash consists of sale of goods and disinvestment of assets, in addition to interest and dividends. The outflow of cash comprises production costs and capital expenditure on purchases of plant, machinery, and other assets, including interest payments on borrowings. The cash flow corporation tax has as its base the excess inflow over outflow of cash. Thus all capital expenditure on fixed assets would be fully deductible, while sales of assets would be taxed in full. Since in the UK 100 per cent depreciation on machinery is already fully allowable in the year of acquisition, and appreciation in stocks is largely deductible under the stock relief scheme, the benefit of full deduction would be extended to outlays on buildings (at present partly deductible), land, and other capital assets and uncovered balances of stock acquisitions.

A corporation tax on cash flows has several advantages. The need for indexation for inflation is eliminated as capital expenditure is immediately allowable for tax deduction. The distinction between capital and revenue loses its significance. The capital gains tax at a concessional rate as at present would no longer be necessary since the entire proceeds of sale of assets would be includible in the taxable inflows. Considering that the acquisition of stocks would be fully deductible, the special scheme of stock relief would become superfluous and redundant. The cash flow corporation tax would be far superior to the existing company tax. Because of the allowance of depreciation at present on a historical cost basis, though mitigated to some extent by the allowance of free depreciation on plant and machinery, the company pays taxes on book profits, while its capital base gets eroded by lack of replacement or modernization of worn-out machinery. Since the inflationary rise in the replacement cost of assets makes it almost impossible for companies to collect funds from their own resources, the dependence on borrowed funds from financial institutions is considerable. The problem is compounded in the case of a country like India where corporate tax liability is high.

Though a cash flow corporation tax in India may initially reduce government revenue, the advantages should outweigh the losses. It would serve as a powerful incentive for industrial growth and enable modernization of machinery out of self-generated funds, thereby greatly reducing the malady of industrial sickness. A diminution in utilization of institutional funds would be accompanied by an increase in the volume of promoter's contribution, leading to greater cost consciousness and restraint in dividends. If it is not considered feasible to adopt a cash flow corporation tax, what government can do is to allow capital expenditure in approved assets in priority industries to be fully deducted for tax purposes (disinvestment being taxable). Such a measure would boost capital formation. As a sequel to stimulated production and income, government revenue would also escalate.

Reserve Bank Study

Certain of the recommendations incorporated in a Reserve Bank study on the 'Impact of Fiscal Policy on the Private Corporate Sector'[2] deserve consideration. The study is rightly critical of the surcharge on corporate tax which introduces an element of instability in the tax structure and should be withdrawn. 'At the same time, corporate income-tax should be reduced in order to induce greater tax compliance and to reduce tax evasion.... Tax reductions have to be combined with a corresponding review and reduction of inummerable tax exemptions and fiscal incentives provided to the corporate sector.' It suggests the retention of tax holiday for new companies, investment or deposit allowance for new investment, rebate for exports, backward areas development, scientific research, and such other important incentives, while others may be withdrawn. Modification of the corporate tax structure along these lines would stimulate investment and inflow of foreign investment capital. However, government has abolished investment allowance and certain other vital allowances as a trade-off with reduction in tax rates.

Rationalization of the tax structure should include reduction in corporate tax levels phased over a period of three years.

TABLE 18.1 — *Existing and Proposed Corporate Tax Rates*

Category	Existing Tax Rates prior to 1990–91	Tax Rates as in Union Budget 1990–91	Tax Rates as in Union Budget 1991–92	Proposed tax structure
			(Percentages)	
Public Companies	50	*40	45	35
Controlled Industrial Companies	55	*45	50	37.5
Small Companies with Profits below Rs 5 lakhs	55	45	50	30
Controlled Investment and Trading Companies	60	*50	50	37.5
Foreign Companies	70	65	65	60

* These rates were also suggested by the aforesaid study.

Despite assurance of stability in the tax structure, the framework of corporate taxation has been subjected to modifications almost every year. Besides, the surcharge on domestic companies with incomes above Rs 75,000 amounts to 15 per cent. The effective tax rate for the assessment year 1991–2 works out to 51.75 per cent for public companies and 57.5 per cent for controlled companies (as compared to 32.5 per cent basic tax rate for companies in the UK). Distinction between trading and investment companies, and other companies has been abolished in this Budget. However, small companies with profits less than Rs 5 lakhs continue to be taxed at the same rate as large companies. It is significant that when the basic tax rate was reduced in the 1990–1 Budget from 50 per cent to 40 per cent for public companies, investment allowance had been withdrawn. It was almost in the nature of a trade-off. But no such allowance was restored in the 1991–2 Budget, even though corporate tax rates were increased.

The tax rates proposed by us would bring the tax structure in closer alignment with the level of taxes prevailing in the UK, where the maximum statutory Corporation tax rate is 35 per cent (reduced to 32.5 per cent in the 1991 Budget) and the US, where it is 34 per cent, and other countries. Besides, what has not been taken cognizance of by the RBI study is that the UK has the imputation system of taxation, whereby shareholders receive credit for part of the taxes paid by corporations. Except for exemption of dividends upto a small limit under Section 80 L, there is double taxation of incomes in India: in the hands of the company and again in the hands of the shareholders. In the case of inter-corporate dividends, the Budget for 1990–91 provides that inter-corporate dividends would be free of tax provided the company distributes an equivalent amount by way of dividend paid. The objective is to encourage genuine investment activity, while discouraging the use of the corporate framework for holding personal wealth.

Concessions have been built into the tax structure in order to promote various extraneous objectives, such as earning foreign exchange, promoting charities, and providing incentives for family planning and for rural development. These concessions have many conditions attached to them, which adds to the complexity of tax laws. If government desires to promote other objectives, it should evolve separate incentive schemes for encouraging them. It would be advisable to further delete some of these provisions from the tax laws, while reducing the effective tax rates, which would result in less evasion and avoidance.

Certain conclusions of the RBI study are significant: (a) it is more advantageous to have a low tax rate with a few well-conceived concessions than to have a seemingly high rate with multifold concessions; (b) the effective tax rate on companies in India was lower than in the UK and US till the first half of eighties; while this finding is not conclusive, it is implicit that in the second half of the eighties, the reverse is true; (c) the average net rate of return was lower in India than in the UK, US, France, Germany, or Japan; (d) growth rates of companies depend upon various factors such as, *inter alia*, efficiency of capital utilization, technological upgradation, and sound management; and (e) the contribution of depreciation to gross capital formation far exceeded that of retained profits. The study shows that, (a) the corporate tax structure needs to be rationalized and, (b) improvement in operational efficiency, modernization, and induction of better technology are imperative if Indian industry is to remain internationally competitive and generate internal resources for accelerated growth.

DEPRECIATION ON REPLACEMENT COST BASIS

The existing tax system makes provision for depreciation on historical cost basis. Inflation has considerably increased the replacement cost of plant and machinery, and the amount accumulated through depreciation over the life of the plant is insufficient to meet the cost of replacement, not to speak of upgradation of technology. Several textile, jute, paper, sugar, cement, and steel industrial units were established decades ago and many of the plants have outlived their utility. Most companies do not have adequate funds for replacement and industries suffer from obsolescence of machinery and technology. Certain European countries have adopted inflation accounting and depreciation is being allowed for income tax purposes on the replacement cost of machinery.

During an inflationary era, when prices are rising, (1) historical cost accounts do not show the correct values to the business of the company's assets; (2) historical cost profit includes unrealized profit from appreciation in the value of stocks, better described as holding gains. (It has been estimated that in the UK, in 1974, holding gains from stock appreciation amounted to almost half the gross trading profits of companies); (3) depreciation on historical cost basis is inadequate, in that it does not cover the replacement cost of assets; and (4) historical cost profit is higher than the real profit, which needs to be arrived at after providing depreciation on replacement cost basis, so that the value of assets is maintained.

The European Cement Association, 'Cembureau',³ stated that it was urgently necessary to maintain the financial integrity of the cement industry in the context of severe inflation. Financial statements prepared on the conventional basis failed to represent the true position. As tax and dividends were paid out of profits which did not provide depreciation on replacement cost of machinery and other assets, there was erosion of capital; inflation accounting had become absolutely necessary.

There are two alternatives. The simplest method is to revalue buildings, plant, machinery, and other fixed assets on replacement cost basis and to provide depreciation on the enhanced values, so that profit is arrived at after taking into account depreciation on replacement cost. The other method is to prepare financial statements which incorporate not only revaluation of fixed assets, but also adjustment to cost of sales and working capital. Obviously, the statement is more complicated and needs expert accounting advice. Inflation accounting has not yet been adopted by industrial concerns in India, although certain companies are attaching as addendum financial statements prepared on replacement cost basis. The problem of replacement cost of machinery can no longer be ignored if the viability of industry and its competitive position in international markets is to be maintained. Depreciation on replacement cost basis should be allowed as deduction from corporate incomes.

Government, however, earlier revised depreciation rates upwards, particularly for plant and machinery,* but the measure is far from adequate to solve the problem of modernization. It is suggested that an allowance equal to 10 per cent of profits for transfer to modernization and rehabilitation reserve may be permitted for selected industries, whose machinery was purchased more than ten years ago. Such reserves would constitute the nucleus capital to finance modernization schemes. With upgraded technology, their cost of production and international competitive capacity would improve.

---

* The 1991–92 Budget however has reduced such depreciation from 33.33 per cent to 25 per cent.

Minimum Tax on Book Profits (115J)

The Income Tax Act provided that with effect from accounting year 1987–8, where the total income of a company computed under the Act after deduction of allowances is less than 30 per cent of its book profit, the taxable income shall be taken as 30 per cent of such book profit. This provision is intended to subject the so-called 'Zero-tax companies' to a minimum tax, even though they may not have any tax liability for the previous year under the provisions of law. The tax is inequitable; besides it is not realized that the term 'Zero-tax companies' is a misnomer. Many of these corporate entities constitute the élite of the corporate sector and pay large amounts in excise duties, sales tax, and other indirect taxes, the quantum of which far exceeds whatever income tax may be payable. They contribute substantially to GNP by increasing production, private employment, earn foreign exchange and through expansion of capital equipment, add to the capital stock in the economy. If they do not have income tax liability, because of their entitlement to depreciation and investment and other allowances, why should that be grudged? After all, allowances are provided for the social and economic purpose of development, and these companies effectively perform this function. To term this avoidance, and tax it through minimum tax provisions in law, is to place initiative and efficiency at a discount.

Government, in order to enforce payment of minimum tax by profit-earning companies, switched over to taxation of book profits. The scheme suffered from several flaws and complexities. The companies had to bear tax on 30 per cent of book profits, even though they may have had brought forward losses. Besides, a company may have long-term capital gains exempt under law by depositing the entire consideration from the sale of property or assets for three years with Unit Trust under Section 54E; yet such gains would be includible in book profits and subjected to minimum tax.

Where a concern has brought forward losses, but turns the corner, the quantum of tax payable by it, say over a period of three years, would be considerably more than the tax liability on present basis. This is essentially so because the tax on book profits is not adjustable against the tax conventionally payable, and earlier losses are ignored. The various allowances and rebates would also not be available. Sick and new companies would experience difficulty in achieving viability. Besides, the dual concept of book profit and taxable profit adds to the complexity of tax laws. To the extent that the quantum of tax on book profits would reduce reserves, the debt–equity ratio would be affected and borrowing capacity for financing expansions eroded. The viability of many units would be affected. And if the management switches over to written-down value basis from straight-line basis of depreciation, the distributable profits would be reduced, with consequent deleterious effect upon share prices. N. A. Palkhivala expressed the view that it was constitutionally illegal, economically disastrous and discriminatory between companies and other categories of taxpayers. Fortunately, government has withdrawn the minimum tax on book profits with effect from accounting year 1990–1.

Section 80 I provides for deduction of 25 per cent of profits from taxable income for eight years for new industrial undertakings (other than non-priority industries). The Union Budget 1990–1 has extended the deduction to 30 per cent of profits for companies for a period of ten years. It is however unfortunate that the backward areas development allowance has been withdrawn in the Union Budget 1990–1. It will adversely affect the development of backward districts. Actually the rebate should have been extended to expenditure for infrastructural development in backward regions by companies. If a company spends money on development of roads, railway sidings, trucks, housing, provision for water and electricity, the capital expenditure should be eligible for such allowance at 15 per cent of the investment. Undistributed profits tax rebate would stimulate corporate savings and lead to a higher incremental savings ratio in the corporate sector. This has been discussed in detail in Chapter 20. Tax credit certificates for additional production should be restored, and made applicable to basic and important industries. The rebate may be given as a deduction from excise duty payable. This would lead to better utilization of installed capacity and improve the capital–output ratio.

MERGERS AND SET-OFF OF LOSSES OF SICK COMPANIES

It would be readily appreciated that one of the best methods for rehabilitation of sick industrial units is to merge them with healthy companies. Section 72A of the Income Tax Act provides that in case of amalgamation of a company, the brought forward depreciation and losses of the amalgamating company would be allowed to be set off against the profits of the amalgamated company, if the sanction of the specified authority is obtained. The procedure for obtaining the sanction was cumbersome and time-consuming, and it discouraged mergers. According to the new Sick Industries Regulations, such amalgamation can be sanctioned by the BIFR.[4] It is suggested that Section 72A should be amended to simply provide that in cases of such mergers, the brought forward depreciation and losses of the merging company would be allowed to be set off against the profits of the healthy company, provided both are industrial companies. This would remove a prime constraint in regard to rehabilitation of sick units. The number of sick units in the country is so large that it is not possible for the BIFR to deal with the large number of cases of small and medium sick units. This change in income tax law would provide an inbuilt device for the rehabilitation of sick units, and contribute to the resolution of this intractable problem.

CONDITIONALITIES

Certain incentives are provided in the income tax law. These are designed to promote certain objectives, and are formulated after due consideration. Such incentives should not be hedged by various procedural and other conditionalities, making it difficult for assessees to claim them. Whatever may be the quantum of allowance, the scheme should be simple and definite, and there should be no room for exercise of discretion by the officer to disallow it.

The yield from corporation tax amounted to Rs 1,377 crores in 1980–1 and was budgeted at Rs 4,099 crores in 1988–9. It works out to 10.5 per cent and 9.6 per cent of gross tax revenue in the respective years. With rationalization and accelerated industrial growth, corporate tax yield should also improve. The corporate tax structure has grown in a haphazard way and taxes are high both by international standards and for promoting capital formation. It needs to be rationalized if it is to serve as an instrument of growth and is to fulfil certain social objectives such as not being unattractive for foreign capital (with high technology), growth of backward areas, and diminution of regional imbalances.

REFERENCES

1. J. A. Kay, 'Tax Policy: A Survey', *The Economic Journal*, March 1990, Royal Economic Society Basil Blackwell Ltd., p. 27.
2. K. C. Sharma, *Reserve Bank of India, Occasional Papers*, vol. 9, no. 3, Sept. 1988, pt. VI, pp. 262, 263.
3. Cembureau, The European Cement Asscn., *Inflation Accounting*, Paris, July 1981, Introd. p. 1.
4. BIFR = Board of Industrial and Financial Reconstruction.

19

Tax-free Reserves as an Instrument of Stabilization in the Economy: The Swedish Case

The rigours of corporate taxation in certain West European countries were mitigated by the allowance of tax-free reserves. Integrated with the scheme of accelerated depreciation and investment allowances, such funds, a part of which usually had to be deposited with the country's central bank, served as fiscal instruments for influencing levels of investment and employment in the economy. With an imaginative approach a similar scheme of tax-free reserves could be improvised for this country; it could afford some tax relief, while control over the direction and timing of the use of those funds could be retained by the authorities.

The Scandinavian countries and Switzerland provided for substantial tax-free amounts; in Sweden they were christened business cycle equalization reserves. A Swedish company could create a tax-free reserve for business activities upto 40 per cent of its assessable profit before tax, provided it deposited 46 per cent of the amount—broadly corresponding to the corporate rate of taxation—into an account with the country's central bank (Riksbank). The residue could be invested by the company at its own discretion. The company could be directed by government to use the blocked amounts for certain purposes, in which case it was allowed a deduction from profits equal to 10 per cent of the amount invested; or after the expiry of five years since its creation, 30 per cent could be used for approved purposes without government sanction and the rest with official acquiescence. Government could also allow its utilization (as also of future creation) for investment in industries or works of national importance upto 75 per cent of the total outlay on those projects. Such utilization in the last two cases, however, did not qualify for the 10 per cent special deduction. Approved purposes included depreciation of plant and machinery, construction, conversion, and repairs of buildings and ships, workers' housing, manufacture and acquisition of stocks, raw and finished, and exploration for minerals. Failure to comply with the law and government instructions entailed taxation of the reserve and an additional 10 per cent penalty. Besides, the assets purchased out of it were treated as having been written off to tax.

The privilege of creating tax-free reserves was available to corporate entities in Norway up to 20 per cent of profits before tax for future acquisition of assets; and in Denmark up to 15 per cent for replacement of worn-out plant and machinery. The entire amount of this in Norway and 50 per cent in Denmark had to be deposited with the country's central bank or in a blocked account with a commercial bank for specified periods. Corporate entities could be directed by government to use the blocked amounts for specified or approved purposes. While Denmark relied on a penal clause to enforce its utilization in desired channels, an appreciable degree of direct control, besides penalty, was exercised by the government in Norway for this purpose. The total quantum of reserves with the central bank, the direction and timing of the use of which it could determine, was sizable enough to constitute it a weapon in its armoury to regulate to business cycles and to channelize investment into desired sectors and development areas.

Government kept a watchful eye on the economic conditions and levels of employment. During periods corresponding to an upward swing of the business cycle, government was chary of releasing the blocked funds for investment; and when there was a decline in business activity, and investment, incomes, and employment tended to fall off, not only released them for investment, but also issued directives for their use, for specified purposes, in which case they qualified for additional tax rebate. Government, at times, found it advantageous to use this fiscal device rather than undertake direct investment itself. Generally, however, the timing and use of this instrument was coordinated with other steps to normalize economic activity and mitigate the severity of the impact of cyclical fluctuations upon the economy.

OPERATIONS IN SWEDEN

Although investment fund legislation in Sweden originated in 1938, it was only during the quinquennium 1958–63, when the economy faced recession, that the scheme was applied practically as a constituent part of economic and employment policies, and could be regarded as having attained maturity. The quantum of funds at the beginning of 1962 amounted to about kr. 2400 million, of which permission for utilization of funds to the extent of kr. 700 million was granted for building construction projects between September 1962 to April 1963. The effect on employment during this period may be gauged from the fact that about 10,000 workers were employed on private investment projects (excluding housing) in the 'controlled sector'; this constituted 31 per cent of the employment on private building works.

The scheme was applied to the industrial sectors also. During November 1962, recessionist tendencies became visible in the engineering and shipbuilding industries, which experienced a decline in the inflow of fresh orders. The Labour Market Board promptly decided to grant permission for utilization of such funds for investment in those industries, and stipulated that orders were to be placed within May 1963. Release of funds for investment in machinery and other equipment steadily gathered momentum, and upto April 1963 permission had been granted for investments aggregating to about kr. 300 million. This move was supplemented by an acceleration in government's purchases of engineering goods. The use of the investment fund scheme in conjunction with orthodox fiscal and other stimulants during the recession of 1958–69 and 1962–3 was marked by an appreciable degree of success. Mr Curt Canarp, an economist, expressed the view, in a quarterly review of *Skandinaviska Banken*, that

we in Sweden seem to have succeeded in creating a system which gives the administrative and financial resources for the pursuance of an active economic policy in the sphere of investments during a recession.... As regards influencing private investments, the investment fund legislation has proved to give wide administrative and financial possibilities.

SCHEME FOR INDIA

The present author, as early as in 1968, had suggested in an article in *The Economic Times* that the Indian government should consider measures that would provide tax relief without appreciable loss of revenue. Properly evolved, a scheme of tax-free reserves, basically as prevalent in West European countries, could be forged into a useful multi-purpose fiscal instrument. Investment, in the process of growth, often needs to be channelized in certain industrial sectors, to which capital, on account of the risk factor or projections of low return, may not be willing to flow without inducement. Such a scheme could be geared to directing invest-ment, (a) into industrial sectors which need to be buttressed; (b) to underdeveloped regions; and (c) for replacement of worn-out or obsolescent plant and machinery.

Government may permit the transfer, it was also suggested, of 20 per cent of the assessable profit to a tax-free reserve, out of which, say, 50 per cent could be required to be deposited with the Reserve Bank of India. Within a period of three years, government might release the blocked reserve with such directive for invest-ment as was deemed necessary in the national interest. While the corporate sector would be benefited by the tax relief, government would acquire control over a substantial part of the money for a certain period and its ultimate disposition. The authorities need not adhere to a fixed schedule with regard to the timing of release. It could be integrated with other fiscal and monetary measures for pre-determined objectives, including regulation of the total flow of investment in the economy during any given period.

Provision for creation of tax-free amounts of varying magnitudes existed in the taxation laws of a number of West European countries, but they were improvised to serve varying objectives. Greece aimed at covering possible future losses, while Switzerland encouraged companies to stagger their investment evenly over booms and depressions. West Germany and Spain provided for tax-free reserves in order to stimulate investment in underdeve-loped countries. The reserves, however, were later taxed. The tax laws in West Germany incorporated incentives for investment in specified developing countries in the form of capital equipment or actual capital for industries, conducive to the development of the investee economy. Besides an initial allowance of 15 per cent of the investment in the first year, tax-free reserves could be created to the extent of 42.5 per cent the total investment. After six years, this reserve was taxed in six annual instalments of equal magnitude. Companies formed in Spain with the sanction of government for holding shares and debentures in foreign companies were eligible for exemption from corporate taxes, as also tax on capital gains. Fees for registration and increase in capital were reducible upto 60 per cent of the amount.

ASSETS REVALUATION

Most European countries in the post-war period have experienced inflation, and this phenomenon made its impact felt upon the basis of depreciation allowed under the tax laws. While the normal basis is historical cost, various countries including Holland and Germany in 1948 after currency reform, Italy in 1962, and Austria in 1954 allowed a writing up of assets so as to enable more realistic depreciation allowances out of profits before tax. This measure strengthened the corporate structure, making it easier for companies to cope with rising costs of machinery and other assets. The Netherlands allowed continuous revaluation of assets on the basis of replacement costs. In India, certain industries, notably sugar and paper, had represented for rehabilitation allowance on the basis of enhanced replacement cost of machinery in the computation of prices of their products; the claim does not appear to have been conceded so far. In Income-tax law also, provision does not exist for depreciation on replacement cost basis, despite an almost continuous upward surge in capital costs since the War.

Most countries, including the United Kingdom, granted acceleration of depreciation in respect of specified assets by initial allowances; these could be allowed in the first year or spread over a number of years. Investment allowances in addition were permitted by the UK, Sweden, Italy, and some Swiss cantons, among others. Initial allowance in Sweden was also granted on a discretionary basis, thereby mobilizing it as a constituent part of the overall strategy to regulate investment and employment in the economy. An initial allowance of 30 per cent and an investment allowance of 10 per cent on acquisition of new plant and machinery were improvised; the availability of such allowance to industry, however, was rendered contingent upon the state of unemployment or the location of the industrial undertaking in specified development districts. Enhanced depreciation and investment allowance against investment in difficult regions could, in India also, constitute a useful device for promoting selective regional development. The scheme of tax-free reserves as a tool for realization of fiscal and economic objectives has been successfully implemented in Western Europe; a similar scheme designed to serve as a fiscal instrument for stabilization and growth in India, along the lines of the Swedish system, appears to be required.

20

Corporate Nucleus Capital Super-Multiplier as an Instrument of Fiscal Policy*

Economic growth and employment are functions of aggregate investment in the economy. Net investment in economic terms, according to J. M. Keynes,[1] means 'the net addition to all kinds of capital equipment, after allowing for those changes in the value of the old capital equipment which are taken into account in reckoning net income. Investment, thus defined, includes, therefore, the increment of capital equipment, whether it consists of fixed capital, working capital or liquid capital.' The entrepreneur is the key figure in mobilizing various factors of production for investment. Capital is one of the principal factors for establishment of industry. The major portion of the nucleus capital or the promoter's contribution is derived from corporate funds mobilized by the entrepreneur, since personal savings through progressive taxation are relatively small. Indeed, even the entrepreneurial function these days, in some cases, is taken over by corporate managements; certain large companies are promoted by a group of two or three corporations.

The central point in our thesis here is that an increase in the reserves of corporations takes place as a consequence of reduction in corporate taxes. This leads to an addition to the pool of funds available for providing nucleus capital for investment in new projects. Actually, if there is an addition to corporate reserves, it induces the management to undertake promotional activity in the establishment of new projects or expansion of existing plant or modernization, which leads to an increase in capital formation equal to several times the increase in corporate reserves. This is on

* With reference to developing economies.

account of what we call the 'Corporate Nucleus Capital Super-Multiplier' effect, which may be explained.

A reduction in the corporate tax rate would initially result in an increase in the post-tax profits of a company by an amount equal to the quantum of tax relief. This accretion to profits would either be transferred to reserve or distributed as dividends. For the present we assume that additional distribution of dividends does not take place, and the entire amount of tax relief is transferred to reserves. In other words, on the basis of this assumption, *the quantum of reduction in corporate tax is equal to the increase in corporate reserves*. The accretion to reserve in the case of the principal 500 industrial companies would mostly be utilized for providing nucleus capital for expansion or for establishment of new projects or diversification into new lines of activity or modernization. Taking an overall view of utilization or accretion to reserves, it would be safe to conclude that not more than 10 per cent of the accretion to reserves would remain idle or be used for extraneous purposes. Another 15 per cent may be used as margin money for working capital.

An analysis of Sources and Uses of Funds in the case of 417 ICICI[2] assisted companies reveals that during 1986–7, Gross fixed assets increased by Rs 3121 crores and Investment by Rs 141 crores, aggregating Rs 3262 crores. Working capital (Inventories Rs 633 crores, Receivable and Advances Rs 1079 crores, less current liabilities Rs 1003 crores) amounted to Rs 709 crores, while Cash and Bank balances were Rs 433 crores. Addition to Fixed Assets and Investments worked out to 74.1 per cent, working capital 16.1 per cent, and Cash and Bank balances 9.8 per cent of the Net Outlay. This analysis is useful for our purposes inasmuch as it provides confirmation that the ratio of investment of funds in working capital to fixed assets and investment is roughly 1:5, and that it would be appropriate to take utilization of Incremental reserves for nucleus capital at 75 per cent, working capital at 15 per cent, and funds kept idle or used for extraneous purposes at 10 per cent.

INTEGRATED EFFECT OF BOTH MULTIPLIER AND ACCELERATOR

Our Theory of Corporate Nucleus Capital Super-Multiplier incorporates the integrated effects of both the 'multiplier' and the 'accelerator'. Although these concepts are well known in economics, they may be briefly explained for the benefit of the lay reader. Assuming that there is unemployment in the economy, government spends an additional one crore of rupees on investment. This amount increases the income of the workers in the invested industries and they spend a substantial portion of the extra income on purchase of consumption goods. Since they would spend only part of the incremental income, the marginal propensity to consume would be less than unity. This gives a fillip to industries manufacturing consumer goods and the incomes of the workers in consumption goods industries increase, who in turn spend a considerable part of their extra incomes on additional consumer goods. Thus the initial extra expenditure of rupees one crore by government results in increase in the income of the community by several crore rupees. This is the multiplier effect, which was developed by R. F. Kahn in the early 1930s; J. M. Keynes used it as an integral part of his theory of employment. In effect, the multiplier expresses the relationship between the increase in investment and the number of times there is an ultimate increase in income.

The accelerator or acceleration principle states that if the demand for consumption goods increases, it would increase the derived demand for the factors of production, such as plant and machinery. In response to the demand, investment in machinery will rise at a proportionately higher rate than the initial increase in demand for consumption goods. The accelerator indicates a functional relationship between the demand for consumption goods and the demand for the factors of production, such as plant and machinery, with which these goods are manufactured. Thus the accelerator makes the level of investment a function of the rate of change in the demand for consumption goods. In the case of our theory of the CNC Super-Multiplier, both the multiplier and the accelerator come into effect in an integrated way. Hence, in order to distinguish the CNC effect from both the multiplier and the accelerator, we have termed it CNC Super-Multiplier.*

CORPORATE NUCLEUS CAPITAL SUPER-MULTIPLIER
(CNC SUPER-MULTIPLIER)

Incremental corporate reserves (less amounts used as margin for

---

* We must acknowledge that the term 'Super-Multiplier' was suggested by Prof. Alak Ghosh to distinguish it from the multiplier and the accelerator, both of whose integrated effects are incorporated in our theory of the CNC Super-Multiplier.

working capital or extraneous purposes) provide the bulk of the promoter's contribution in new industrial projects established with such incremental reserves. It is our contention that, in given circumstances, a definite ratio termed by us Corporate Nucleus Capital Super-Multiplier can be established between, (1) the quantum of reduction in corporate taxes, leading to an equivalent increase in accretion to corporate reserves, and (2) investment, arising out of the utilization of such accretion to reserves as nucleus capital which according to the economic definition given earlier, includes capital assets, working capital, and liquid funds, being the project outlays of new industrial projects.

The CNC Super-Multiplier is determined by: (1) the fraction of incremental corporate reserves (on reduction in tax rate) utilized as nucleus capital for new projects; (2) percentage of promoter's contribution to equity capital of new projects; and (3) the debt–equity ratio. The value of the CNC Super-Multiplier, that is, the number of times the quantum of investment in new projects on account of this factor would increase in relation to the incremental corporate reserves can be worked out as follows:

The Super-Multiplier would be equal to the *product* of the fraction of Incremental reserves utilized as Nucleus capital or promoter's contribution, the reciprocal of the percentage of Promoter's Contribution to Equity Capital of new projects, and the sum of Debt–Equity Ratio plus One (Equity part).

Assuming:

I   = Addition to Private Investment (taken as Outlay on New Projects) over a period of time, arising out of nucleus capital from Accretion to Reserves.

Ct   = Reduction in Corporate Taxes on Lowering of Corporate Tax Rate.

R   = Corresponding Increase in Corporate Reserves (including Balance carried forward on Profit and Loss Account).

M   = Corporate Nucleus Capital Super-Multiplier.

f(R) = Fraction of Accretion to Reserves on Reduction in Tax Rate, utilized as nucleus capital or promoter's contribution for New Projects or Expansion of existing projects.

Nc   = Percentage of Nucleus Capital or Promoter's Contribution to Equity Capital of New Projects.

DEr = Debt–Equity Ratio according to Norms of Financial Institutions.

The formulae for calculating the CNC Multiplier and Addition to Investment are:

$$M = 1 \times f(R) \times \frac{100}{Nc} \times (DEr + 1)$$

$$I = Ct \times f(R) \times \frac{100}{Nc} \times (DEr + 1).$$

Assuming further:

1. Reduction in Corporate Taxes at Rs 100 crores on reduction in corporate tax rate; (2) Utilization of Reserves as Nucleus Capital at 75 per cent; (3) Promoter's Contribution at 40 per cent; and (4) Debt–Equity Ratio at 2:1, we arrive at the values of the CNC Multiplier and Investment as follows:

$$M = 1 \times f(R) \times \frac{100}{Nc} \times (DEr + 1)$$

$$= \frac{75}{100} \times \frac{100}{40} \times (2 + 1)$$

$$= 5.625.$$

$$I = Ct \times f(R) \times \frac{100}{Nc} \times (DEr + 1)$$

$$= 100 \times \frac{75}{100} \times \frac{100}{40} \times (2 + 1)$$

$$= Rs\,562.50 \text{ crores.}$$

In the case of capital-intensive industries such as cement, fertilizers and petrochemicals, the Debt–Equity Ratio may be 4:1, in which case the Super-Multiplier is considerably higher, as also Addition to Investment. Taking tax relief Ct = Rs 100 crores, we have:

$$M = 1 \times f(R) \times \frac{100}{Nc} \times (DEr + 1)$$

$$= 1 \times \frac{75}{100} \times \frac{100}{40} \times (4 + 1)$$

$$= 9.375.$$

$$I = Ct \times f(R) \times \frac{100}{Nc} \times (DEr + 1)$$

$$= 100 \times \frac{75}{100} \times \frac{100}{40} \times (4 + 1)$$

$$= Rs\,937.50 \text{ crores.}$$

We made an initial assumption that the quantum of reduction in corporate tax is equal to accretion to reserves, on the basis that accretion to profits would not be distributed as dividends. An analysis of financing of companies financed by the ICICI for the year 1985–6 shows that retained profits as percentage of profits after tax amounted to 69.4 per cent in 1986–7 and dividends amounted to 30.6 per cent of profits after tax. These figures are largely representative and the ratio of profits transferred to reserves and distributed as dividends is often in the vicinity of 70:30, although there can be no hard and fast rule. It would appear that with a reduction in taxes, if the post-tax profit increases, dividends may be increased, but the general experience is that a hike in dividends in response to lower taxes is less than the proportion of reduction.

Undistributed Profits Tax Rebate[3]

We would suggest that in order to maximize the incremental savings ratio in the corporate sector, a tax rebate of 20 per cent of the amount of transfer to reserves (undistributed profits) should be given. This would be an added incentive to managements to restrain distribution of dividends and to plough back profits as much as possible. Taking the corporate tax at 50 per cent and undistributed profits at 70 per cent of post-tax profits, the undistributed profits rebate would come to 7 per cent. In other words, the overall rate of effective taxation would then be 43 per cent instead of 50 per cent.

We are of the opinion that if an Undistributed profits rebate is provided, there would be an inbuilt automatic check on dividends, and the entire amount of reduction in tax may be ploughed back. However, it may be pointed out that in spite of an undistributed profits rebate, if part of the increase in profits due to reduction in corporate tax is used for increasing dividends, the formulae for calculating the CNC Super-Multiplier and Addition to Investment would be as follows:

$$M = f(1) \times f(R) \times \frac{100}{Nc} \times (DEr + 1),$$

$$I = f(Ct) \times f(R) \times \frac{100}{Nc} \times (DEr + 1),$$

where $f(Ct)$ represents the fraction of tax relief (post-tax profits) transferred to Reserves, that is, 'Accretion to Reserves'. *Note*: $(1-f(Ct))$ would be the fraction of post-tax profits distributed as dividends out of tax relief.

Assuming that Tax reduction is Rs 100 crores; 30 per cent of Incremental Reserves are distributed as Dividend; 70 per cent of Incremental post-tax profits are transferred to Reserves; 75 per cent of Incremental Reserves are utilized for providing Nucleus capital; 40 per cent is the Promoter's contribution; and 2:1 is Debt–Equity Ratio, we have:

$$M = \frac{7}{10} \times \frac{75}{100} \times \frac{100}{40} \times (2 + 1)$$

$$= 3.94,$$

$$I = \frac{100 \times 7}{10} \times \frac{75}{100} \times \frac{100}{40} \times (2 + 1)$$

$$= Rs\,393.75 \text{ crores.}$$

In the case of capital-intensive industries, with debt–equity ratio at 4:1, the Super-Multiplier and Addition to Investment would work out as follows:

$$M = \frac{7}{10} \times \frac{75}{100} \times \frac{100}{40} \times (4 + 1)$$

$$= 6.56,$$

$$I = \frac{100 \times 7}{10} \times \frac{75}{100} \times \frac{100}{40} \times (4 + 1)$$

$$= Rs\,656.25 \text{ crores.}$$

In developing the Theory of the CNC Super-Multiplier, we have isolated the Accretion to reserves on account of reduction in corporate taxes from: (a) the general pool of funds in a company existing on account of capital, reserves and borrowings, and

(b) addition to corporate funds on account of normal profits after tax and depreciation during the year. This is necessary to emphasize the effect of a cut in corporate taxation in increasing the quantum of investment in the economy to the extent of a number of times the actual tax cut. Actually, this relationship between corporate tax cuts and addition to investment is expressed by the CNC Super-Multiplier. The utility of the CNC Super-Multiplier may now be indicated:

1. The Super-Multiplier indicates the number of times addition to investment takes place in response to a reduction in corporate taxes by government. Thus, the super-multiplier constitutes an instrument in fiscal policy which is useful, (a) for assessing the effect of corporate tax reduction on additional investment, and (b) for promoting investment through corporate tax cuts.

2. Two of the determinants of the Super-Multiplier are the percentage of promoter's contribution to equity capital and debt–equity ratio. A reduction in the promoter's contribution to equity capital would substantially increase the value of the CNC Super-Multiplier and the quantum of addition to investment.

Increase in the debt–equity ratio also increases the Super-Multiplier and the addition to investment. The debt–equity ratio is much higher in Japan, and this contributed substantially to stepping up industrial growth and the rate of increase in GDP. In India and other developing countries also, the debt–equity ratio should be increased, and this may be combined with more intensive monitoring by Financial Institutions. As we have already seen earlier, the value of the CNC Super-Multiplier is higher at 6.56 in the case of capital-intensive industries, in whose case the institutional norm for debt–equity ratio is 4:1 as compared to 3.94 in the case of other industries with debt–equity ratio of 2:1.

3. The Theory of CNC Super-Multiplier has highlighted the need to provide undistributed profits tax rebate to companies. With a small sacrifice in revenue, this measure could ensure the maximization of the incremental-savings ratio in the corporate sector. It would provide a powerful instrument to induce corporations to plough back resources and restrict distribution of dividends.

We have referred to the need to provide tax rebate on undistributed profits of corporations. In West Germany and Japan corporate tax rebate is provided in respect of amounts distributed as dividends. This induces increase in dividend distribution to the maximum. While this may be justified in the case of developed economies, the postulates of growth for developing countries are different. Capital accumulation is of prime importance. The Undistributed profits tax rebate would provide an incentive to managements to plough back the greater part of their profits, while maintaining dividends at a reasonable rate, ensuring maximization of the incremental savings ratio in the corporate sector. An objection may be that high dividends contribute to an increase in share prices and facilitate raising share capital, and should not be discouraged. But an analysis of yields on share markets in India today shows that dividend yield on blue chip shares is between 2 to 4 per cent. This bears evidence that it is not dividends which determine share prices, but prospects of bonus issues and right shares in good companies. Of course, a certain level of dividends is expected to be maintained. The undistributed profits tax rebate would only provide a tool for inducing managements to refrain from excessive dividend distribution and frittering away corporate tax relief.

ADDITIONAL EXCISE REVENUE AND ACCELERATED INVESTMENT

We have seen that reduction in corporate tax results in an increase in overall investment in the economy by 3.94 times such relief, but this is not the end of the story. New projects go on stream within about two to three years. In the private sector, the ratio of sales to capital employed is generally about 1.5:1. Thus, if investment in new enterprises increased by about Rs 400 crores, sales would amount to Rs 600 crores, say in the third year. Taking Excise duty at 20 per cent, government would obtain additional Excise duty of about Rs 120 crores per annum from these concerns, besides other taxes. Further, the overall receipts of the companies to the extent of about Rs 600 crores would be distributed among the various factors of production. These amounts would provide further demand for wage-goods and other consumer products, depending upon the marginal propensity to consume, emanating from the recipients of incomes. With a satisfactory investment climate and adequate inducement to invest (and other relevant factors), consumer goods, as also other industries, would be stimulated. Provided unemployed resources are available, accelerated investment would take place in various sectors of the economy.

REFERENCES

1. J. M. Keynes, *The General Theory of Employment, Interest and Money*, Macmillan & Co., London, 1947, p. 75.
2. ICICI (Industrial Credit and Investment Corporation of India), *Financial Performance of Companies, ICICI Portfolio 1986–87*, Table 7, p. 11.
3. *Vide* Ch. 16.

21

Equity and Growth: Synthesis of Approaches to Eighth Plan Necessary

Composed as the Planning Commission was, *inter alia*, of eminent social scientists and Gandhian economists, their overwhelming concern for poverty alleviation through increased employment and welfare, rural development, and decentralization was understandable. The Commission proposed in the new Approach Paper to the Eighth Five Year Plan (1990–5)[1] the adoption of a new employment-based growth model, rejecting the traditional model of growth, so as to correct the 'aberrations of lopsided development in the economy'. It appeared that the Commission's basic approach was to rely on a trade-off between employment and growth. Actually, the need was for a synthesis of the two approaches, and for more challenging growth targets—which were attainable—even while recognizing the validity of the Commission's basic objectives.

The reconstituted Planning Commission was of the view that increase in employment during the eighties has not been commensurate with the accelerated growth, and that the Eighth Plan should radically alter the direction of public spending, investment, and choice of techniques, thereby launching a frontal attack on unemployment and poverty. It rejected the 'trickle-down model of growth' involving centralized planning and the need for rapid growth of capital goods industries, in which the poor had to wait for long periods for the benefits of growth to percolate to them.

GROWTH PATTERN

The Commission was critical of past economic policies in regard to a growth pattern that ignored growing unemployment, inadequate support to the small-scale industrial sector, rising levels of internal and external borrowings and imbalances, and uncontrolled imports, and encouragement to a consumption pattern that catered to the urban rich, while the per capita availability of mass consumption goods and essential commodities remained stagnant. In its revised Approach Paper, the Commission focused on decentralization, guaranteed employment, revitalization of local bodies, rural development, and area planning. It proposed to give priority to accelerating agricultural growth, stimulating agro-processing industries, and restructuring the industrial policy framework to provide for harmonious development of cottage and small-scale industries with medium-sized and large-scale units. It stated that the thrust would be on employment and not growth *per se*.

Stressing that the average annual rate of growth during the eighties was 5.3 per cent, the Approach Paper suggested 5.5 per cent as the targeted annual growth rate. The savings rate would be increased to 22 per cent from 20.3 per cent, external resource inflow would be 1.5 per cent of GDP, and export growth in volume terms 12 per cent every year. It emphasized that growth in employment would be targeted at 3 per cent per annum to create on an average an additional ten million jobs annually for the next five years. Other quantitative targets regarding incremental capital–output ratio, overall size of the Plan, public sector investment, and various sectoral targets, however, were conspicuous by their absence. Besides, there was lack of consistency in the targets that had been indicated. While targeting for 5.5 per cent growth rate, the Approach Paper was seeking to increase employment elasticity from 0.36 to about 0.55, that is by 0.19, which was almost a 50 per cent increase. It also envisaged the investment of plan funds of about 50 per cent to employment generation, rural development, and welfare. It is doubtful if employment could be increased by 3 per cent per annum as envisaged by the Planning Commission with a 5.5 per cent growth rate; besides, the proposed pattern of allocation of resources would lead to erosion of public sector investment in the core sector and sunrise industries, large-scale power and other infrastructural projects, and other necessary develomental expenditure. Succinctly, it would distort investment priorities, and adversely affect orderly development.

INFLATIONARY IMPLICATIONS

Besides, the danger of inflation loomed large. Despite good

agricultural and industrial production during the last two years, the annual rate of inflation, which was 10.6 per cent during the drought year 1987–8 and had come down to 5.7 per cent in 1988–9, remained high, signifying the existence of latent inflationary forces in the economy. The Wholesale Price Index increased by about 10 per cent on a point to point basis in December 1990. The seasonal decline in prices that usually manifests itself, commencing from September, was delayed. According to an assessment by the *Economist*, London, inflation may rise to 10 to 12 per cent during 1990–1, and even higher if serious security problems arise. Essentially, this was attributable to an average growth of money supply of above 17 per cent[2] during the last two years as against the safe limit of 14 per cent suggested by the Chakravarty Committee. The paper was critical of the extraordinary inversion of real economic priorities, in that recurrent budget deficits were beeing financed by capital budget surpluses.

The White Paper on the Economy stated that while higher production may help in checking supply side pressures on prices, the general pressures of inflation are attributable to the imbalance between aggregate demand and supply, and the overhang of liquidity from earlier years. The Budget deficit for 1989–90, worked out to Rs 11,750 crores and net RBI credit to the Central Government till 17 November 1989 that year amounted to Rs 12,403 crores. Money supply to that date rose by about 12 per cent as against 10.7 per cent, and currency with the public increased by 12.6 per cent as against 8.9 per cent in the corresponding period of 1988–9. The growth in money supply during 1989–90 was estimated at 19.9 per cent.

The pattern of resource allocation proposed by the Planning Commission had inflationary implications. The expenditure on generation of employment, rural development, and welfare on a massive scale would generate considerable purchasing power in the hands of the people with high propensity to consume, while corresponding increases in supply of goods and services on the requisite scale to balance such demand would not be available. It would lead to double digit inflation. Government, however, was making a Herculean effort to control administrative and other expenditure and reduce budgetary deficits and public sector borrowings. All investment and outlays, including expenditure for stimulating employment, must be productivity oriented. Production of mass consumption wage goods on a massive scale would no doubt assist in checking inflation. Basically, however, the imbalance between aggregate demand and aggregate supply needed to be corrected and increase in money supply (M3) and RBI credits to government restricted, if inflation was to be controlled.

Dr I. G. Patel[3] was critical of the tendency in some quarters in India to denigrate the importance of economic growth. An increase in the average growth rate from 3.5 per cent which prevailed for nearly three decades, to 5 per cent or more was a creditable achievement. With population growth of 2 per cent, this doubled the rate of growth of per capita incomes from 1.5 per cent to 3 per cent. This would reduce the period for doubling per capita incomes by half from some 48 years to 24 years. Conservatively, if the rate of growth is 5.5 per cent during the next decade, it would be modest in comparison to the increase in the growth rate during 1980–7 achieved by a number of countries, including China (10.4 per cent), Korea (18.6 per cent), Pakistan (6.6 per cent), Egypt (6.3 per cent), Thailand (5.6 per cent), Hong Kong (5.8 per cent), and Oman (12.7 per cent).

Decrying the aversion to the so-called 'trickle-down theory', Dr Patel observed, 'A degree of equality as well as a measure of inequality are inherent in a process of steady and significant growth. But a higher growth rate at least provides the means for alleviating extreme poverty; and here too the majesty of the compound rate of growth provides the only binding redress over time.' The pattern of investment may be changed, but if those who have benefited from growth cannot be adequately taxed, the situation cannot be remedied by 'railing against trickle down metaphors or against luxury production', or by redirecting investment where it has low or no productivity. Improvement in the standards of living of the poor could be effected by giving them land or capital and training them to employ them productively. Technological upgradation and product improvement are necessary both for the poor farmer and the handloom weaver. Simply proliferating employment-generation schemes without any return on investment will not alleviate poverty, only prepetuate it.

MORE CHALLENGING GROWTH TARGETS NEEDED

The Planning Commission, in attempting to move away from 'growthmanship', committed some crucial mistakes and the chances of success with this model of development are slim. The broad growth figures indicated seemed deliberately modest, projecting economic deceleration and stagnant saving ratios. Any planning exercise that does not project more challenging targets than those that have already been achieved by the economy become questionable. Besides, the Planning Commission's strategy of development postulated the existence of representative and effective local bodies. These did not in actuality exist in many areas. It would in all probability take about twelve to eighteen months to build up the infrastructure of local bodies, which would delay the implementation of the Plan.

Indeed, an economic model of development directed at employment and welfare creation by itself has little chance of success. That these objectives need to be given special importance in Plan formulation and the pattern of allocation needs to be modified is true, but without substantial growth in national income, neither adequate welfare measures nor transfer payments are feasible. Accelerated growth of the modern large-scale industrial sector is necessary to generate revenues which would finance such programmes on the scale envisaged. If there was sizeable diversion of funds to the rural sector, development of industry and infrastructure, as also revenues, would suffer, and it would be difficult to sustain the programmes in subsequent years. Besides, what is of greater relevance for the purpose of rural development and increase in employment is proper utilization of funds allocated for these purposes, rather than a significant diversion of scarce economic resources from other development purposes. A suitable machinery needs to be evolved to effectively monitor such expenditure at the district level, so that money substantially reaches the target groups and maximum benefits are derived in terms of employment and welfare.

Employment-generation schemes, unrelated to productivity and return on capital employed, could hardly solve the employment problem or alleviate poverty. *The two approaches need to be synthesized*, and while targeting for a higher growth rate, the pattern of resource allocation should be so constituted as to promote rapid industrial and agricultural development, as also production of mass consumption goods, employment-generation and welfare schemes, and labour intensive small- and medium-scale industries (as ancillaries to large-scale units and utilizing modern technology).

Recognizing the limitations of the trickle-down theory, M. Nara-simham,[4] former RBI governor, called for direct affirmative action towards poverty alleviation and provision of gainful, productive employment. To translate growth into improved material well-being for the people, there was need to redesign investment priorities towards the production of goods and services that would ensure basic human well-being and restructure the framework of 'policies of planning, investment and management of the economy'. However, such redirection of investment and expansion of public expenditure towards these ends postulates an expanding resource base which only a vigorously growing economy can provide. Both equity and growth are necessary. 'The quantum of growth needs to be expanded, even as its content needs to be improved.'

During the first four years of the Seventh Five Year Plan, the Indian economy expanded by about 5.9 per cent per annum. The rate of growth during 1988–9, following the drought year 1987–8, was spectacular at 10.6 per cent. Agricultural production recorded an increase of 20.8 per cent, while industrial production rose by 8.8 per cent. Infrastructure (power) increased by 9.5 per cent, and exports surged ahead by 28.9 per cent. Industrial production, which had slackened during the first half of 1989–90, picked up the tempo of growth during the last quarter of the year. In the agricultural sector, food production amounted to 166 million tonnes in 1988–9, working out to an increase of 20.3 per cent over the previous year's production of 130 million tonnes. Cotton and oilseeds production increased by 23 per cent and 30 per cent respectively. All these items had a weightage of 82.1 per cent in the index of agricultural production. Food production during 1989–90, the terminal year of the Plan, targeted at 175 million tonnes, amounted to a record 170.6 million tonnes. The services sector was estimated to have grown by about 8 per cent during 1988–9.

The Indian economy built up a remarkable momentum of growth during the periods of the Sixth and Seventh Plans; the need of the hour is to take maximum advantage of such momentum and to accelerate it. 'There is a tide in the affairs of men: Which, taken at the flood, leads on to fortune.' So it is with nations. The economy at this juncture is at the cross-roads. If the momentum of growth can be accelerated, there will be an upsurge in national income, production and revenues, and with all-round expansion, the economy could progress towards, if not transcend, the stage of self-sustaining growth. The targets, while formulating plans, should always be challenging, and efforts should be directed at stimulating growth beyond what has been achieved. If that is not done, the economy may lose the momentum that has been built up, and a fine opportunity for vigorous development may be lost.

It appears that with the existing parameters, and the sound structural framework of policies and the state of the economy, it is possible to plan for a cumulative annual growth rate of 6 per cent for the Eight Plan. The World Bank,[5] in its *Annual Report 1989* also stated,

Given the acceleration of economic growth, it will be possible for the government to aim at a 6 per cent growth target for the eighth-plan period (1991–95). However, tighter control of domestic demand, especially more stringent fiscal management, will be necessary to avert inflationary pressures that can jeopardize achievement of growth targets. Also crucial will be the continuation of the steady progress in industrial and trade reforms.

The ICOR could be brought down to around 4:1 with higher utilization of installed capacity and effective use of resources through improved monitoring of plan and non-plan expenditure; savings raised to about 23 per cent from 21 per cent in 1988–9; and foreign aid plus *inflow of foreign investment capital* taken to 2.5 to 3 per cent, aggregating 25 to 26 per cent investment. According to the *RBI Annual Report for 1988–89*, the ratio of net resource inflow from abroad to GDP increased to about 2.9 per cent in 1988–9, resulting in aggregate gross investment in the economy of 23.9 per cent.

Considering the widespread criticism of the new Planning Commission's Approach Paper and its deficiencies, the portents were that crucial targets, parameters, and figures would have to be indicated to render it acceptable to government and people. The Planning Commission may vary the pattern of public investment in order to subserve the priorities it had listed, but it is imperative that it adopts a dynamic and progressive approach, and provides for a framework of policies which are conducive to the stimulation of inflow of foreign equity investment with modern technology in chosen fields—for which there is tremendous scope—and allocates a larger role and greater developmental responsibility to the private sector, which has great potential for stepping up the quantum of investment and·industrial expansion. The Commission should raise its sights and formulate a plan which not only stimulates employment, rural development, and welfare, but is also bold and challenging, targeting for adequate growth, consistent with past achievements, current strengths and resources, and future potential.

REFERENCES

1. Planning Commission, *Approach Paper to Eighth Five Year Plan 1990–91*.
2. *Vide* Table Ch. 2.
3. Dr I. G. Patel, 'IDBI Silver Jubilee Commemoration Lecture 1990', delivered at Bombay on 20 April 1990, *Economic Times*, Calcutta, 25 and 26 April 1990.
4. M. Narasimham, Presidential Address at IDBI Seminar on 1 May 1990, *Financial Express*, 16 May 1990.
5. World Bank, *Annual Report 1989*, Washington, p. 118.

22

Policy Liberalization 1991—An Overview

Cataclysmic changes, like revolutions, be they economic or political, did not originate in a vacuum; over a period of years a complex set of factors and circumstances created the climate and environment conducive to them, while some immediate compulsions triggered the events. The entire gamut of trade reforms, industrial policy changes, and fiscal measures pronounced by the Finance Minister in July 1991 constituted an economic revolution of sorts that could lead to transition from a command economy to a market economy, and change the tone and tenor of industrial and economic development in the country. The package of economic reforms were necessitated by the imperatives of the crisis arising out of the Gulf War, a serious foreign exchange crunch, and compulsions of macroeconomic adjustments considered appropriate to defuse the crisis and facilitate IMF loans, short-term and long-term. But in actuality, enhanced liberalization of the framework of economic policies, entry of the private sector in state reserved sectors and reduction in the state's interventionist role and functions, and the need to create an environment largely in consonance with a global economic climate that would stimulate the exchange of goods, technology, and capital had become almost inevitable.

The Finance Minister initiated bold and historic steps to dismantle at one stroke a vast complex network of controls, including part of MRTP legislation, institute a framework of policies designed to encourage the inflow of foreign investment capital with sophisticated technology, and adopt market-oriented strategies for fostering free markets and stimulating foreign trade—policies which led senior industrialist JRD Tata to remark 'Let the world now say: "A new tiger has emerged in Asia—a tiger uncaged" '.[1] The Finance Minister had indeed brought about what amounted to a revolutionary change.

The international climate has also changed, and the portents are that in the decade of the nineties, economic progress in the world will accelerate, not only in the Western World and Eastern Europe, but also in developing countries. The rapid decline of communism, disintegration of the economic system in many countries that had adopted in a greater or lesser degree the Soviet model of a command economy, and the failure of centralized planning to deliver, brought about a surge of disillusionment and in its wake a turnaround in favour of a 'market-friendly' approach and reduced state intervention. *The World Development Report 1991*, after distilling the lessons of four decades of developmental experience the world over, felt that speedy development called for a reappraisal of the roles of the state and the market. The functioning and operations of government should be confined to areas in which markets did not work; it should reduce its presence to the minimum in areas in which markets did or could operate. Economic growth postulates more productive use of economic assets and better quality of investment—which matters more than the quantity; and both in industry and agriculture, the most appopriate investment decisions flow from entrepreneurs competing with each other and facing international competition. Government intervention should be limited to providing an environment that stimulates productivity. The price mechanism should be allowed to operate freely so that prices reflect scarcities and channelize resources to areas which are most productive. The World Bank's experience of investment projects in developing economies confirms that market incentives work, and the rate of return from projects is higher if policies do not distort prices. The economy should be open to international trade so that competition, both domestic and from the outside world, spurs efficient operation, innovation, and inflow of modern technology which, together with foreign investment capital, is the engine of growth. Japan, South Korea, Singapore, and even the USA and European countries obtained global competitive advantage through competition. The state too has a positive role; it must provide adequate infrastructure, not only power, communications, irrigation, and the like, but also law and order and an adequate institutional framework, and it must invest in human resources by

providing education and medical facilities. These latter investments are not only socially most useful, but also stimulate
economic growth and productivity through increased skills and
ability to imbibe new technology, and also contribute to reduced
fertility.

Above all, the state must finance public expenditure without
resort to deficit financing and created money, for the latter fuels
inflation, which is counter-productive both in regard to constricting efficient investment and growth, and in exacerbating
social misery and privation. Macroeconomic stability and microeconomic efficiency are linked, and governments could achieve
both these goals by 'reappraising their spending priorities, implementing tax reform, reforming the financial sector, privatizing
state-owned enterprises, and using charges to recover the cost of
some state-provided services'.[2]

With such clear signals emanating from both the international
environment and aid-dispensing institutions, few governments—
particularly in the free world—can remain insulated from these
trends. The framework of policies formulated by the Finance
Minister are in consonance with such trends. The Government
has not just accepted and followed IMF conditionalities; only such
parts of the IMF prescription, which were perceived to be in
the national interest and conducive to a resolution of the critical
problems facing the economy were accepted and adopted.

The Reserve Bank, in order to achieve macroeconomic stabilization and structural adjustment, in the context of the post Gulf-War
crisis, sharply devalued the rupee in two instalments in July 1991
by 18 to 19 per cent against major currencies. The objective was:
'promoting competitiveness of our exports, reducing inessential
imports, minimizing incentives for capital flight, stabilizing the
capital account, and generally restoring viability of country's
balance of payments position'.[3] Devaluation had become necessary
because exports and invisible earnings had slowed down and the
foreign exchange reserves had declined to a low level of US $1.3
billion in July 1991. Besides, some of India's competitors during
the eighties had depreciated their currencies sizeably: China 68 per
cent and Indonesia 65 per cent, while India had reduced the value
of the rupee by only 53 per cent, even though taking price levels
into account, inflation in China and Indonesia was lower at 100 per
cent and 111 per cent respectively as compared to 114 per cent in

India. As C. Rangarajan noted,[4] 'taking all these factors into account, the depreciation of the rupee value by 18–19 per cent seems appropriate'. It has been estimated that the real effective exchange rate (REER) was an important factor in regard to export growth and for one percentage point depreciation of the REER, export volume would increase by 0.66 of one per cent; and the price-sensitivity of manufactured goods—which constituted 70 per cent of Indian exports—was even greater. The price elasticity of demand for imports was also high, although a part of the imports—defence supplies, oil, fertilizers and other bulk goods—necessarily had to be made irrespective of the level of prices. An RBI study showed that price elasticity for machinery, transport equipment, and manufactured goods, which accounted for about 50 per cent of imports, was more than unity. Besides, invisibles were also responsive to exchange rate adjustment, and devaluation should contribute to an increase in their inflow.

India's foreign indebtedness exceeded $71 billion. Government was keen to ensure that it did not default in meeting its short-term obligations of about $6.5 billion and servicing of $10 billion deposits due to NRIs. The seriousness of its intent was reflected in its leasing gold to the Bank of England as a bridging measure, in the event of delay in IMF loan sanction and disbursement, so that loans could be obtained from the former against such gold deposit to meet its obligations. Government sought to stimulate inflow of foreign capital and technology and to make the rupee freely convertible within five years. The various measures taken and IMF assistance should increase the country's credit rating and also improve the scope for short-term commercial borrowings.

Two options, according to Bimal Jalan,[5] were available to countries: 'shock treatment' in the form of once and for all large-scale changes in policy or piece-meal, gradual change. If the disequilibrium was large and persistent, shock treatment might be necessary, even though it may involve high costs in terms of institutional, structural and policy changes, and severe hardship to the people. It would also necessitate large inflows of foreign aid which might not be available. In India's case, the balance of payments disequilibrium has normally been about 1 to 1.5 per cent of GDP; and stimulated exports and invisibles, together with a higher level of inflow of foreign investment capital, should enable the country to achieve viability, provided emphasis is placed upon export-oriented production, necessary structural and administrative changes in the economy are effected, and the policy framework suitably modified.

ABOLITION OF INDUSTRIAL LICENSING

Government initiated drastic changes in its industrial licensing and foreign investment policies as a part of a wider programme of macroeconomic adjustment and fiscal reforms, so that the 'key sectors of our economy are enabled to attain an adequate technological and competitive edge in a fast changing global economy'.[6] The New Industrial Policy 1991 stated that industrial licensing would be abolished for all industries except 18 strategic ones, irrespective of levels of investment. Automatic clearance for projects requiring imported capital goods would be available from April 1992, where the foreign exchange component had been covered by foreign equity; or the value of such goods was lower than 25 per cent of the total cost of plant and machinery or rupees two crores. These limits however are inadequate and need to be relaxed. Projects involving release of foreign exchange of a larger magnitude for capital goods would require sanction from SIA.[7] Other relaxations included blanket provision enabling existing industries to effect substantial expansion; withdrawal of all registration schemes, including those with government (apart from filing a memorandum of information); and abolition of the mandatory convertibility clause in respect of term-loans by financial institutions for new projects. The modifications were commendable, particularly in regard to the substantial expansion and convertibility clause. The latter had inhibited certain companies from initiating schemes for modernization and technological upgradation, and even expansion and diversification, thereby adversely affecting industrial development and competitiveness, particularly in the case of MRTP companies.

FOREIGN INVESTMENT POLICY

The changes in foreign investment regulations are of far-reaching import, and will contribute to making Indian industry more competitive and efficient. Since international competitiveness and technological advancement postulate speedy response to fast-changing external conditions, the new industrial policy goes a long way in removing the shackles that have bound industry and inhibited the inflow of foreign investment capital, joint venture foreign collaborations, and transfer of technology. Automatic approval to direct foreign investment upto 51 per cent of equity in industrial concerns in high priority industries will be available, provided the foreign exchange component of project cost is covered by foreign equity. Remittance of dividends will, however, be monitored by the Reserve Bank to ensure that they are covered by earnings of foreign exchange over a period of time. Foreign technology agreements complying with specified norms are also eligible for automatic permission. Besides, there is to be no discrimination between foreign and indigenous industries in the import of raw materials and intermediate goods, and payment of know-how fees and royalties. Free from pre-determined parameters, a new specially empowered Board will negotiate and secure the inflow of capital and technology, as also entry of large foreign export houses.

The above package marks a radical transformation of government policies and should attract multinational investment in India, and also enable Indian entrepreneurs to import advanced foreign technologies to enhance their international competitiveness. It must however be said that there are other important prerequisites for stimulating inflow of foreign equity investment if India is to attain a level somewhat closer to that of the NIEs of South-East Asia. These include, *inter alia*, political stability and a satisfactory law and order situation, adequate availability of infrastructure, rates of taxation largely in alignment with international levels, and an active capital market. The investment climate in India is healthy and propitious for fresh investment and foreign collaborations, except in certain border states. However, government will need to strive to augment the availability of infrastructure—principally a domain of the public sector—and rationalize tax levels. The capital market is buoyant, while other postulates for development such as supply of skilled labour and technicians, sound institutional framework of law, administration, defence, and economic stability exist in adequate measure. It is true that Eastern Europe, including East Germany and the Soviet Union, may attract Western capital in large measure, and the total international pool of funds is somewhat limited, but even then the portents are that with the existing liberalization, the inflow of foreign investment capital into India is likely to be greatly stimulated.

REFORM OF MRTP LAW

The New Industrial Policy has candidly recognized that with 'the need for achieving economies of scale for ensuring higher productivity and competitive advantage in the international market, the interference of the Government through the MRTP Act in investment decisions of large companies has become deleterious in its effects on Indian industrial growth'.[8] The threshold limits of assets in respect of MRTP companies and dominant undertakings are to be abolished, and it will no longer be necessary for MRTP houses to obtain prior government sanction for investment decisions, establishment of new undertakings, expansion, amalgamation, takeover, and appointment of certain directors. However, certain restrictions will continue. While the concept of dominant undertakings is to be determined on the basis of the market share of the company and not the assets limit, government retains its power to direct severance of the interconnection between dominant undertakings under Section 27 of the Act, if considered necessary in public interest or in the interest of the industry or undertaking. Provisions regarding restrictions on acquisition and transfer of shares by market-dominant undertakings are to be transferred to the Companies Act.

The retention of these clauses of the MRTP Act is hardly consistent with the policy of effective liberalization and freeing the economy of discretionary controls. It may also prove to be the thin end of the wedge and open the way for reimposition in the future of some bureaucratic controls by a government not equally liberal in its outlook. Besides, the implementation of the restrictive trade practices sections of the Act would be given a sharper edge to control and regulate monopolistic restrictions, unfair trade practices, and exploitation of the consumer.

The MRTP law, enacted in June 1970, shackled large industrial houses and decelerated industrial development in the country. While a large number of applications for establishment of new industries and expansion of existing units were rejected, establishment of projects in approved cases was considerably delayed by the time taken in processing applications. Owing to inflationary rise in prices of capital equipment, the MRTP Act also contributed to increased project costs. Certain vital sectors of industry could not be fully developed, nor economies of scale secured, as the requisite sanctions were not forthcoming, while non-MRTP industrial houses were not in a position to garner the requisite capital to set up large-scale capital-intensive industries. The reforms constitute a positive stimulus to industrial development, and the momentum of growth is bound to be accelerated.

PUBLIC SECTOR

The New Industrial Policy document stated that the public sector had established public enterprises in key sectors of the economy, adopting new areas of technology, but had developed certain weaknesses. Recognizing its deficiencies and the low rate of return on overall capital employed, the policy document stated that the portfolio of public sector investments would be reviewed. It was envisaged that the public sector would concentrate on development of strategic, high-tech. and essential infrastructure; and there would be no bar to entry of the private sector on a selective basis. Budgetary support to public enterprises might also be reduced.

Public undertakings which were chronically sick would be referred to the BIFR or a similar institution for formulation of revival schemes. Workers affected by rehabilitation packages would be provided a social security net. An important decision was to privatize part of the shareholding of certain public enterprises. This was expected to yield about rupees 2500 crores. Priority sector undertakings and those generating profits would be strengthened, and autonomy through Memoranda of Understanding would be provided to them. The new policy displayed a degree of realism, but its success postulates successful implementation. Two questions arise: will the government have the political will and clout to privatize a part of the public sector; and will it be able to retrench surplus labour in overstaffed undertakings? The leftist (and even other principal) parties in Parliament are not likely to easily acquiesce to these measures. The resolution of these and other related problems are crucial to the success of the new policy.

DIFFICULTIES IN IMPLEMENTATION

The Finance Minister initiated various steps to restore equilibrium to the current account (BOP) position, and reduce budgetary and fiscal imbalances. While the progress in implementation of trade policy has been adequate, measures to reduce revenue account deficit are not easy to implement. In a regime of liberalization, administrative controls and licences relating to foreign trade were reduced, imports largely linked with exports, decanalization of certain import and export items permitted, and facilities afforded to exporters to open foreign exchange currency accounts. These measures are directed at stimulating exports and increasing competition and initiative. Besides, cash compensatory support (CCS), which cost the government a hefty sum of about rupees 1500 crores a year in the form of subsidy, was abolished. Exporters will be issued Exim scrips to the extent of 30 to 40 per cent of the value of exports, and imports will be permitted against the scrips, which are freely tradeable. The profit on sale will be exempt from income-tax. The linkage of imports with exports conveyed a clear message to industry that it must export and earn foreign exchange if it required it; and this may be made obligatory in times to come if industrial enterprises fail to take the cue. The trade reforms should bring about a transformation from an inward-looking, controlled economy into one conducive to free markets and foreign trade. An end to the regime of import control should reduce red-tape and its attendant evils.

Government sought to reduce the fiscal deficit from 8.6 per cent to 6.5 per cent of GDP, but its options were limited. Efforts are being made to cut government expenditure by 5 per cent in the case of ministries, and Financial Advisors have been asked to identify areas for reduction of outlays. The ministries may face constraints in effecting the proposed cuts, and the degree of success achieved, if past experience is any guide, may be limited.

As regards the proposed reduction in fertilizer subsidy and the concurrent increase in fertilizer prices, the reduction had to be diluted in the face of pressure from farmers' lobbies. The States were recalcitrant in implementing the scheme whereby richer farmers were to pay discriminatory higher prices while the marginal farmer was subsidized. Besides, procurement prices of foodgrains had to be increased, adding to the momentum of inflationary forces in the economy. Reduction in food subsidies seemed a remote possibility. Defence expenditure in real terms was stated to have been marginally reduced, but in view of border hostilities, the scope for sizeable cuts appeared to be limited. As regards interest charges, borrowings could be minimized and money used more productively in the future, so that the interest burden does not rise inordinately. Augmenting revenues to reduce current budgetary deficits is a multi-dimensional problem, presenting various difficulties discussed in earlier chapters. It may, however, be emphasized that efforts to raise the ratio of direct taxes to indirect taxes will not provide the solution in the context of a fiscal structure where a small proportion of the population bears the bulk of direct taxes. The feasibility of taxing agricultural incomes is remote because of political factors, and evasion is rampant partly due to high tax levels and administrative constraints.

Even at the cost of some repetition, it needs to be emphasized that besides cutting wasteful expenditure and outlays, it is necessary to enforce strict simultaneous monitoring to ensure that funds are utilized effectively, leakages are obviated, and moneys reach the target groups. Reduction in PSBR is a necessary concomitant of any exercise to cut fiscal deficit and this postulates rationalization of expenditure and plan outlays, and efficient implementation, return flow of funds to the budget from public enterprises through generation of surpluses, and efforts by all echelons of government to achieve economy and efficiency in expenditure.

Unfortunate though it is, the linkage between devaluation and inflation is bi-directional. Inflation often constitutes one of the principal factors necessitating devaluation. On the other hand, devaluation reinforces inflation by increasing the costs of imports, with a cost–push effect, while a larger quantum of exports reduces the availability of goods for domestic consumption, leading to higher prices. Inflation, currently running at about 15.6 per cent, has partially neutralized the effect of 18 per cent devaluation, and the competitive edge of the latter had been somewhat blunted, giving rise to doubts whether there could be another round of devaluation. The RBI, however, categorically denied the possibility. But control of inflation has become imperative if the liberalization package is to be successfully implemented—and at minimum of cost in terms of human suffering.

The liberalization package also needs to be extended to effecting a dimensional change in labour policies and devising a suitable exit policy for sick industries. Wages should be linked to productivity. Multiple trade unions in industry, and political leadership from outside, should be eschewed if industry is to run smoothly, production maximized and industrial sickness minimized. Government has not crystallized thinking on the right of employers to close down sick industrial units, and payment of compensation to labour. A national renewal fund, however, was proposed to be set up for rehabilitation of retrenched workers.

The dismantling of controls and various liberalization measures contributed to almost euphoric conditions, which were reflected in an inordinate rise in share prices on the stock exchange. These measures overshadowed the burden imposed on the corporate sector, in that corporate tax liability had been substantially increased by a direct hike in the tax rate by 5 per cent and reduction in allowance for depreciation from 33 to 25 per cent. Working capital costs had been sizeably enhanced by an almost unbridled increase in interest rates by banks. The costs of establishing new industrial projects and initiating programmes of modernization and upgradation of technology had considerably escalated as a result of the higher cost of imported machinery after devaluation; high interest rates ranging between 18 to 20 per cent charged by financial insitutions on term-loans; 25 to 40 per cent premium on REP licences; steep rise in prices of petroleum and oil products, and the consequential effect upon prices of industrial raw materials and intermediate goods; and the cost–push effect of increase in administered prices of coal, power, and steel, and higher price of cement.

The expectation was that as a countervailing measure to devaluation, import duty on capital goods would be sizeably reduced, but the cut was only marginal from 85 to 80 per cent. The extent of the burden could be gauged from the fact that the price of machinery originally worth rupees ten crores increased due to devaluation to rupees 11.8 crores, and duty at 80 per cent escalated it to rupees 21.2 crores (as compared to rupees 18.5 crores prior to devaluation). Thus, machinery costing rupees ten crores to foreign industry abroad will entail an outlay of rupees 21.2 crores to Indian industry, reducing the latter's competitive capacity in foreign markets.

The Finance Minister's proposals to this extent are not growth-oriented, although there are certain mitigating factors: the liberalization and dismantling of controls and stimulated flow of equity investment capital with sophisticated technology should boost overall industrial growth; and the Finance Minister recognized that 'the rates and structure of corporation taxation have to be consistent with the needs of an economy aiming to become internationally competitive,'[9] which engenders the hope that tax rates in the near future will be brought to levels prevailing internationally. NRIs have been permitted to establish ventures in infrastructure, housing, and real estate on a non-repatriable basis; and they are to be afforded facilities to establish new industries, although destabilization of the management structure of existing industries will not be allowed.

The corporate sector appears to have taken these factors in its stride, and there is hardly any deceleration in corporate activity for expansion and diversification. We would emphasize that Indian industry has acquired such strength, resilience, and momentum that despite all difficulties and vicissitudes, it will continue to expand, modernize, and progress. Its rate of growth in real terms during the five years of the Seventh Plan period has ranged between 7.5 per cent and 9.1 per cent; it was 8.6 per cent in 1989–90 and 8.4 per cent in 1990–1. However, 1991–2 has witnessed a setback in industrial production, and recession in certain sectors of industry. This has occurred principally due to excessive tightening of monetary and credit policies, and high interest rates—designed to check inflation. The future outlook for industrial growth is nevertheless promising, and this is reflected by the bouyancy of the stock markets—a good barometer of business confidence.

REFERENCES

1. J. R. D. Tata, Statement on Industrial Policy in *The Economic Times*, Calcutta, 1 Aug. 1991.
2. *World Development Report 1991*, World Bank/OUP, New York, p.9.
3. Reserve Bank of India, *Annual Report 1990–1*, p. 2.
4. C. Rangarajan, 'Devaluation: Causes and Consequences', in *Economic Times*, Calcutta, 5 Aug. 1991.
5. Bimal Jalan, *India's Economic Crisis: The Way Ahead*, OUP, New Delhi, 1991; *Economic Times*, Calcutta, 18 Aug. 1991.
6. Dr Manmohan Singh, Finance Minister, *Budget Speech 1991–92*, 24 July 1991, GOI, Pt A, Para 9.
7. SIA = Secretariat of Industrial Approvals.
8. *New Industrial Policy 1991*, Ministry of Industry, GOI, 1991, Para 37.
9. Dr Manmohan Singh, *Budget Speech 1991–92*, Pt B., Para 92.

Appendix 1
Galenson and Libenstein's Marginal Per Capita Reinvestment Quotient Criteria*

Galenson and Libenstein argue that allocation of investment resources should be so ordered that 'per capita output, or average income, either over time, or at some time in the future' is maximized. Since capital is the principal determinant of growth and output per capita, and the objective is to maximize output per head at some future time, investible surplus should be maximized in the present, and investible resources should be so allocated as to provide each worker in the future with the maximum possible capital per head. This implies that capital-intensive projects, which minimize the use of labour and the wage-bill, should be given a much larger allocation. Inevitably, in such an economic model, the present level of output and employment would suffer, while greater quantum of investment would be available for stimulating production and output per head in the future. Galenson and Libenstein have christened this principle of allocation marginal per capita reinvestment quotient criterion (MPCRQ), and the goal is to secure allocation of investment resources in such a way that from each productive unit or use, the MPCRQ is equalized.

The magnitude of MPCRQ would depend upon certain factors:† the direction of reinvestment and allocation of resources; the gross productivity per worker and the per capita consumption of wage goods; decline in fertility and mortality rates; increase in efficiency of workers unrelated to the use of capital; and the replacement and maintenance of machinery and productive apparatus in which capital is invested.

The MPCRQ could be expressed in the form of a formula. Taking p as net value added *output* from investment;

   e   as number of workers attached to the investment;

   w as real wage;

   k   as cost of investment; and

   r   as the growth rate; we have

---

* *Vide* Ch. 6.

† *Vide* A. P. Jhirlwell, *Growth and Development*, ELBS, Macmillan, London, 1986, pp. 197, 198.

$$r = \frac{p - ew}{k}$$

$$r = \frac{(p)}{(k)} \cdot \frac{(p - ew)}{(p)}$$

$$r = \frac{(p)}{(k)} \cdot \left(1 - \frac{ew}{p}\right).$$

Assuming that the entire amount of the wage-bill is consumed by the workers, and all the profits are reinvested, the growth formula is equivalent to the reinvestment formula, s representing savings ratio and c denoting ICOR.

Now $s = \dfrac{(p - ew)}{p}$ and $c = \dfrac{k}{p}$

$$r = \frac{(p)}{(k)} \cdot \left(1 - \frac{ew}{p}\right).$$

Hence, $r = \dfrac{1}{c} \cdot s$

$$r = \frac{s}{c} = g$$

$$r = g.$$

In Harrod's growth model, the 'warranted' growth rate is Gw and Cr is the capital co-efficient or capital–output ratio; and

$$Gw = \frac{s}{Cr} = s \cdot \frac{1}{Cr}.$$

In the Galenson–Libenstein formula, $s = \dfrac{p - ew}{p}$ and $Cr = \dfrac{k}{p}$

$$r = \frac{p}{k} \times \left(1 - \frac{ew}{p}\right).$$

Hence $r = \dfrac{1}{Cr} \times s$

$$r = \frac{s}{Cr} = Gw.$$

The long-run rate of growth is maximized by significantly

increasing the rate of reinvestment or the rate of generation of investible surplus by channelizing resources into capital-intensive projects which generate greater surplus of output over consumption. In other words, investment should be made in projects which have higher MPCRQ. This theory has been criticized on the grounds that such allocation of resources to capital intensive projects may accentuate inequality of incomes; and present consumption is sacrificed to future consumption which is likely to cause great hardship to the common people in the present. This is hardly advisable for developing countries where standards of living are low and poverty is extreme.

Appendix 2

Note on Utilization of Corporate Funds*

Let us consider the use to which corporate reserves can be put. The additional reserves may be utilized for the following purposes:

(1) Expansion of existing project.
(2) Formation of a new company—same line of industrial activity or diversification.
(3) Modernization project.
(4) Working capital or repayment of working capital.
(5) Purchase of machines on deferred payment basis.
(6) Inter-corporate loans or their repayment.
(7) Extraneous loans or other purposes.
(8) Money kept idle.

Where schemes are framed for expansion of existing projects, formation of a new company or modernization project, a project report would be prepared incorporating a scheme of outlay and its financing. Negotiation with financial institutions would take place for providing term loans for projects, underwriting shares offered to the public, and other assistance. The promoter's contribution in the form of equity and loan, and debt–equity ratio, would be decided in accordance with institutional norms. With regard to equity capital, the promoter's contribution may be 40 per cent and 60 per cent may be offered to the public. In the case of joint sector projects, 25 per cent would generally be the promoter's contribution, 26 per cent of equity would be taken up by the public sector partner (state and/or promotional or financial institutions), and 49 per cent would be offered to the public. The debt–equity ratio is normally 2:1, but may be higher, say 4:1, in the case of capital-intensive industries like cement and fertilizers. The accretion to reserves, accumulated reserves or capital, and the promoter's own contribution and that of his associates, would generally provide the nucleus capital.

A company may choose to purchase machines on deferred payment basis. Usually down payment has necessarily to be made to the extent of about 5 per cent to 25 per cent of the value of the machine, and the balance is payable in instalments over a period of years. The initial payment is made out of the funds of the company.

* *Vide* Ch. 20.

Part of the funds may be utilized for working capital, in which case there may be addition to inventories, book-debts and other current assets. The company usually provides out of its funds, or the promoter's funds, the margin money for working capital which is in effect five to six times the margin. As regards repayment of working capital, taking an aggregate view of the entire corporate sector, the repayments by some companies would be set off against the working capital raised, and the net amount of working capital would constitute additional capital formation. Part of the funds may also be used for extraneous purposes, although loans given to group companies in the form of inter-corporate loans, are generally utilized for supplementing temporary shortage of working capital by the recipient company.

It is possible that certain managements may have lost their dynamism or are unable to utilize the reserves for further expansion and development. It is also possible that due to depression in the economy, the return on capital employed may not be sufficiently attractive, or the investment climate may not be regarded as congenial. In such a situation, the accretion to reserves may lie dormant or idle with the company. The act of investment is central to economic and industrial growth, whether in a developing or developed economy; and it is equally vital to our theory of CNC Super-Multiplier. If Accretion to reserves are not utilized as nucleus capital for industrial projects, modernization or working capital, but are allowed to remain idle or used for extraneous purposes, it does not lead to Addition to Investment, and in a way may be regarded, over the period of time they are not so utilized, as 'leakage' of investible funds from the overall flow of funds for Investment. It may however, be pointed out that, (1) idle funds do not yield income; (2) in an inflationary era, costs of production continuously go on increasing; and (3) newer competing industries with improved technology come into existence, producing goods at lower prices. All these and other factors make it incumbent upon corporate managements to either expand their activity in the same business, establish new plant, or to diversify into other industries where the profitability is greater. Most progressive managements in response to increase in reserves, would utilize additional funds for investment. Companies which do not expand or diversify, stagnate and may ultimately become sick. In such a situation, it is not likely that accretion to reserves would remain surplus or idle with companies for long periods.

Bibliography

Adiseshiah, Malcolm S. (ed.), *Seventh Plan Perspectives*, Lancer International, Delhi, 1985.

Ahluwalia, Isher Judge, *Industrial Growth in India*, OUP, Delhi, 1989.

Banuri, Tariq (ed.), *Economic Liberaliazation: No Panacea*, Clarendon Press, Oxford, 1991.

Chelliah, Raja J., *Fiscal Policy in Underdeveloped Countries*, George Allen & Unwin Ltd., London, 1960.

Chakravarty, Sukhamoy, *Development Planning*, OUP, Delhi, 1987.

Erhard, Ludwig, *Prosperity Through Competition*, Thames & Hudson, London, 1958.

Friedman, Milton & Rose, *Free to Choose*, Secker & Warburg, London, 1980.

Galbraith, J. K., *A History of Economics*, Hamish Hamilton, London, 1987.

Ghosh, Alak, *New Horizons in Planning*, World Press Pvt. Ltd., Calcutta, 1982.

Halm, George N., *Economic Systems*, Oxford & IBH Publishing Co., Calcutta, 1965.

Hicks, Ursula K., *Development Finance*, Clarendon Press, Oxford, 1965.

Jha, L. K., *Economic Strategy for the 80's*, Allied Publishers Pvt. Ltd., Delhi, 1980.

Kahn Herman, *The Emerging Japanese Superstate*, Penguin Books, Harmondsworth, 1973.

Kay, J. A. and M. A. King, *The British Tax System*, OUP, Oxford, 1978.

Keynes, John Maynard, *The General Theory of Employment, Interest and Money*, Macmillan & Co., London, 1947.

Lewis, W. Arthur, *The Theory of Economic Growth*, George Allen & Unwin Ltd., London, 1957.

Lucas, Robert E.B. and Gustav F. Papanek (eds.), *The Indian Economy*, OUP, Delhi, 1988.

Lange, Oskar and Fred M. Taylor, ed. by B.E. Lippincot, *Economic Theory of Socialism*, University of Minnesota Press, Minneapolis, Minnesota, 1938.

Marshall, Alfred, *Principles of Economics*, Macmillan & Co., London, 1947.

Meade, J.E., *The Structure and Reform of Direct Taxation*, Report of Committee Chaired by J.E. Meade (U.K.), George Allen & Unwin Ltd., London, 1978.

Musgrave, Richard A. & Peggy B., *Public Finance in Theory & Practice*, McGraw Hill Book Co., Int. Students Edn., Singapore, 1984.

Nurkse, Ragnar, *Problems of Capital Formation in Underdeveloped Countries*, Basil Blackwell, Oxford, 1955.

Mishan, E.J., *The Economic Growth Debate—an assessment*, George Allen & Unwin, London, 1977.

Pigou, A.C., *A Study in Public Finance*, Macmillan & Co. Ltd., London, 1956.

Roll, Eric, *A History of Economic Thought*, Faber & Faber Ltd., London, 1954.

Rostow, W. W. , *The Stages of Economic Growth*, Cambridge University Press, Cambridge, 1960.

Rostow, W. W., *The Economics of Take-off into Sustained Growth*, Macmillan, London, 1963.

Samuelson, Paul A. and D. Nordhaus, *Economics*, Mcgraw Hill Book Co., Int. Edn., Singapore, 1985.

Seth, M. L., *The Theory and Practice of Economic Planning*, S. Chand & Co. Pvt. Ltd., Delhi, 1971.

Schumpeter, Joseph A., *Capitalism, Socialism and Democracy*, George Allen & Unwin Ltd., London, 1959.

Thirlwall, A.P., *Growth and Development*, ELBS, Macmillan Education Ltd., London, 1983.

Government Publications, Journals & Newspapers:

Cembureau, The European Cement Assn., *Inflation Accounting*, Paris, July 1981.

Direct Tax Laws Committee (Choksi Committee) *Final Report*, Ministry of Finance, Sept. 1978.

Economic Impact, No. 49, 1985/1, Int. Communication Agency, USA, Washington DC.

Economic Journal, Royal Economic Society, London, March 1990.

The Economist, various issues; and some figures from issues in 1984 and 1987 relating to the British Economy.

The Economic Times, Calcutta, 25 & 26 April 1990; also 1, 5 & 18 August 1991.

Finance & Development, IMF/World Bank, Sept. 1983.

Financial Express, 16 May 1990.

Government of India, *Economic Survey, Delhi, 1987–88, 1988–89, 1989–90 & 1990–91.*

ICICI, *Financial Performance of Companies*, ICICI Portfolio, Bombay, 1986–7.

Newsweek, 28 March 1988; 8 Aug. 1988.

OECD, *Economic Surveys, Japan*, 1976.

Reserve Bank of India, Annual Reports, 1987–8, 1988–9, 1989–90, 1990–1.

Reserve Bank of India, Occasional Papers, vol. 9, no. 3., Sept. 1988.

The Sunday Times, London, 20 March 1988.

Tax Bureau, *An Outline of Japanese Taxes*, Ministry of Finance, Japan, Tokyo, 1980.

Taxation Enquiry Commission Report, vols. 1 & 2, Government of India, Delhi, 1955.

World Bank Annual Report, 1989 & 1990.

World Development Report, 1987, 1988, 1989, 1990 & 1991, World Bank/OUP, New York.

Index